JOE FAMULARO

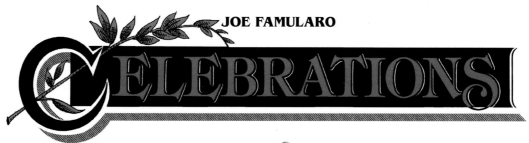

CELEBRATIONS

Sumptuous Meals *for* Festive Occasions

BARRON'S

Acknowledgments

There are many people who help make a book like this possible; I couldn't do it alone.

My sincere thanks and appreciation to:

Cathy and Peter Morrell for their wine suggestions. • Annie Nadler, Miriam Bernstein, and Lydia Moss for their special menus. • Katherine Eisenhauer Thomas for her wedding cake. • Susan and Howard Kaskel for their "Doral" recipes. • Marie McCormick and Kathryn Levy for their computer help. • Bill Halpin for rescuing parts of the manuscript. • Lorraine De Pietro and Grace Freedson for their editorial guidance, and Manuel Barron for his publishing expertise.

And to family and friends (in alphabetical order) with whom I share cooking successes and failures:

Leticia Maria Bondurant, Don Cameron, Marion Cleveland, Sandy Daniels, my brother Judge "Jerry" Famularo, Cathy Franztsis, Connie Freeman, Betty and John Hettinger, my sister and brother-in-law Louise and John Imperiale, Bernie Kinzer, Dennis O'Hara, Dana and Bob Ornsteen, Georgiana and Armando Orsini, Lucy Abel-Smith, Marguerite and Tom Whitney, JerryAnn and Gene Woodfin.

And to my sister Mary Tassiello, who taught me to enjoy and give meaning to celebrations of all kinds.

Cover and Book Design: Milton Glaser, Inc.

All inquiries should be addressed to:
Barron's Educational Series, Inc.
250 Wireless Boulevard
Hauppauge, New York 11788

Library of Congress Catalog Card No. 93-10731

International Standard Book No. 0-8120-6275-2

Library of Congress Cataloging-in-Publication Data

Famularo, Joseph J.
    Celebrations : sumptuous meals for festive occasions /
Joe Famularo.
        p.   cm.
    Includes index.
    ISBN 0-8120-6275-2
    1. Holiday cookery. 2. Table etiquette. I. Title.
TX739.F267   1993
641.5'68—dc20   93-10731
                                        CIP

PRINTED IN HONG KONG
3456   9927   987654321

Contents

Introduction

"The pleasures of the table are of all times and all ages, of every country and of every day."

—Brillat-Savarin

When Belshazzar, the King of Babylon, gave a party, nothing was too much trouble. To keep domestic tranquility, he had to invite hundreds of warriors and priests; the table service and supplies to accommodate them could have bought a small kingdom. The noise of laughter and music was such that a volcano could have erupted unnoticed among the revelers. Imagine the perfumed air of Babylon's hanging gardens filling the banquet rooms, blending with the clashing of cymbals, the clapping of the dancing maidens, and the eerie strains of reed flutes. Consider the menu: dark red wines served by eunuchs, intoxicating brews of barley, river perch cooked whole with ginger and coriander, cornucopias overflowing with carrots, leeks, onions, and turnips, roasted ducks and geese sauced with mint and mustard. Wooden trays the size of rafts carried lettuces, cress, and endive, to be followed by sweet barley cakes. What a celebration!

Times may have changed, but not entirely. Today the simplest get-together can become a celebration, especially when it is spiked by the host's own delight—even if he is not the King of Babylon. Hospitality is so embedded in our culture that the spirit of joyous sharing comes naturally to most of us. Nonetheless, as with so many of life's activities, significant changes have occurred in the way we entertain. Stylish kitchen parties, imaginative get-togethers on the back porch, and gala cookouts are a few examples of what one might call the "new formulas." There are no rigid rules that spell out what makes a celebration get off the ground. But there are guidelines, especially where food is concerned, and that's what this book is all about.

In past centuries, the dinner party was formal and limited to certain people—mostly the affluent or the politically powerful. Nowadays, we invite those people with whom we really want to share food and time. Because planning a meal is more than looking up recipes, or buying a pound of smoked salmon and some pumpernickel, the emphasis in this book is on menus—in other words, the balancing act of bringing together various dishes to form a harmonious whole.

I'm often asked what makes a meal memorable. The answer is never simple, but I do know that there have to be enough textures, flavors, colors, and shapes to please the palate, the eye, and the sense of smell. Toss in a bit of the unexpected, and the result will whet the appetite and add to everyone's appreciation of the meal. Putting some emphasis on seasonal food is also important. What is more welcome than fresh asparagus in the springtime or thick potato slices baked with rosemary in the winter?

Foods should contrast and complement each other in texture and flavor, but they should also look good together. Mashed potatoes and boiled cauliflower florets don't look as if they were meant for each other. Is it wise to follow a cream soup with a creamy turkey pot pie? I think not, and have avoided such pitfalls in designing these celebratory menus.

Menus are usually simple these days, but we all want something a little more elaborate for a birthday, a holiday, any special event. Two desserts are offered in some of the menus; you may want to use both, but choosing one will not destroy the meal. In many menus, an alternative, usually fish, is given for the meat course—again, with a balance of flavors, textures, and tastes in mind.

Some people cook the same menu for virtually every big occasion. If the meal is good, there's nothing wrong with it—but something other than pork roast with green beans or grilled chicken with sliced tomatoes can surely be imagined and executed. Often the problem is just that we get lazy and don't want to plan a different meal. The purpose of this book is to get the ideas flowing.

A special section on pages 196 to 203 describes the important accoutrements to a good meal. The tablesetting, for one, should be as artful as you can make it. You'll discover that creative centerpieces are not always Tiffany tureens, but can be vegetables, antique accessories befitting the occasion, or other items suggested on these pages. For years I have enjoyed two old porcelain rabbits, each carrying a basket on its shoulder, which I use for Easter table centerpieces. I fill the baskets with dyed eggs, or chocolate ones—or sometimes just with jelly beans or brightly colored excelsior. One year they were even filled with just-picked crocuses. Once I had to improvise a summertime centerpiece for a last-minute lunch for the celebrated food writer Craig Claiborne. I ended up with two fresh broccoli bunches and several bunches of scallions standing in an antique straw basket.

Everyone loves informal gatherings for food and wine, and buffets, kitchen parties, and lawn parties are still popular. But there seems also to be a desire to return to something more formal—to sit-down dinners with appropriate table coverings and attractive china and silverware. Food and menus for such occasions are included here; most comprise a first course, main course, salad, and dessert. Such menus are manageable if steps can be done ahead.

All food doesn't have to be hot to be good. A cold salad with hot rolls makes an interesting combination. Vegetables, grilled early in the day and served at room temperature, get a boost when a hot-from-the-oven corn pudding is served at the same meal. It's important to read and reread the recipes to get a better understanding of what is involved in a specific meal. Most of the recipes give information on do-ahead preparation steps.

This book has been on my mind for years. The more involved I have become with cooking, be it through reading, writing, teaching, or simply entertaining at home, the more I realize how much good food means to special events. I always do my best cooking when I've planned a Christmas dinner, an Easter lunch, an intimate and special birthday party, or a major fourth of July cookout for family and friends. I believe the same can be said for all of us: We do our best cooking when the event is special—in other words, a celebration!

Ring out the old, ring in the new,
   Ring, happy bells, across the snow:
   The year is going, let him go;
Ring out the false, ring in the true.

—from *In Memoriam*, Section CVI, by
Alfred Lord Tennyson (1809–1892)

Long ago, the New Year was celebrated in early spring. There were only ten months to a year, and the old Roman New Year fell on the first day of March. January and February came into being when Julius Caesar added them to the calendar. January was named for the Roman god Janus, whose name came from *janua*, meaning "door." Janus was pictured with two faces—one looking forward, one backward. From ancient Roman times to the present, all the customs of this holiday have been connected with bidding good-bye to the past and welcoming a new and better future.

Today, many people ring in the year with dancing, noisemaking, and "Auld Lang Syne" at a ballroom or restaurant. Many others enjoy staying at home to watch the proceedings on television while entertaining friends. To help keep the good times rolling, this chapter presents a moderately formal dinner for your New Year's Eve celebration.

New Year's Eve

DINNER MENU FOR 8

ONION TART

BROILED SALMON WITH MUSTARD
MINT SAUCE

STEAMED SNOW PEAS

SPINACH, MUSHROOM, PEPPER,
AND CORN SALAD

VANILLA ICE CREAM WITH SAMBUCA
AND INSTANT ESPRESSO

Salmon With Mint Sauce

FOOD PREPARATION

Serve the onion tart as an appetizer on individual plates before dinner. The dinner plates should hold the salmon, mint sauce, and snow peas; the salad should be served on individual salad plates.

1 day ahead:
- Prepare pastry for tart
- Make mustard mint sauce
- Prepare salad greens and dressing

Serving day:
- Bake tart
- Broil salmon
- Cook snow peas
- Dress salad
- Make dessert

WINE SUGGESTIONS

Greet your guests with Veuve Clicquot Brut Champagne. Serve Carbout Rosé Brut with dessert and also to ring in the new "vintage" year. During the meal, serve the delicate Ferrari Carano Alexander Valley Chardonnay.

ONION TART

8 Servings

1 pâte brisée crust (page 193)

5 tablespoons butter

1½ pounds onions, thinly sliced

1 tablespoon all-purpose flour

2 eggs, lightly beaten

pinch of nutmeg

salt and pepper

1. Fit the pastry into a 10 × ¾-inch round tart pan with removable bottom, crimping the pastry edge about ¼ inch higher than the rim of the pan. Cover and refrigerate until needed.

2. In a large skillet, melt 4 tablespoons butter over medium heat and cook the onions uncovered until soft and lightly colored, about 30 minutes. Sprinkle the flour over the onions, stir well and cook 2 minutes longer. Remove from heat and let cool for 15 minutes. Add the eggs, nutmeg, and salt and pepper.

3. Preheat oven to 350°F. Spread onion filling in the tart shell and bake on the lowest oven rack until nicely browned, about 40 minutes.

4. Melt the remaining tablespoon of butter and brush over the tart. Let stand 10 to 15 minutes. Serve warm.

Onion Tart

BROILED SALMON WITH MUSTARD MINT SAUCE

Have the fishmonger fillet two sides of a fresh salmon and remove all the skin. In most cases, he will not remove the bones, but this is easy to do at home. Simply run your fingers over the fillet to locate them, then remove each bone with tweezers or needle-nosed pliers. Each side should produce six fillet pieces, about 2 inches wide.

8 Servings

2 filleted sides of salmon, each weighing about 2 pounds, bones removed

⅔ cup sugar

6 tablespoons coarse salt

6 tablespoons juniper berries, ground

2 teaspoons freshly ground pepper

2 tablespoons grated orange zest

olive oil

Mustard Mint Sauce (see next page)

1. Set the whole salmon fillets on a piece of waxed paper large enough to wrap them completely. (They should not be cut into individual servings at this point.)

2. Combine all remaining ingredients except the olive oil and sauce and rub the mixture over both sides of the fillets. Wrap well and refrigerate for 4 to 12 hours. Bring the salmon to room temperature before broiling.

3. Preheat broiler to high. Brush the fish lightly with olive oil and cut the fillets crosswise into individual servings. Arrange on a baking sheet and broil 4 to 5 inches from the heat source just until the salmon becomes opaque, about 7 to 9 minutes; there is no need to turn the fish. Serve immediately with Mustard Mint Sauce.

MUSTARD MINT SAUCE
Makes about 1¼ cups

6 tablespoons olive oil

6 tablespoons peanut oil

3 tablespoons white wine vinegar

1½ tablespoons Dijon-style mustard

1½ tablespoons coarse-grained mustard

¼ cup finely chopped fresh mint

1. Combine the oils in a glass measuring cup and set aside.

2. In the bowl of a processor, blend the vinegar, mustards, and mint. With the machine running, pour in the oil very slowly and process until sauce is the consistency of mayonnaise.

STEAMED SNOW PEAS

8 Servings

1 pound fresh snow peas

2 tablespoons butter, softened

salt and pepper

1. Trim the ends of the snow peas and pull away strings if necessary. Rinse in cool water. Cook in a large steamer set over boiling water until barely tender, about 3 to 5 minutes. Drain the peas and pat dry.

2. In a serving bowl, toss the snow peas with the butter and salt and pepper to taste. Serve right away.

3. If you prefer, steam the snow peas ahead of time. To reheat, melt the butter in a large skillet, add the cooked snow peas, salt and pepper, and sauté over high heat for 2 to 3 minutes to heat through.

SPINACH, MUSHROOM, PEPPER, AND CORN SALAD

The roasted sesame oil and soy sauce in this salad provide an exciting flavor. This is as it is prepared by Chef Ron Hook at the Doral Saturnia Spa in Miami, Florida. Wholewheat croutons are easily made at home; dice slices of bread and toast in the oven until crisp, or buy them packaged in most markets.

8 Servings

1 pound fresh spinach, stemmed

2 cups sliced mushrooms

1 cup corn kernels

½ cup diced red or yellow bell pepper

½ cup alfalfa sprouts

whites of 4 hard-boiled eggs, chopped

1 cup Sesame Dressing (see below)

4 ounces wholewheat croutons

Wash the spinach in several changes of water and dry well. Arrange the vegetables and egg whites on individual plates. Top with the dressing and croutons.

SESAME DRESSING

This dressing goes nicely with spinach and other mild greens but is not good with assertive, bitter greens such as radicchio, arugula, or endive. Leftover dressing can be refrigerated for up to two months.

Makes 3 cups

1⅓ cups red wine vinegar

¾ cup water

½ cup Oriental sesame oil

½ cup low-sodium soy sauce

Combine all ingredients in a jar and shake to blend. Chill.

VANILLA ICE CREAM WITH SAMBUCA AND INSTANT ESPRESSO

Add a little more Sambuca and espresso granules if you wish, but be sure to serve this dessert in your best porcelain shallow soup bowls or in crystal champagne glasses.

8 Servings

1 quart vanilla ice cream

8 tablespoons Sambuca

⅓ cup instant espresso granules

Place 2 small balls of ice cream in each plate or glass. Pour 1 tablespoon Sambuca over each serving and dust with instant espresso.

Spinach and Corn Salad

On New Year's Eve and Day we toast each other with a "wassail," which comes from the Anglo-Saxon words *wes hael,* meaning "be in good health." Our American custom of open house parties is synonymous with the great tradition of the wassail bowl. Dutch wives in New Amsterdam put on their fanciest dresses, made their best punches, and baked their lightest cakes and most delicate cookies to receive guests on New Year's Day. Rarely used parlors were freshened and opened up for hospitality from early morning to early evening.

The custom was not limited to New Yorkers. Dashing young men in Baltimore carried lists of homes to visit lest they offend any one particular lady and miss out on invitations the rest of the year. Hostesses vied for prestigious guests and even advertised their open house hours. In Atlanta, ladies staggered their parties to be sure that the most eligible bachelors would appear at each home. Callers presented personal cards that were intricately designed with flowers and birds, Cupids and gardenias, baskets and bows.

George and Martha Washington held open house for the public during the seven years that the national capital was in Philadelphia. Although John and Abigail Adams moved into the White House before it was completed, they held a reception there on New Year's Day in 1800. From Thomas Jefferson on, it became customary to have presidential receptions at the White House on New Year's Day open to all citizens. Today, New Year's Day celebrations survive in such festivities as the Mummers' Parade in Philadelphia and the Tournament of Roses in Pasadena, California.

Here is an informal New Year's Day buffet, American style, where food and drink are festive and plentiful.

New Year's Day

BUFFET MENU FOR 12

SOLE AND SALMON MOLD WITH
HAPPY NEW YEAR BALLOONS

COLD BUFFET SHRIMP

PASTA SHELLS WITH GREEN PEAS
AND BASIL

SPINACH SALAD WITH SESAME
DRESSING

MERINGUE CAKE WITH CHAMPAGNE
SABAYON AND CHOCOLATE
RASPBERRY SAUCE

Sole and Salmon Mold

FOOD PREPARATION

Except for the pasta, which should be made the morning of the buffet and reheated, most of this food may be prepared one or two days ahead. The salad greens can be rinsed and dried a day ahead and dressed at buffet time.

WINE SUGGESTIONS

Serve Fetzer Sundial Mendocino Chardonnay and Beaulieu Vineyards Beautour Napa Cabernet Sauvignon, so both good yet inexpensive red and white are available to complement the variety of dishes.

SOLE AND SALMON MOLD WITH HAPPY NEW YEAR BALLOONS

Serve this with a basketful of toasted bread thins.

12 Servings

2 ¾ cups Fish Aspic (see next page)

1 pound fillets of lemon sole or other white-fleshed fish

1 cup dry white wine

3 tablespoons butter

3 tablespoons all-purpose flour

¾ cup fish stock or clam juice

2 tablespoons fresh lemon juice

¾ cup heavy cream, whipped

¼ pound smoked salmon, cut into 1 x ¼-inch strips

salt and white pepper

4 large fresh radishes, sliced

6 to 8 fresh chives

1. Pour 2 cups of the fish aspic into an 8-inch square pan. Refrigerate until firm.

2. Liberally oil a 6-cup charlotte mold or other deep mold (a 3- or 4-inch-deep springform works well here also) and set aside.

3. Rinse the fish in cool water and pat dry. Place the fish and wine in a saucepan and bring to simmer. Lower heat, cover, and cook just until fish becomes opaque, about 5 minutes; do not overcook. Drain. Transfer to a processor bowl and puree to a thick paste. Transfer to a large mixing bowl.

4. Heat the butter in a small saucepan until bubbling. Add the flour and whisk 2 minutes. Add the fish stock and lemon juice and whisk until the sauce is thick and smooth, about 3 to 4 minutes. Remove from heat and allow to cool.

5. Stir the cooled sauce into the bowl with the fish. Add the remaining liquid fish aspic and mix well. Fold in the whipped cream, salmon strips, salt and pepper. Spread the mixture in the prepared mold. Cover tightly and refrigerate. This may be made two days ahead.

6. Run a sharp knife around the inside of the mold. Place a hot towel briefly on the bottom and invert the mold onto a serving platter. If using a springform mold, carefully loosen and remove the side. Arrange half a dozen or so radish slices, more or less together, on the upper half of the mold to resemble a cluster of balloons. Make "balloon strings" of the chives, gathering them on the lower half of the mold. Remove the jellied aspic from refrigerator and cut into ½-inch cubes. Spoon around the edge of the mold.

FISH ASPIC
Makes 3 cups

2 egg whites

3 cups fish stock or clam juice

2 eggshells, crushed

1½ tablespoons unflavored gelatin

⅓ cup cool water

1. Beat the egg whites until soft peaks form. Transfer to a 1½- to 2-quart saucepan. Add the fish stock and crushed eggshells.

2. Sprinkle the gelatin over the water in a small heatproof bowl and let stand a few minutes until gelatin is softened. Set the bowl in a small saucepan containing an inch or so of water and stir over low heat until the gelatin is dissolved.

3. Add gelatin mixture to the fish stock. Place over medium-high heat and bring to boil, stirring frequently. Immediately reduce heat and simmer without stirring until a crust forms on top and the liquid below is clear, about 15 to 20 minutes (check by separating the egg crust with the point of a knife). Carefully pour the aspic into a bowl through a strainer lined with a double thickness of cheesecloth.

Cold Buffet Shrimp

COLD BUFFET SHRIMP

This flavorful dish is ideal for a buffet because it is made ahead.

12 Servings

2 tablespoons mixed pickling spice

2 garlic cloves, halved

juice of 4 lemons

12 whole peppercorns

3½ pounds shrimp

3 garlic cloves, pressed or minced

6 tablespoons olive oil

2 tablespoons dry vermouth

1 teaspoon dill seed

3 tablespoons Dijon-style mustard

2 tablespoons salt

pepper

1. Combine the pickling spice, halved garlic, juice of 1 lemon, and peppercorns in a large saucepan. Add about 2 quarts water. Bring to boil and cook briskly for 5 minutes.

2. Add the shrimp and cook just until they turn pink, about 5 minutes; do not overcook or they will shrivel and toughen. Immediately remove shrimp from the boiling water and plunge into ice water. When cool enough to handle, remove the shells and devein if necessary. Place the shrimp in a large bowl.

3. In a bowl, combine all remaining ingredients. Add to the shrimp and toss thoroughly. Cover and marinate overnight in the refrigerator.

4. Remove the shrimp from the refrigerator 10 to 15 minutes before serving.

PASTA SHELLS WITH GREEN PEAS AND BASIL

For New Year's Day, "basil taketh away melancholy and maketh merry and glad."
from *The Great Herbal*, 1526 (author unknown)

12 Servings

4 cups canned plum tomatoes

6 tablespoons olive oil

2 onions, chopped

2 garlic cloves, minced

2 packages (10 ounces each) frozen peas, cooked and drained

1 pound pasta shells, cooked and drained

salt and pepper

20 basil leaves, chopped

1 cup grated Parmesan cheese

1. Reserve several of the tomatoes and cut into chunks, removing as many seeds as possible. Put the remaining tomatoes through a food mill.

2. In a large saucepan, heat the oil and sauté the onions until they begin to soften and color. Add the garlic and cook 2 minutes longer. Add the tomato puree and chunks and simmer 15 minutes.

3. Add the peas, pasta, and salt and pepper to the tomato mixture and bring to boil. Remove from heat. Transfer to a large bowl or platter. Sprinkle with basil and toss lightly. Serve with the Parmesan.

Spinach Salad with Sesame Dressing

12 Servings

2 pounds fresh spinach

¼ cup sesame seeds

1 teaspoon sugar

4 teaspoons light soy sauce

¼ cup chicken or vegetable stock or broth

1. Rinse the spinach several times and let stand in cool water for 15 minutes or so. Drain and rinse once again. Discard the thick outer leaves and any coarse stems. Spin the spinach dry or blot with paper towels. Tear into small pieces. Refrigerate in a plastic bag until ready to use.

2. Toast the sesame seeds in a dry skillet over low heat until golden, stirring and shaking the pan. Immediately transfer the seeds to a bowl. Add the sugar, soy sauce, and stock and mix well. Pour over the spinach, toss, and serve.

Meringue Cake with Champagne Sabayon and Chocolate Raspberry Sauce

The following ingredients will fill two 8-inch round pans, each serving approximately eight persons. The meringues are presented as individual "cakes" and sliced. To serve, spread 1 tablespoon of the chocolate raspberry sauce on each plate, put a piece of cake on top of the sauce, and liberally dollop with the champagne sauce.

MERINGUE CAKE
12 to 16 Servings

6 egg whites

½ teaspoon cream of tartar

1⅔ cups confectioner's sugar

½ cup coarsely chopped pecans

1. Line two 8-inch cake pans with sheets of foil large enough to use for pulling out the baked meringue. Spray each with vegetable cooking spray.

2. Whip the egg whites in the largest bowl of an electric mixer at maximum speed until frothy. Add the cream of tartar and whip until soft peaks begin to form. Add the sugar a tablespoon at a time and whip until all is incorporated and the egg whites are stiff and shiny.

3. Preheat oven to 300°F. Divide the meringue between the prepared pans and smooth lightly with a rubber spatula. Sprinkle evenly with pecans. Bake until light brown, about 1¼ hours. Remove meringues from the pans by carefully lifting the foil. Allow to cool.

CHAMPAGNE SABAYON SAUCE
Makes about 2 cups

5 egg yolks

¼ cup sugar

⅔ cup champagne

⅔ cup heavy cream

CHOCOLATE RASPBERRY SAUCE
Makes about 1 cup

3 ounces semisweet chocolate, coarsely chopped

¾ cup heavy cream

1 tablespoon butter

3 tablespoons framboise (raspberry liqueur)

FOR THE CHAMPAGNE SAUCE

1. Whisk the yolks and sugar in the top of a double boiler over simmering water until blended. Add the champagne and whisk until thickened, about 10 minutes. Remove from over water and set over a pan of ice water to cool, whisking occasionally.

2. Whip the cream to soft peaks and fold into the cooled sabayon.

3. Cover and refrigerate. The sauce can be made a day ahead of time.

FOR THE RASPBERRY SAUCE

1. In a small saucepan, combine the chocolate and cream. Cook over low heat, stirring constantly, until the chocolate has melted. Remove from heat and stir in the butter. Fold in the liqueur.

2. This may be made ahead and kept warm in the top of a double boiler over hot water.

Meringue Cake

GONG HAY FAT CHOY:
Wishing you a prosperous New Year celebration.

Chinese New Year, which falls between January 21 and February 19, is one of the most colorful celebrations in the calendar. In the Chinatowns of San Francisco and New York, streets are filled with crates of vegetables and boxes, jars, and cans of imported delicacies. The flower stands seem to have been staged by Monet for a painting. The festival is loud and boisterous with firecrackers and celebrants who scare away evil spirits. During the dragon parade, the sidewalk is filled with hundreds of children who buy sweetmeats, wrapped in Chinese red paper, with their good luck money.

As a rule, New Year's Eve is a time of abstinence from meat. On the following day, families visit their temples or stay at home. The feast comes the next day, when presents are exchanged. Alexandra von Nagel, an old friend, has always had a Chinese New Year's party at her home. When we can, we meet in New York to view the great dragon parade with the lion and other floats, the firecrackers, and lanterns. The local populace greet each other with *gong hay fat choy*, which means "Wishing you a prosperous New Year celebration."

Chinese New Year

MENU FOR 8

SHRIMP AND EGG SOUP

DEEP-FRIED GARLIC SHRIMP

STIR-FRIED SIRLOIN WITH BROCCOLI
OR SPARERIBS, SCALLIONS, AND
GINGER COOKED IN A WOK

SPICY CHICKEN IN STAR ANISE
SAUCE *OR* HOT STIR-FRIED CELERY
AND CHICKEN WITH WALNUTS

SZECHUAN NOODLES *OR*
BAKED RICE

CUCUMBER SESAME SALAD

ORANGES IN SWEET GRAPEFRUIT
SAUCE

FORTUNE COOKIES

Shrimp and Egg Soup

FOOD PREPARATION

1 or 2 days ahead:
- Make the soup but do not add the spinach or custard until ready to serve.
- Cook one of the chicken dishes
- Cook the spareribs if you chose this dish
- Make the noodles if you chose this dish
- Prepare vegetables for other dishes to be cooked the next day
- Make orange dessert

Serving day:
- Deep-fry the shrimp
- Stir-fry the sirloin if you chose this dish
- Bake the rice if you chose this dish
- Make the salad
- Reheat dishes made the day before

WINE SUGGESTIONS

The spicy flavors of Chinese cuisine are complemented by the fruitiness of the Riesling grape. Serve an Alsatian or Pacific Northwest throughout the meal.

SHRIMP AND EGG SOUP

8 Servings

4 eggs, beaten

2 teaspoons sugar

1 teaspoon salt

6 tablespoons dry sherry

10 cups defatted chicken stock or broth

8 shrimp

2 teaspoons fresh lemon juice

1 tablespoon light soy sauce

16 leaves fresh spinach, stemmed and thinly sliced

1. Blend the eggs, sugar, salt, sherry, and 1¼ cups stock in the top of a double boiler. Cover and steam over simmering water for 15 minutes or until the mixture forms a custard. Remove from over water and set aside.

2. Bring 2 cups water to boil in small saucepan or skillet. Add the shrimp and lemon juice and cook just until the shrimp turn pink, 3 to 4 minutes. Drain and rinse under cool water. Remove shells and veins, and halve the shrimp lengthwise. Place 2 shrimp halves in each of 8 bowls.

3. Bring the remaining stock to boil with the soy sauce. Add the spinach and cook 2 minutes. Distribute among the soup bowls.

4. Turn custard out onto a plate and cut into ½-inch squares. Gently drop 2 pieces into each bowl and serve.

DEEP-FRIED GARLIC SHRIMP

Although no condiment is essential, these are delicious served with jalapeño jelly—not Chinese, to be sure, but a Western contribution.

8 Servings

2 pounds large shrimp

4 garlic cloves, minced

1 teaspoon salt

2 cups bleached all-purpose flour

1½ tablespoons baking powder

⅔ cup vegetable oil

1¼ cups water

2 quarts oil for deep-frying

1. Remove the shrimp shells, leaving the tails on. Devein the shrimp and rinse well; pat dry. Place in a bowl with the garlic and ½ teaspoon of the salt. Toss well, cover, and let stand 30 minutes.

2. In a bowl, combine the flour, baking powder, and remaining ½ teaspoon salt and mix well. Slowly add ⅔ cup oil, stirring until the dough forms a ball and cleans the sides of the bowl. Gradually add the water, stirring constantly until the mixture resembles pancake batter.

3. Heat the 2 quarts of oil in a deep-fryer, wok, or large saucepan to 350°F. Test the temperature of the oil by adding a drop of batter; it should sizzle, puff up, and float.

4. Take a shrimp by the tail, immerse it in the batter, and drop immediately into the hot oil. Repeat with the remaining shrimp, without crowding the pan. As each shrimp browns, remove it with tongs and drain on paper towels. Serve immediately, or keep the cooked shrimp warm in a 200°F oven for up to 1 hour.

STIR-FRIED SIRLOIN WITH BROCCOLI

8 Servings

⅓ cup light soy sauce

¼ cup dry sherry

1 tablespoon sugar

1 teaspoon finely chopped fresh ginger

2 scallions, thinly sliced

2 tablespoons cornstarch mixed into ⅓ cup water

½ cup chicken stock or low-salt broth

3 tablespoons peanut oil

2 pounds boneless sirloin (all visible fat removed), chilled and thinly sliced

1½ pounds broccoli, stems removed, divided into small florets

4 large black Chinese mushrooms, soaked, drained, and sliced

1. In a bowl, combine the soy sauce, sherry, sugar, ginger, scallions, cornstarch mixture, and chicken stock. Mix well and set aside.

2. Heat the oil in a wok over high heat until sizzling. Add the sirloin and stir-fry for 2 to 3 minutes. Add the broccoli and stir-fry 2 to 3 minutes longer. Add the mushrooms and stir-fry 2 minutes.

3. Add the soy sauce mixture and stir-fry 2 minutes. Serve immediately.

Sirloin With Broccoli

SPARERIBS, SCALLIONS, AND GINGER COOKED IN A WOK

8 Servings

2 teaspoons sugar

1 tablespoon cornstarch

1 tablespoon salted black beans, rinsed

2 tablespoons soy sauce

¼ cup water

1 teaspoon salt

2 pounds spareribs (1 slab), cut into riblets about 2 inches long

2 tablespoons peanut oil

2 garlic cloves, minced

3 thin slices ginger, minced

1 cup chicken stock or low-salt broth

½ cup thinly sliced scallions

1. Mix the first five ingredients and set aside.

2. Bring about 1 quart water to boil. Add the salt and spareribs and return to boil. Reduce heat and simmer 5 minutes. Drain and dry the ribs well.

3. In a wok, heat the peanut oil and stir-fry the ribs over high heat until browned. Add the garlic and ginger and stir-fry another minute. Add the chicken stock, cover, and cook 5 minutes.

4. Add the cornstarch mixture, cover, and cook another 5 minutes. Sprinkle with the scallions, toss, and serve.

SPICY CHICKEN IN STAR ANISE SAUCE

One of the components of the Chinese "five spice" mixture is star anise, available in Chinese, Hispanic, and food specialty shops, and in many supermarkets.

8 Servings

4 large chicken breasts with bone in (about 2 pounds)

¼ cup dry sherry

¼ cup corn oil

⅓ cup light soy sauce

1 tablespoon Oriental sesame oil

6 scallions, trimmed and cut into ½-inch pieces

8 dried Chinese mushrooms

3 tablespoons grated fresh ginger

4 small whole red chilies

4 dried star anise

1 tablespoon sugar

1. Cut away at least half of the skin from each chicken breast. With a heavy cleaver, chop breasts (including bone) into 2-inch pieces. Arrange in one layer in a stainless steel, ceramic, or glass dish.

2. Combine all remaining ingredients and mix well; pour over the chicken. Turn the meat to coat all sides. Cover and refrigerate overnight, turning two or three times. If there isn't time to marinate overnight, let stand at room temperature for 3 hours, turning two or three times.

3. If refrigerated, bring the chicken to room temperature. Preheat broiler or prepare charcoal grill. Arrange the pieces on skewers and broil or grill about 4 inches from the heat source, basting two or three times. Broiling time should not exceed 15 minutes; test for doneness by removing a piece and cutting it

4. Bring the leftover marinade to boil; boil for a few minutes. Remove the hot chilies. Spoon over the chicken and serve.

HOT STIR-FRIED CELERY AND CHICKEN WITH WALNUTS

8 Servings

2 cups celery cut into ¾-inch dice

1½ cups bamboo shoots cut into ¾-inch dice

1 cup onion cut into ½-inch dice

12 water chestnuts, thinly sliced

1 pound skinless, boneless chicken breasts

juice of ½ lemon

2 tablespoons light soy sauce

2 tablespoons cornstarch

1 teaspoon salt

1 teaspoon sugar

2 teaspoons dry sherry

¼ teaspoon red pepper flakes

6 tablespoons peanut oil

½ cup chicken stock or low-fat broth

1½ cup walnut meats

1. Combine celery, bamboo shoots, onion, and water chestnuts in a bowl. Toss and set aside.

2. Trim the chicken breasts of all fat and cartilage (scissors are helpful to accomplish this). Place in a bowl. Sprinkle with the lemon juice, toss well, and let stand for 10 minutes. Drain and pat dry. Flatten the breasts and cut into ¾-inch squares. Set aside.

3. Combine the soy sauce, cornstarch, salt, sugar, sherry, and pepper flakes. Add the chicken pieces and toss to coat well.

4. Place 3 tablespoons oil in each of two woks or large skillets. Set over high heat. Add the vegetables to one of the woks or skillets and stir-fry until lightly browned but still crisp, about 5 minutes.

5. Add the chicken and marinade to the other wok and stir-fry over high heat until cooked through. Add the chicken stock and the vegetables, using a slotted spoon. Remove from heat.

6. Return the wok to the heat and add a few drops of oil if needed. Sauté the walnuts until browned, about 1 minute. Add to the chicken mixture and place over high heat for 2 to 3 minutes to blend flavors. Serve immediately.

SZECHUAN NOODLES

Somen noodles are Japanese and available in most large supermarkets. They're fun to work with.

8 Servings

1 package (10 ounces) somen noodles

⅓ cup hot water

⅓ cup chunky peanut butter or sesame paste

2 teaspoons light soy sauce

2 teaspoons rice vinegar

2 teaspoons Oriental sesame oil

2 scallions, finely chopped

2 garlic cloves, minced

1 teaspoon sugar

4 drops chili oil

1. Prepare the somen noodles according to package directions. Drain and rinse in cold water. Transfer to a serving bowl or plate.

2. Combine the hot water and peanut butter. Add all remaining ingredients except a small handful of chopped scallions. Pour the sauce over the noodles and toss well. Top with the reserved scallions and serve at room temperature.

BAKED RICE

For this meal, plain rice—that is, rice cooked in water instead of meat broth—is fine. Cooking the rice in a flavored liquid is not necessary because of the many flavors in the other dishes. Baking the rice instead of boiling it saves time.

8 Servings

2 cups uncooked white rice

1½ cups cold water

4 teaspoons fresh lemon juice

1. Preheat oven to 350°F. Thoroughly wash the rice in a colander or strainer under cold running water. Place in a covered baking dish or casserole with the water and lemon juice.

2. Bake for 40 minutes. Stir the rice with a fork. If it seems dry, add 1 to 2 tablespoons water. Reduce heat to 325°F, cover again, and bake until fluffy and fully cooked, 5 to 10 more minutes.

Buffet for 8

CUCUMBER SESAME SALAD

8 Servings

3 small, thin cucumbers

2 tablespoons peanut oil

1 tablespoon rice vinegar

1 teaspoon Oriental sesame oil

3 drops chili oil

juice of ½ lemon, strained

salt

1 teaspoon toasted sesame seeds

1. Trim the ends from the cucumbers and peel the skin in lengthwise strips. Run the tines of a fork down the cucumbers. Slice thinly and place in a bowl.

2. Combine all remaining ingredients except the sesame seeds. Mix well and pour over the sliced cucumbers. Toss to coat well.

3. Refrigerate the salad until well chilled. Sprinkle with the sesame seeds just before serving.

Oranges in Grapefruit Sauce

ORANGES IN SWEET GRAPEFRUIT SAUCE

Make this one day ahead, cover tightly, and refrigerate overnight.

8 Servings

½ cups fresh grapefruit juice

¼ cup sugar

1 tablespoon grenadine

1 2-inch piece vanilla bean, split

8 large seedless oranges, peeled, white pith removed

1 tablespoon finely chopped candied ginger

1. Combine the juice, sugar, grenadine, and vanilla bean in a small nonaluminum pan and bring to boil. Cook until reduced by half.

2. Thinly slice oranges and overlap on a large plate. Pour sauce over and dot with ginger. Cover and chill.

There are several theories about the origin of St. Valentine's Day, although it would be difficult to prove any of them.

In about 270 A.D., a Roman priest called Valentine was martyred during the persecution of the early Christians. He was canonized, and his feast day was set for February 14.

There are also claims that Valentine was a priest during the reign of Claudius, a cruel emperor who was detested by his subjects. Valentine performed beautiful temple services and people of all ages and social classes flocked to him. Claudius needed to recruit warriors for his armies but found it difficult because the men didn't want to leave their wives and sweethearts. In retribution, Claudius ordered a stop to all betrothals and marriages. Thinking this unkind to young people, Valentine secretly went ahead with some nuptials, and when discovered by the emperor, was thrown in jail only to die there.

Another story is that St. Valentine was jailed for helping Christians. While incarcerated, he cured the jailer's daughter of blindness—and he fell in love with her, writing her letters signed, "From your Valentine." Infuriated, Claudius had him beheaded; the date of this sad event was February 14 in A.D. 269. About 200 years later, Pope Gelasius designated the date as St. Valentine's feast day. This new Christian holiday celebrated Valentine as the patron saint of lovers, and his feast as the specific time for exchanging expressions of affection. The idea that the first person you see on Valentine's Day will be your true love still lingers. In Shakespeare's *Hamlet*, Ophelia hopes to catch Hamlet's eye on that morning as she says:

> Good morrow! 'tis St. Valentine's Day
>   All in the morning betime,
> And I a maid at your window
>   To be your Valentine.

Valentine's Day

DINNER MENU FOR 2

Smoked Salmon Horseradish
Slices with Heart Beets

Spicy-Sweet Cornish Hens

Glazed Celery in Mustard
Sauce

Brown Rice a la Doral

Frozen Strawberry Yogurt
with Raspberry Coulis

Salmon With Heart Beets

FOOD PREPARATION

This menu for two can be doubled, tripled, or quadrupled as necessary. The raspberry sauce is easy to prepare and can be made well ahead of time; the frozen yogurt may be purchased at your favorite ice cream shop or grocery store. The first course may be made two or three days ahead; the hens can be marinated overnight in their spicy-sweet coating. However, this is a simple dinner that can easily be prepared on the day it is to be served.

WINE SUGGESTIONS

Serve Sonoma Cutrer Russian River Chardonnay (half-bottle) with the first course, Clos du Bois Sonoma Merlot (half-bottle) with the cornish hen, and Moët et Chandon Brut (half-bottle) with dessert.

SMOKED SALMON HORSERADISH SLICES WITH HEART BEETS

This may be made ahead and covered with plastic wrap until ready to serve.

2 Servings

2 medium to large beets

1 teaspoon cumin seeds

¼ cup vinaigrette (page 193)

¼ pound sliced smoked salmon

¼ cup heavy cream, whipped

1 tablespoon prepared horseradish

salt and pepper

2 teaspoons finely chopped chives

1. Cut off the beet greens, leaving about 1 inch of stem so beets do not bleed during cooking. In a saucepan, cover the beets with salted water; add cumin seeds. Simmer until beets are tender, about 40 minutes.

2. Cool beets in cold water. Slip off skins. Cut into ¼-inch-thick slices and place in a small glass bowl. Add vinaigrette and toss lightly to coat. This may be done 1 to 2 days ahead. Refrigerate the beets, but bring to room temperature before serving.

3. Arrange the slices of smoked salmon on a work surface to make a 4-inch square. Mix about 3 tablespoons whipped cream with the horseradish, salt and pepper. Spoon this mixture along the edge of the salmon square. Carefully roll the salmon to enclose the filling. Wrap in plastic and freeze 1 to 2 hours.

4. Remove salmon roll from freezer about 30 minutes before serving. Let stand about 20 minutes to soften slightly. Cut the roll into 6 slices. Cut the larger beet slices into heart shapes and arrange on two plates. Drizzle with vinaigrette. Place 3 salmon slices on each plate and sprinkle liberally with chives; be sure the filled salmon slices are thawed before serving.

SPICY-SWEET CORNISH HENS

To prepare these a day ahead, coat the hens with some of the sauce, wrap tightly in plastic, and refrigerate overnight.

2 Servings

*2 Cornish hens,
1¼ to 1½ pounds each*

salt and pepper

½ cup lime jelly

3 tablespoons fresh lime juice

1 tablespoon Worcestershire sauce

1 teaspoon minced canned jalapeño peppers

1. Preheat oven to 500°F. Split the hens in half and remove the backbones; rinse and dry. Season with salt and pepper.

2. In a nonaluminum saucepan heat the jelly, juice, Worcestershire and jalapeños until jelly is melted. Coat the hens with some of the sauce. Roast skin side down on a rack in a roasting pan, basting 3 or 4 times with the remaining sauce, until juices run clear, about 30 minutes. Serve hot.

Spicy Cornish Hen

GLAZED CELERY IN MUSTARD SAUCE

2 Servings

5 celery stalks

¾ cup chicken stock or low-salt broth

1 tablespoon butter

sugar

3 tablespoons heavy cream

1 teaspoon Dijon-style mustard

salt and pepper

1. Rinse celery and remove any coarse strings with a vegetable peeler. Cut off leaves, chop finely, and reserve. Cut the stalks into ½-inch-thick diagonal slices and place in a large skillet.

2. Add the stock, butter, and 1 teaspoon sugar and bring to boil. Cook, stirring, until the liquid is reduced to a glaze.

3. Combine the cream and mustard and add to the skillet. Lower heat and cook until the sauce is thickened, seasoning with salt and pepper.

4. Preheat broiler. Divide the mixture between 2 individual ramekins. Sprinkle a little more sugar over the top of each. Broil until the top is flecked with brown. Sprinkle with the chopped celery leaves and serve.

Strawberry Yogurt With Raspberry Coulis

BROWN RICE A LA DORAL

Traditional recipes call for cooking rice with the lid on, but Chef Ron Hook at the Doral Saturnia Spa in Miami, Florida, cooks it uncovered to keep it from becoming sticky. Brown rice has more nutrients and fiber than white rice.

Makes 2 cups

1 cup short-grain brown rice

1 ½ cups chicken stock or low-salt broth

1. Rinse the rice in cold water and drain well. Place the rice and chicken stock in a saucepan, cover, and bring to boil.

2. Uncover, lower the heat, and simmer until the stock is absorbed, about 20 minutes. Remove from heat, cover, and let stand for 5 minutes before serving.

FROZEN STRAWBERRY YOGURT WITH RASPBERRY COULIS

2 Servings

½ cup fresh or thawed frozen raspberries

¼ cup Grand Marnier or other orange liqueur

1 pint frozen strawberry yogurt

2 mint leaves or several strawberry slices (garnish)

1. Puree the raspberries in a processor or blender. Strain to remove seeds. Stir in liqueur. Divide sauce between two dessert plates.

2. Top the pool of sauce with a scoop of yogurt. Garnish with a mint leaf or 2 or 3 thin strawberry slices.

Passover commemorates the Jews' liberation from slavery in Egypt. The Book of Exodus tells how, 31 centuries ago, each Israelite family gathered to eat roast lamb with unleavened bread and bitter herbs, sandals on their feet and staffs at hand, prepared for the flight from Egypt that foreshadowed Israel's great march through the centuries in search of freedom. Every year, during the first one or two nights of the eight-day Passover holiday, Jewish families gather to recall the experience of slavery, and to celebrate their liberty and the hope of freedom for all peoples.

The Passover table always centers around the seder dish, a platter that holds several symbolic items: a roasted egg, representing the renewal of life and hope; bitter herbs, recalling the bitterness of the Jews' enslavement in Egypt; haroset, an apple-and-nut paste that suggests the mortar used by Israelite laborers during their captivity; parsley, representing the hard labor the Jews did in Egypt; and a lamb shank bone, representing the offering, the sacrifice of a lamb.

Miriam Bernstein prepared the Passover seder for family, friends, and close relatives for many years, first on Long Island and for the last 25 years in the Florida Keys. Now she joins her two sons in cooking the meal.

Passover

MENU FOR 8

Haroset

Miriam's Homemade Gefilte Fish

Miriam's Chicken Soup
with Matzo Balls

Roast Turkey with Vegetable
Sauce

Roast Brisket of Beef

Whipped Yams

Asparagus, Scallions, and
Green Beans with Dill

Baked Beets in Lettuce Cups
with Lemon-Pepper Dressing

Passover Chocolate Walnut
Cake

Pineapple Ice with Strawberry
Sauce

Baked Beets in Lettuce Cups

FOOD PREPARATION

1 week ahead:
- Make pineapple ice and sauce and freeze

3 days ahead:
- Cook the chicken soup

2 days ahead:
- Make the haroset, whipped yams, and gefilte fish

1 day ahead:
- Bake the beets and make the salad dressing
- Roast the brisket and make the sauce
- Bake the cake

Serving day:
- Roast the turkey and make the sauce
- Cook the asparagus and other vegetables
- Reheat dishes prepared in advance

WINE SUGGESTIONS

These wines are kosher, so serve both: Baron Herzog Chenin Blanc and Hagafen Cellars Cabernet Sauvignon.

HAROSET

This appears on the seder dish to represent the mortar used by Israelite laborers during their captivity in Egypt. Accompany it with small pieces of matzo.

Makes about 1½ cups

1 McIntosh or Golden Delicious apple, peeled, cored, and sliced

½ cup chopped walnuts

2 tablespoons cinnamon

3 tablespoons red wine

Combine all ingredients in the bowl of a processor and blend for several seconds. Add more apple, wine, or nuts if necessary to achieve a pastelike consistency.

MIRIAM'S HOMEMADE GEFILTE FISH

Served cold as an appetizer with the jellied fish stock alongside. Pass the horseradish in separate bowls.

Makes 12 to 15 pieces

3 pounds whole whitefish

2 pounds whole yellow pike

3 large onions

4 eggs

¼ cup matzo meal

½ cup cold water

1 teaspoon sugar

salt and pepper

3 carrots, sliced

1 cup prepared white or red horseradish

1. Remove the head, tail, skin, and bones from the fish, or have your fishmonger do this, and reserve.

2. Grind or finely chop the filleted fish and the onions. Add the eggs one at a time. Add the matzo meal, water, sugar, and salt and pepper. Divide the mixture into 12 to 15 portions and form into oval cakes with wet hands. Set aside.

3. In a large pot, bring 5 quarts water to boil with the fish heads, tails, bones, and skin. Boil 10 minutes. Add the fish cakes, lower the heat, and simmer, covered, for 2 hours. Add the carrot slices and simmer 1 more hour; the fish cakes will become light and fluffy.

4. Remove the fish cakes and carrots with a slotted spoon. Arrange the cakes on a large dish and place a carrot piece atop each. Cover with plastic wrap and chill.

5. Strain the fish stock into a glass dish, cover with plastic, and chill.

MIRIAM'S CHICKEN SOUP WITH MATZO BALLS

Make this soup the day before, refrigerate it, and then remove every trace of solidified fat. Reheat the clear broth and serve it piping hot.

8 Servings

1 large hen (about 5 to 6 pounds)

2 beef shoulder bones

2 carrots, coarsely chopped

1 parsnip, coarsely chopped

1 large onion, peeled and quartered

6 celery stalks, including leaves, thickly sliced

salt and pepper

Matzo Balls (see next page)

1. Combine all ingredients except matzo balls in a large soup pot and add water to cover. Bring to boil. Lower heat and simmer until the hen is tender, about 2 hours. Remove the cooked chicken and reserve for another use, such as chicken salad.

2. Strain the broth, discarding the vegetables and shoulder bones. Refrigerate until well chilled.

3. Reserve ⅓ cup of solidified fat on the surface of the broth. Discard remaining fat and reheat the broth. Transfer to individual bowls or a tureen, add the matzo balls, and serve.

MATZO BALLS

The matzo meal must be marked "kosher for Passover"; otherwise, it is forbidden for use during the holiday.

Makes 15 to 20

4 eggs, beaten

⅓ cup rendered chicken fat, melted

½ teaspoon salt

pinch of pepper

1 tablespoon chopped parsley

1 cup matzo meal

½ cup water

1. In a bowl, combine the eggs, chicken fat, salt, pepper, and parsley. Stir in matzo meal, then the water. Cover and refrigerate for several hours.

2. Dipping your hands frequently in cold water to prevent sticking, form the mixture into balls the size of walnuts. Matzo balls will expand as they cook.

3. Bring 2 quarts salted water to boil in a large saucepan. Drop in the matzo balls, cover tightly, and cook until they float to the surface, about 20 minutes. Remove with a slotted spoon.

ROAST TURKEY WITH VEGETABLE SAUCE

Cook the neck and giblets in the roasting pan with the turkey, as they will be used for making the sauce.

8 Servings

1 turkey (about 12 to 14 pounds), rinsed and dried

¼ cup margarine, melted

½ cup red wine

salt and pepper

2 onions, thickly sliced

4 celery stalks, thickly sliced

1. Preheat oven to 350°F. Place the turkey on a rack in a roasting pan and add the giblets. Combine the butter and wine and brush over the turkey inside and out, reserving some of the mixture for basting the turkey as it roasts. Salt and pepper the bird inside and out.

2. Add the onions and celery to the pan around the turkey. Pour water into the pan to a depth of about 1 inch.

3. Roast the turkey 20 minutes per pound or according to the instructions on the wrapper, basting frequently with the wine mixture.

4. Remove the cooked giblets. Pour off and degrease the juices from the roasting pan. Remove the meat from the turkey neck and coarsely chop the giblets. Combine the neck meat, giblets, vegetables, and pan juices in a food processor and puree, thinning with water if necessary. Reheat the vegetable sauce if desired and serve with the turkey.

Roast Turkey With Yams and Asparagus

ROAST BRISKET OF BEEF

Ask your butcher to give you a "first cut" of brisket.

8 to 12 Servings

6-pound lean brisket of beef

2 onions, sliced

2 carrots, sliced

½ green bell pepper, coarsely chopped

2 fresh tomatoes, peeled, seeded, and chopped

3 celery stalks

3 garlic cloves, coarsely chopped

salt and pepper

1. Preheat oven to 350°F. Place the brisket in a roasting pan and add water to come halfway up the sides of the meat. Add the vegetables and season with salt and pepper. Cover with foil and roast 1½ hours. Remove the foil and check to see if more water is needed; if so, add another cup or two.

2. Continue to roast uncovered until the meat is well browned and easily pierced with a fork, 1 to 1½ hours longer.

3. Pour off and degrease the pan juices. Combine the juices and cooked vegetables in a food processor, in batches if necessary, and puree to make the sauce. Season with salt and pepper to taste.

4. Let the brisket cool for 15 to 20 minutes. Reheat the sauce. Slice the meat and serve with the sauce.

WHIPPED YAMS

These can be made a day ahead, covered with foil, and reheated in a hot oven for 20 minutes before serving.

8 Servings

6 large yams, unpeeled

½ cup margarine

2 tablespoons firmly packed brown sugar

salt and pepper

1. Rinse the yams and place in a large saucepan. Cover with water. Bring to boil, reduce heat, and simmer until the yams are tender, about 45 minutes. Drain, cool, and peel.

2. Mash the yams, incorporating the margarine and brown sugar. Season with salt and pepper. Beat with an electric mixer until fluffy.

Asparagus and Other Vegetables

ASPARAGUS, SCALLIONS, AND GREEN BEANS WITH DILL

8 Servings

1½ pounds fresh asparagus, trimmed

2 bunches scallions, trimmed

1 pound fresh green beans, trimmed

6 tablespoons margarine, melted

2 tablespoons fresh lemon juice

2 tablespoons finely chopped fresh dill

salt and pepper

8 thin rings red or yellow bell pepper

1. Rinse the asparagus and cut into 5- to 6-inch lengths. Lay flat in a skillet, layering if necessary, and cover with water. Cook uncovered about 7 minutes. (To microwave, place the stalks in a microwave-safe dish, add ¼ cup water, cover with plastic, and cook on High for 5 minutes. Drain well and set aside.) Cook the scallions the same way as the asparagus, but for only 4 minutes. (To microwave the scallions, follow the same directions given for asparagus, but cook for only 2 minutes.)

2. Bring 1 quart salted water to boil in a saucepan. Add the beans slowly so as not to lose the boil; if you do, cover the pan just until the water resumes boiling. Cook beans uncovered until crisp-tender, 10 to 15 minutes. Drain well.

3. Combine the vegetables in a baking dish, mounding some of each at a time, juxtaposing the asparagus tips and the scallion heads so some face north and south, or east and west.

4. Combine the margarine, lemon juice, dill, and salt and pepper. Pour over the vegetables. Keep warm in a low oven. Just before serving, overlap the pepper rings on top of the vegetables.

BAKED BEETS IN LETTUCE CUPS WITH LEMON-PEPPER DRESSING

8 Servings

4 medium beets

4 medium tomatoes, cored and cut into ½-inch cubes

1 cup thinly sliced celery heart

½ cup finely chopped onion

½ cup finely chopped fresh mint

½ cup vegetable oil

juice of 2 lemons

½ teaspoon each salt and black pepper

8 to 16 inner leaves of Boston, Bibb, or leaf lettuce

1. Preheat oven to 450°F. Leave the roots on the beets; trim all but 1 inch of the tops. Do not puncture the skins. Rinse, dry, and wrap each beet in foil. Bake on the center rack for 1½ hours. Peel beets and cut into ½-inch cubes.

2. Combine beets, tomatoes, celery, onion, and mint, and toss.

3. In a small bowl, combine the oil, lemon juice, and salt and pepper. Pour over the vegetables and toss well. Adjust salt and pepper to taste; the salad should be peppery.

4. On a large platter, form cups with the lettuce leaves and spoon some of the vegetable mixture into each. This may be refrigerated for 1 to 2 hours, but bring to room temperature for 10 minutes before serving.

Seder Traditions

PASSOVER CHOCOLATE WALNUT CAKE

8 to 12 Servings

8 eggs, separated

1½ cups sugar

¼ cup orange juice

¼ cup red wine

½ cup Passover cake meal

¼ cup potato starch

2 tablespoons unsweetened cocoa powder

½ teaspoon salt

1 cup chopped walnuts

1. Beat the egg yolks well. Gradually add the sugar, beating until light and fluffy. Beat in the orange juice and wine.

2. Preheat oven to 350°F. Combine the cake meal, potato starch, cocoa, and salt. Sift onto the yolk mixture. Using clean beaters, whip the egg whites until stiff. Fold into the batter with the cocoa mixture and nuts.

3. Pour the batter into an ungreased 10-inch springform pan. Bake until a tester inserted in the center comes out clean, about 50 minutes.

4. Invert the cake onto 4 cups or mugs, positioned to support the pan by the edges. Let cool completely.

5. Turn the cake right side up and loosen from the pan with a spatula or sharp knife. Remove the side of the springform (do not remove the bottom) and place the cake on a serving plate.

PINEAPPLE ICE WITH STRAWBERRY SAUCE

Make the ice and the sauce one week ahead and freeze. Thaw the sauce before serving.

8 Servings

3¾ cups unsweetened pineapple juice

1½ cups sugar

1 tablespoon unflavored gelatin softened in ⅓ cup water

1½ tablespoons fresh lemon juice

Strawberry Sauce (see below)

16 1-inch squares fresh pineapple

1. In a nonaluminum saucepan, bring 1½ cups pineapple juice to boil. Reduce heat to low. Add the sugar and gelatin mixture and cook until both sugar and gelatin are dissolved. Remove from heat and let cool.

2. Add the lemon juice and the remaining pineapple juice. Refrigerate until well chilled. Transfer to an ice cream maker and process according to the manufacturer's directions.

3. Spoon some sauce onto individual plates. Top with a scoop of ice and 2 pieces of pineapple.

STRAWBERRY SAUCE

This will keep for two days if covered and refrigerated, longer if frozen.

Makes about 3 cups

2 12-ounce bags frozen unsweetened strawberries, thawed

½ cup sugar

¼ cup strawberry preserves

Puree all ingredients in processor and strain through fine sieve.

Easter Sunday, the celebration in honor of Christ's resurrection, is thought by many to be the world's most significant religious observance. Easter has no fixed date, but for the last 1600 years it has been celebrated on the first Sunday following the full moon that appears on or after the spring equinox, about March 21. Therefore, Easter can be celebrated between March 22 and April 25, a spread of 35 days. In spite of repeated attempts, consensus has never been achieved on fixing a single date for the holiday.

Brightly colored and intricately patterned eggs have become symbols of Eastertime. They represent resurrection, for they hold the seeds of new life. Medieval English priests blessed eggs, which were then eaten "in thankfulness for the resurrection of our Lord." And in certain parts of France, abstaining from eggs at Eastertime meant that one would be bitten by a snake sometime during the year. Eggs were colored in ancient times by the peoples around the Mediterranean—some say in anticipation of spring colors, other to imitate the colors of the aurora borealis. The Christians in the Catacombs colored them red for the blood of Christ and his resurrection.

It was the Germans who invented the idea of the Easter bunny; since rabbits are the most prolific of animals, it made sense that they would represent fertility. Some French children were told that the hare had to go to Rome for its eggs; others were taught that eggs were brought not by rabbits but by bells, which flew to Rome after Mass on Holy Thursday, fetched the eggs, and dropped them into the children's homes on their return. As no Mass is held and no bells are rung between Holy Thursday and Easter Sunday, it seemed a reasonable assumption that the bells were away fulfilling this task.

Easter Sunday

DINNER MENU FOR 8

LEMON-PEPPERED MUSHROOM
SALAD

HERBED ROAST LEG OF LAMB

JERUSALEM ARTICHOKE AND RED
BELL PEPPER CONDIMENT

GRILLED ONION CUSTARD WITH
GREEN PEPPER STRIPS

ASPARAGUS WITH DIJON
VINAIGRETTE

EASTER RICOTTA PIE IN
ORANGE-FLAVORED CRUST

Herbed Roast Leg of Lamb

FOOD PREPARATION

1 day ahead:
- Make Jerusalem artichoke condiment
- Bake ricotta pie

Serving day:
- Roast the lamb
- Make onion custard, asparagus, and mushroom salad

WINE SUGGESTIONS

A French red bordeaux is the traditional complement to lamb. Serve Barton & Guestier Merlot de Bordeaux, an ideal soft varietal to accompany the classic flavors here.

LEMON-PEPPERED MUSHROOM SALAD

8 Servings

1 pound fresh mushrooms, wiped clean and sliced as thinly as possible

2 tablespoons fresh lemon juice

¼ cup finely chopped parsley

¼ cup olive oil

juice of 2 lemons

salt and freshly ground pepper

8 Bibb lettuce or curly endive leaves, rinsed and dried

8 very thin Parmesan cheese shavings, about 2 x 3 inches

1. Toss the mushrooms with 2 tablespoons lemon juice. Cover and refrigerate several hours.

2. Shortly before serving, toss the mushrooms with the parsley.

3. Add the oil to the remaining lemon juice, whisking until emulsified. Season with salt and a liberal amount of pepper. Pour over the mushrooms and toss.

4. Place a lettuce leaf on each plate; divide the mushrooms among them. Top each salad with a Parmesan shaving.

HERBED ROAST LEG OF LAMB

8 Servings

1 5- to 6-pound leg of lamb

8 garlic cloves

3 tablespoons dried rosemary

1 ½ tablespoons salt

1 ½ teaspoons pepper

about ¾ cup olive oil

1. Ask the butcher to remove as much fat as he can from the lamb and to remove the skin. With a small sharp knife, cut 8 slits in the lamb.

2. Cut 2 of the garlic cloves into 4 slices each. Insert each slice into a slit in the lamb. Mince the remaining garlic.

3. Combine the minced garlic, rosemary, and salt and pepper in the bowl of a mini-processor or in a mortar. A tablespoon at a time, blend in enough olive oil (about ½ cup) to make a thick but spreadable paste.

4. Spread the paste all over the lamb and rub in well. Cover and refrigerate overnight.

5. Bring the lamb to cool room temperature. Preheat oven to 375°F. Roast the lamb for 1 hour (rare) to 1½ hours (medium rare), basting with remaining ¼ cup olive oil 3 or 4 times during roasting. Let the lamb rest for 10 minutes before slicing.

JERUSALEM ARTICHOKE AND RED BELL PEPPER CONDIMENT

Wear rubber gloves while preparing the jalapeño pepper, or be sure to wash your hands thoroughly afterward. Jerusalem artichokes are often packaged as "sunchokes."

Makes about 3 cups

1½ pounds Jerusalem artichokes

2 red bell peppers

¼ cup olive oil

¼ cup minced red onion

1 jalapeño pepper, seeded and minced

¼ finely chopped parsley

salt and pepper

1. Peel the artichokes and cut into ½-inch cubes. Place in cool water until ready to use. Seed and devein the bell peppers; cut into ½-inch pieces.

2. Pat the artichoke cubes dry. In a skillet, heat the oil and sauté the artichokes until light brown, about 6 to 8 minutes. Remove with a slotted spoon and transfer to a bowl.

3. In the same skillet, sauté the red peppers for 3 minutes. Add the onion and jalapeño and cook 3 minutes longer. Return the artichokes to the skillet and toss. Remove from heat and add the parsley, and salt and pepper. Toss well and serve.

Easter Ricotta Pie

GRILLED ONION CUSTARD WITH GREEN PEPPER STRIPS

If you will be using a barbecue grill, slice the onions ¼ to ½ inch thick. Grill directly on the oiled grid or enclose the slices in foil packets with some butter and grill for 10 to 15 minutes. Or broil them as below.

8 Servings

3 tablespoons butter

4 cups sliced white onions

1 green bell pepper, seeded, deveined, and cut into thin lengthwise strips

4 eggs

1 cup half-and-half or light cream

pinch of freshly grated nutmeg

salt and pepper

1. Preheat broiler. Spread the butter over a 15 × 10-inch jelly-roll pan. Spread the onions over the butter. Arrange the pepper strips to one side. Broil until the onions begin to color and soften. Transfer to processor bowl and puree. Let cool. Set the pepper strips aside.

2. Preheat oven to 375°F. Combine the eggs, cream or half-and-half, and salt and pepper in a bowl and whisk until well combined. Add the onion puree and adjust the seasoning. Divide the mixture among 8 well-buttered custard cups or flat-bottomed ½-cup timbales.

3. Arrange the cups in a baking pan just large enough to hold them. Pour enough hot water into the pan to reach halfway up the sides of the cups. Bake until the custard is firm and the point of a knife inserted in the center comes out clean, about 40 minutes.

4. Remove the cups from the hot water and let stand for 4 to 5 minutes, then turn custards out. Decorate each custard with 2 strips of grilled green pepper, arranged in a cross on top of the mold. Serve hot.

ASPARAGUS WITH DIJON VINAIGRETTE

8 Servings

2½ pounds fresh asparagus

lettuce leaves

1 cup vinaigrette (see page 193)

1. Snap off the lower end of each asparagus stalk at the point where it breaks naturally. Use a vegetable peeler to peel the lower part of the remaining stalk. Soak the asparagus in cool salted water for at least 30 minutes to remove grit. Drain and rinse again.

2. Stand the cleaned stalks upright in a narrow, deep vessel, such as an asparagus steamer or coffee percolator. Add boiling water to come up to the bottoms of the asparagus tips. Cover and cook just until the asparagus are tender, no more than 10 minutes; do not overcook. Drain and cool.

3. Arrange the asparagus on 8 salad plates lined with lettuce leaves. Spoon the vinaigrette over and serve.

EASTER RICOTTA PIE IN ORANGE-FLAVORED CRUST

Serve with a dollop of whipped cream if you like.

8 Servings

PASTRY

1½ cups all-purpose flour

¼ teaspoon salt

6 tablespoons cold butter, cut into ¼-inch cubes

2 tablespoons cold vegetable shortening, cut into small pieces

1 egg yolk

2 tablespoons ice water

2 tablespoons grated orange zest

FILLING

1½ pounds fresh ricotta cheese or 1½ containers (15 ounces each)

2 tablespoons grated lemon zest

¼ cup all-purpose flour

1 tablespoon vanilla extract

⅓ teaspoon salt

4 eggs

1 cup sugar

FOR THE PASTRY

1. Combine the flour, salt, butter, and shortening in a large bowl and blend with your fingertips or a pastry blender until crumbly. Alternatively, combine the flour and salt in a processor bowl and blend 2 seconds; with the motor running, add the butter and shortening through the feed tube and blend until the mixture resembles meal.

2. In a small bowl, beat the egg yolk and water. Blend into the flour mixture just until the dough pulls together, adding a little more ice water if needed. If using a processor, add the egg and water through the feed tube and blend just until the dough begins to cohere; do not overprocess. With floured hands, flatten the dough into a round. Wrap in waxed paper and refrigerate at least 30 minutes.

3. Roll the dough out on a floured surface into a 12-inch circle. Fit into a 9 x 1½-inch round cake pan or a 10-inch tart pan with removable bottom. Sprinkle the orange zest evenly over the bottom and press in lightly. Refrigerate while preparing the filling.

FOR THE FILLING

1. Preheat oven to 350°F. In a large bowl, combine the ricotta, lemon zest, flour, vanilla, and salt and blend well.

2. In another bowl, beat the eggs until foamy. Add the sugar and beat until thick and fluffy. Stir into the ricotta mixture and blend until smooth. Pour into the pastry-lined pan and bake until the filling is firm and the pastry is golden, 50 to 60 minutes.

3. Let cool for 30 minutes, then remove from the pan.

Lemon-Peppered Mushroom Salad

May 5 is not Mexico's Independence Day. It is, instead, a celebration of the day in 1862 that the Mexicans successfully opposed, though only for a short time, an invasion of their country by the French. The Mexican General Zaragosa held them off with only one-third the troops that the French had engaged.

Mexican cuisine is dominated by the indigenous foods of the Americas: corn, peppers, beans, avocados, chocolate, peanuts, potatoes, squash, tomatoes, vanilla. On the other hand, Europeans, mostly the Spanish and French, brought cattle, pigs, chickens, cheeses, citrus fruits, pastries, herbs, and spices.

When I think of Mexican food, my heart and stomach rush to that country's Bajío area, where a number of times I have made the circuit of important colonial towns—from Guanajuato to Irapuato, from Querétaro to San Miguel de Allende, to Dolores Hildalgo and back to Guanajuato.

A visit to the main market in Guanajuato is a good way to come to know the ingredients used in Mexican cuisine. The market is in a huge building with a curved ceiling of glass panes. The view of the main floor from the balcony is a vivid Rivera painting, alive with the smells of onion, cilantro, and ripe fruit. Guanajuato is one of the most beautiful colonial cities in Mexico. The city is cradled in a ravine, and buildings march up and down the sides of the surrounding mountains. Homes are painted in bright colors and soft pastels, their balconies filled with hanging plants. Most of the streets are cobbled or laid with pavement stone.

Cinco de Mayo

MENU FOR 6

MARGARITAS

GUACAMOLE

CHILI SHRIMP WITH CILANTRO
AND RED ONIONS

GREEN CHICKEN ENCHILADAS

FLAN WITH STRAWBERRIES

Margaritas

FOOD PREPARATION

This is easily prepared on the day it is to be served, except for the shrimp, which needs overnight marination. Still, there are a few things you can do ahead if you wish.

1 day ahead:
 • Cook shrimp and marinate overnight
 • Roast poblano chilies if not using canned ones
 • Make flan and prepare strawberries

Serving day:
 • Make guacamole and enchiladas

BEVERAGE SUGGESTION

Serve cold beer.

MARGARITAS

The salt-rimmed cocktail glass is considered essential by cognoscenti, but I often omit it. Also, I find it difficult to make this in batches, so I make one at a time.

1 Serving

salt (optional)

4 ounces crushed ice

2 ounces white tequila

1½ ounces fresh lime juice

1 ounce Cointreau or Triple Sec

1. If desired, dip the rim of a cocktail glass or champagne coupe into cold water, then into salt to form a ¼-inch-wide edge.

2. Combine all remaining ingredients in a blender or small food processor and blend until frothy. Pour into the glass and serve immediately.

GUACAMOLE

The quality and ripeness of the avocado in this dish are important. Use the smaller dark green avocados labeled Hass. They should be ripe (soft to the touch), and may have to be left at room temperature to ripen at home for several days. Serve the guacamole with crisp tortilla chips.

Makes about 2 cups

2 tablespoons fresh lemon juice

2 garlic cloves, minced

½ teaspoon salt

4 or 5 dashes hot pepper sauce

¼ cup finely chopped onion

2 avocados, pitted and mashed

1. Combine the lemon juice, garlic, salt, hot sauce, and onion in a small bowl and let stand for 10 to 15 minutes for the flavors to develop.

2. Coarsely mash the avocados with a fork; do not puree. Add the garlic mixture to the avocado and blend thoroughly. Cover tightly and chill.

CHILI SHRIMP WITH CILANTRO AND RED ONIONS

6 Servings

1½ pounds uncooked medium shrimp, peeled and deveined

¾ cup olive oil

⅓ cup white wine vinegar

3 tablespoons fresh lemon juice

2 tablespoons Dijon-style mustard

1½ tablespoons tomato puree

2 teaspoons chili powder

salt and pepper

1 red onion, thinly sliced into rings

¼ cup finely chopped cilantro

1. Drop the shrimp into a large pot of boiling water and cook just until light pink, about 4 minutes (they will marinate overnight and the vinegar and lemon juice will "cook" them further). Rinse in cool water and pat dry. Place the shrimp in a shallow glass dish.

2. Combine the oil, vinegar, lemon juice, mustard, tomato puree, chili powder, and salt and pepper until well blended. Pour over the shrimp and toss well. Cover with plastic wrap and refrigerate overnight.

3. Arrange the shrimp and marinade on a serving plate. Place the onion rings on top and sprinkle the cilantro over all. Serve chilled.

GREEN CHICKEN ENCHILADAS

Poblanos are green chilies, which must be roasted and peeled before use (see page 193). They are available in cans already roasted and peeled. Do not substitute green bell peppers, which taste quite different. Tomatillos are small green tomato-like fruits with papery husks. They are available in most supermarkets, fresh or canned. Do not use regular green tomatoes.

6 Servings

3 cups chopped cooked chicken

¼ cup chicken stock or broth

5 poblano chilies, roasted and peeled, or canned whole green chilies

1 jalapeño pepper, seeded and coarsely chopped

1 can (13 ounces) tomatillos, drained

2 large garlic cloves, minced

¼ cup cilantro leaves

salt

1 cup heavy cream

1 egg

vegetable oil

12 corn tortillas

½ cup sour cream, whisked

1. Place the chicken in a saucepan or skillet. Add the chicken stock and keep warm over low heat.

2. Combine the poblanos, jalapeño, tomatillos, garlic, and cilantro in the bowl of a processor and puree. Add salt to taste. Transfer to a skillet.

3. Beat the cream with the egg until blended. Add to the puree. Place over low heat to keep warm.

4. Heat a little oil in a skillet and briefly fry one tortilla to soften. Dip one side of the tortilla in the puree. Spoon some chicken onto the coated side. Roll up tightly and place in a baking dish just large enough to fit 12 enchiladas. Repeat with the remaining tortillas, puree, and chicken.

5. Preheat oven to 350°F. Pour the remaining puree over the enchiladas. Bake until the enchiladas are heated through, about 15 minutes.

6. Drizzle the sour cream over the enchiladas and serve hot.

Chili Shrimp With Onions

FLAN WITH STRAWBERRIES

6 Servings

1 pint fresh strawberries

1 ½ cups sugar

3 cups milk

4 eggs

¼ teaspoon salt

1 teaspoon vanilla extract

½ cup heavy cream, whipped

1. Rinse and hull the berries. Slice them into a bowl and sprinkle with 2 tablespoons of the sugar. Toss well. Cover with plastic and refrigerate until ready to serve.

2. Measure ½ cup sugar and reserve. Place the remainder of the sugar in a saucepan and melt over low heat until it becomes amber and syrupy. Quickly pour the syrup into a 9-inch glass or ceramic baking dish, tilting it so the syrup covers the bottom.

3. Preheat oven to 350°F. Scald the milk. Meanwhile, beat the eggs with the reserved ½ cup sugar until light and thick. Slowly beat in the warm milk. Add the salt and vanilla. Pour this mixture into the baking dish. Set the dish into a larger pan and add warm water to the outer pan to come halfway up the sides of the dish. Cover the flan with foil. Bake until a knife inserted in the center of the flan comes out clean, 1 hour or longer, removing the foil after 45 minutes. Remove from the water bath and refrigerate for several hours.

4. Run a knife around the outer edge of the flan. Invert a plate over the flan and unmold it. To serve, spoon the flan onto individual plates, add some strawberries to the side, and top with a dollop of whipped cream.

Liz Ducas Bonham, who lives in Wiltshire, England, tells me that England observed Mother's Day long before we did in America. On "Mothering Sunday," young household workers who earned their living in towns distant from their homes returned home to visit their churches and mothers. Such visits were especially popular in Gloucestershire. It was customary in the 18th and 19th centuries for the firstborn son to bring "mothering cake," usually a rich, heavily decorated fruitcake, which the family enjoyed together.

In America, Mother's Day was first officially celebrated in 1914. In practice, however, Mother's Day was observed as early as 1908 in Philadelphia and in Grafton, West Virginia. It was at this time that the practice of wearing white and red carnations took hold. White was worn if one's mother was deceased, red if she was living.

From this point on, Mother's Day observances spread all over the country. Although the celebration has been commercialized, the fact remains that it is still a moving observance for mothers and their children. Usually this day in May is sunny, with forsythia beginning to bloom and tulips showing their heads. The sun streaming in is especially uplifting as it highlights the spring flowers on the table.

Mother's Day

MENU FOR 6

SPRINGTIME ASPARAGUS TART

GRILLED SALMON WITH
CHARDONNAY BUTTER,
MUSHROOMS, AND LEEKS

BOW-TIED VEGETABLE BUNDLES
WITH VINAIGRETTE

GRAND MARNIER CAKE

OJOS DE SUEGRA
(MOTHER-IN-LAW'S EYES)

Asparagus Tart

FOOD PREPARATION

Most experienced cooks can prepare this meal on the day it is to be served, but many steps can be done ahead of time.

3 or 4 days ahead:
- Make the cake, cover tightly with plastic, and refrigerate. Bring to room temperature before serving.
- Make mother-in-law's eyes. Place in a covered tin or other container lined with waxed paper or paper doilies.

1 day ahead:
- Prepare vegetable bundles to the point of dressing, wrap securely, and refrigerate
- Mix salad dressing but do not add until 1 to 2 hours before serving
- Bone the salmon; prepare vegetables for cooking and refrigerate in plastic bags

Serving day:
- Make asparagus tart
- Cook salmon, leeks, and mushrooms
- Sauce vegetables bundles

WINE SUGGESTION

Serve Swanson Napa Valley Chardonnay throughout the meal.

SPRINGTIME ASPARAGUS TART

This is made with phyllo pastry, which is now available frozen in most markets. Phyllo dries out quickly, so you should work fast once it is out of the refrigerator. If you are lucky enough to live near a Greek bakery, buy the pastry leaves fresh there. In Manhattan, excellent phyllo is available from the Poseidon Pastry Shop at 629 Ninth Avenue.

6 Servings

24 asparagus stalks

1 cup low-fat yogurt

1 cup part-skim ricotta cheese

2 eggs, lightly beaten

½ cup finely chopped onion

¼ cup chopped parsley

1 teaspoon grated orange zest

generous pinch of freshly grated nutmeg

salt and pepper

7 phyllo sheets

¼ cup butter, melted

¼ cup freshly grated Parmesan cheese

1. Snap off the bottoms of the asparagus stalks, leaving a tip at least 4 inches long. Peel with a vegetable peeler. Cook the asparagus in boiling salted water until barely tender; do not overcook. Cut the spears into 4-inch lengths, including the tips. From leftover pieces, cut enough thin slices to make 1 to 1 ½ cups. Set aside.

2. In a large bowl, combine the yogurt, ricotta, eggs, asparagus slices, onion, parsley, orange zest, nutmeg, and salt and pepper. Mix well and set aside.

3. Brush one sheet of phyllo with butter and lay lengthwise in an 8 × 11-inch baking pan. Repeat with a second sheet. Butter 2 more sheets and lay across the width of the pan, perpendicular to the first two. Butter 2 more sheets and lay lengthwise in the pan. (The phyllo will overlap the sides of the pan.) Add the filling, spreading evenly. Fold over the ends of the phyllo to cover. Butter the last phyllo sheet and fold in half crosswise. Lay it on top of the filled tart. Brush the top with the remaining butter.

4. Preheat oven to 375°F. Sprinkle about half the Parmesan over the top phyllo sheet. Bake until the filling is firm and the top is golden, 35 to 40 minutes. Arrange the asparagus spears side by side down one long side of the pan, with the flower tips pointing inward. Repeat along the other side, tips pointing inward. Sprinkle with the remaining Parmesan. Return to the oven for 5 minutes, or pass the tart quickly under the broiler to lightly brown the cheese. Let the tart cool about 5 minutes before cutting and serving.

GRILLED SALMON WITH CHARDONNAY BUTTER, MUSHROOMS, AND LEEKS

Buy a side of salmon, or two if needed, with the skin on. Before cooking, run your hand gently over the salmon and you will feel the bones; use tweezers or needle-nose pliers to pull them out. Cut the side of salmon into six pieces, about 2 inches wide and 1 inch thick at the center. Each piece should be about 6 to 8 ounces. Reserve the end pieces for another use.

6 Servings

6 salmon fillet pieces, as above

3 tablespoons olive oil

pepper

2 tablespoons chopped fresh tarragon or 1 teaspoon dried

2 cups Chardonnay

1 cup (2 sticks) butter, cut into 1-tablespoon pieces

salt

½ pound fresh cremini, shiitake, porcini, or chanterelle mushrooms, cleaned with a towel or soft brush, cut in halves or quarters depending on size

4 medium to large leeks, most of green part removed, washed thoroughly

1. Coat the salmon pieces with olive oil. Season with pepper and half of the tarragon. Cover and refrigerate for several hours. Bring the salmon to room temperature before cooking.

2. Boil the wine in a large saucepan until reduced to ⅓ to ½ cup. Over medium heat, whisk in 12 tablespoons butter, 1 tablespoon at a time. Season with salt and pepper.

3. In a large skillet, heat 2 tablespoons butter. Add the mushrooms and sauté until lightly browned and juices have evaporated. Season with salt, pepper, and the remaining tarragon. Set aside and keep warm.

4. Prepare grill or heat broiler. Cut the leeks in quarters or halves lengthwise, depending on thickness. Coat with the remaining butter. Grill or broil the leeks until browned and tender but not mushy. Set aside. Then grill or broil the salmon, about 3 minutes per side over hot coals or 5 to 7 minutes under the broiler, 4 inches from the heat source.

5. Spoon some of the sauce on each of 6 warm plates and lay a salmon fillet on top. Arrange grilled leeks alongside the fish. Spoon the mushrooms slightly over the salmon, toward the other side of the plate. Serve immediately.

BOW-TIED VEGETABLE BUNDLES WITH VINAIGRETTE

These are to be served with the main course but on a separate plate. Please do not put them on the same dish as the fish; the sauces will run into each other. The ingredients below will make 12 bundles. If you wish, cut the recipe in half to make one bundle per person.

6 Servings

1 large red bell pepper

12 snow peas

2 celery stalks

2 small zucchini

24 green beans

2 carrots

4 scallions

vinaigrette (see page 193)

1. Cut the pepper into ¼-inch-thick strips, then into 2 ½-inch lengths. Place in a bowl of ice water and set aside.

2. Cut the snow peas and celery stalks into ¼ × 2 ½-inch strips. Add to the ice water.

3. Scrub but do not peel the zucchini; trim the ends. Cut into strips the same size as the other vegetables, discarding seedy centers. Steam until barely tender. Transfer to the bowl with the other vegetables.

4. Cut the green beans and carrots into strips to match the other vegetables. Steam each until tender. Add to the ice water.

5. Drain all vegetables and pat dry. Place in a shallow dish. Pour half the vinaigrette over and toss lightly. Let marinate for 2 to 3 hours.

6. Trim the scallions and carefully separate leaves, keeping them as long as possible (each leaf must be long enough to wrap a 1-inch-thick bundle of vegetables). Drop the raw leaves into a large skillet of boiling water. Immediately turn off heat and transfer the leaves to a towel to dry.

7. Place one scallion leaf on a work surface. Over it arrange a variety of vegetables to make a bundle about 1 inch in diameter. Wrap the bundle with the scallion leaf, tying carefully. Arrange in a shallow dish. When all the bundles are assembled, pour more dressing over them. Cover and refrigerate but bring to room temperature before serving.

Grilled Salmon With Leeks

GRAND MARNIER CAKE

This cake will keep in the refrigerator for about a week if well wrapped. Serve it with a dollop of whipped cream and a thin slice of orange as garnish.

12 Servings

CAKE

1 cup (2 sticks) butter, room temperature

1 cup sugar

4 eggs, separated, at room temperature

1 cup sour cream

2 tablespoons minced orange zest

2 cups all-purpose flour

1 teaspoon baking powder

1 teaspoon baking soda

Grand Marnier Syrup (see below)

GRAND MARNIER SYRUP

⅓ cup Grand Marnier or other orange liqueur

juice of 1 orange

juice of 2 lemons

¾ cup sugar

pinch of salt

FOR THE CAKE

1. Cream the butter and sugar until well blended. Add the egg yolks, sour cream, and orange zest and beat until the batter is light and fluffy and a ribbon forms when the beaters are raised.

2. Preheat oven to 325°F. Grease and flour a 9-inch tube pan. Sift the flour, baking powder, and soda into a large bowl. Stir into the butter mixture. Using clean beaters, beat the egg whites until stiff but not dry; fold into the mixture.

3. Pour batter into the prepared pan. Bake until a tester inserted in center comes out clean, about 1 hour. Remove and let cool for 15 minutes. When the pan is cool enough to handle, very carefully loosen the cake around the edge with a sharp knife and invert onto a plate. Drizzle hot syrup over the warm cake, letting it soak in.

FOR THE SYRUP

In a small nonaluminum saucepan, combine all ingredients and bring to boil. Lower heat and simmer until the sugar is dissolved and the liquid is syrupy, about 5 minutes.

OJOS DE SUEGRA (MOTHER-IN-LAW'S EYES)

My friend Bobby Hilguera, who lives in Buenos Aires, tells me that these are served as a party sweetmeat there. It seems appropriate to include them as an extra on Mother's Day. They may be made days ahead and stored in a tightly covered container.

Makes 18

½ pound purchased marzipan or almond paste, room temperature

18 large pitted prunes or dates

¼ cup ground Brazil nuts or walnuts

¼ cup sugar

1. Knead the marzipan until pliable. Stuff the prunes or dates with it.

2. Combine the ground nuts and sugar. Roll each stuffed fruit in the nut mixture to cover. Arrange on a decorative plate and cover with plastic until ready to serve.

Grand Marnier Cake

Memorial Day is a legal holiday in every state except Texas. In some southern states, Confederate Day may also be celebrated. There's an appealing story about the creation of Memorial Day. Right after the Civil War, certain ladies in Mississippi decorated the graves of their own as well as those of the Union Army's fallen soldiers.

On May 30, 1868, the national commander of the Union's veterans organization issued an order that this day be observed "for the purpose of strewing with flowers or otherwise decorating the graves of the comrades who died in defense of their country." The idea became popular across the country; New York State was the first to make the day a legal holiday in 1873. A memorial day is also observed in Puerto Rico, Holland, Luxembourg, Italy, France, the Philippines, the South Pacific islands, and elsewhere.

Between wars, we seem to forget the heroism and sacrifice of many of our fellow countrymen; perhaps this long weekend has lost much of its meaning. Yet the mere existence of Memorial Day emphasizes the freedom we enjoy, made possible by those men and women who sacrificed to make it so. We think of the holiday weekend as a time of rest—or of doing chores to prepare for the upcoming summer and an opportunity for the first big cookout.

Memorial Day

SUPPER MENU FOR 10

ROSEMARY-ROASTED PECANS

KEY WEST PORK TENDERLOINS
WITH SOUR CREAM JALAPEÑO
SAUCE

RAGOUT OF BLACK BEANS,
EGGPLANT, ZUCCHINI, AND
TOMATOES

ARUGULA AND FENNEL SALAD

KEY LIME PIE

Memorial Day Supper

FOOD PREPARATION

1 day ahead:
- Marinate pork and prepare ragout
- Make sauces for pork and salad
- Make pie

Serving day:
- Roast pecans
- Prepare salad and refrigerate in plastic bags until needed
- Bring sauces to room temperature. Reheat ragout. Grill or broil pork.

WINE SUGGESTIONS

The pungent, spicy soft flavors of the Sirah are a perfect complement to the pork, jalapeño sauce, and spicy vegetables. Serve California Petit Sirah or Châteauneuf du Pape.

ROSEMARY-ROASTED PECANS

Makes 4 cups

¼ cup butter

1 tablespoon dried rosemary, crushed

1 teaspoon salt or more to taste

¾ teaspoon cayenne pepper

4 cups pecan halves

1. Preheat oven to 350°F. Melt the butter in the preheating oven in a jelly-roll pan or a large pie plate.

2. Combine all remaining ingredients. Add to the butter and toss to coat. Bake until the nuts are lightly browned, about 10 minutes. Let cool. Store in an airtight container or in the freezer.

Pork and Black Bean Ragout

KEY WEST PORK TENDERLOINS WITH SOUR CREAM JALAPEÑO SAUCE

If outdoor grilling isn't convenient, these may be broiled about 5 inches below the heat source, or roasted in a preheated 350°F oven for about 20 minutes.

10 Servings

4 pounds pork tenderloins

¼ cup jalapeño jelly, melted

2 tablespoons Oriental sesame oil

2 tablespoons olive oil

4 garlic cloves, minced

4 dashes Tabasco or other hot pepper sauce

salt

Sour Cream Jalapeño Sauce (see below)

1. Remove any excess fat from the tenderloins. Wipe the meat with paper towels and place in a glass or ceramic container.

2. Combine the jelly, oils, garlic, and Tabasco. Pour over the meat and turn to coat all sides. Cover with plastic wrap and refrigerate several hours or overnight. Bring to cool room temperature before grilling.

3. Prepare the barbecue. Season the tenderloins with salt. Grill until pink on the inside, about 5 minutes per side depending on heat. Let stand about 5 minutes, then slice diagonally and serve with a spoonful of sauce.

SOUR CREAM JALAPEÑO SAUCE
Makes 1¼ cups

1 cup sour cream

¼ cup jalapeño jelly

salt and pepper

Combine all ingredients and stir until the jelly is thinly streaked throughout the cream. Cover and refrigerate until ready to use.

RAGOUT OF BLACK BEANS, EGGPLANT, ZUCCHINI, AND TOMATOES

This is a very flavorful, easy-to-prepare dish. It will last for about a week in the refrigerator.

10 to 16 Servings

¼ cup vegetable oil

1 medium eggplant (about 1 pound), cut into ½-inch cubes

1 medium-size red bell pepper, seeded and cut into ½-inch squares

4 jalapeño peppers, seeded and cut into ¼-inch squares

1 large onion, cut into ½-inch pieces

6 large garlic cloves, minced

2 rounded tablespoons ground cumin

3 small zucchini, cut into ½-inch cubes

4 cans (16 ounces each) black beans, thoroughly rinsed and drained

1 can (28 ounces) plum tomatoes, put through food mill

¼ cup chopped parsley

juice of 1 lemon or lime

salt

1. Heat the oil in a large saucepan and sauté the eggplant, red pepper, jalapeños, and onion for 10 minutes, stirring frequently.

2. Add the garlic and sauté 1 minute. Add the cumin and zucchini and sauté 5 minutes.

3. Add the beans and tomatoes, cover and simmer for 10 minutes, stirring several times.

4. Add the parsley, lemon juice, and salt to taste. Serve hot.

ARUGULA AND FENNEL SALAD

Prepare the fennel and arugula ahead of time and refrigerate them in a plastic bag.

10 Servings

3 tablespoons fresh lemon juice

1 teaspoon grated lemon zest

salt and pepper

½ cup plus 2 tablespoons olive oil

1 large fennel bulb, thinly sliced and dried

2 to 3 bunches arugula, rinsed and dried

1. Combine the lemon juice, zest, and salt and pepper in a bowl. Slowly add the oil, whisking until emulsified. Keep at room temperature until ready to dress the salad.

2. Place the fennel and arugula in a large bowl. Add the dressing, toss well, and serve.

Key Lime Pie

KEY LIME PIE

Key limes are difficult to find except in south Florida, so feel free to substitute bottled Key lime juice or the juice of fresh regular limes.

10 Servings

4 eggs, separated

1 can (14 ounces) sweetened condensed milk

½ cup Key lime juice

2 teaspoons grated lime zest

1 9-inch pastry shell, baked and cooled

½ teaspoon cream of tartar

⅓ cup sugar

1. Preheat oven to 350°F. Whisk the yolks and stir in the condensed milk. Fold in the lime juice and zest.

2. Stiffly beat 1 egg white and fold into the lime mixture. Transfer to pie shell.

3. Beat the remaining egg whites with cream of tartar until frothy. Add sugar 1 tablespoon at a time, beating until stiff but not dry. Spread on top of pie.

4. Bake until the meringue is golden brown, about 20 minutes. Cool and chill before serving.

The rose is the official flower for Father's Day. As with Mother's Day carnations, a red rose is the celebration of a living father; a white rose is to remember one who has passed away. Father's Day has been observed nationally since 1924, when President Coolidge officially placed it on the third Sunday in June.

I remember my father with a white rose. And I remember him for many other things, one being a recipe for pasta with an Oriental accent. My father cooked this dish religiously and swore it was an ancestral recipe. I used to accuse him of having invented it, for he was born in old New York on Mott Street, which quietly divides Little Italy from Chinatown. On my visits to either neighborhood, I almost always stroll down Mott Street; although the building in which my father was born was torn down a long time ago, I still derive a sense of roots from the visit.

I don't wait until Father's Day arrives to cook this pasta. It's easy to prepare as a versatile appetizer or a main course. I'm including it here as an alternative for the littleneck clams, and also as a way to say "Happy Father's Day" to all other dads.

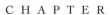

Father's Day

MENU FOR 6

SAVORY BROILED LITTLENECK
CLAMS *OR* PASTA WITH GINGER
AND GARLIC

"BARBECUED" SPARERIBS

CAROLINE'S BAKED ONIONS WITH
BALSAMIC VINEGAR

HAZELNUT CHEESECAKE

Pasta and Clams

FOOD PREPARATION

This meal can easily be prepared on the day it is to be served, except for the cheesecake; make that one or two days before. The pasta can also be made ahead; some people prefer it at room temperature.

Many markets now sell cleaned, prepared, ready-to-cook clams, oysters, and mussels; if you can find them, use them. Otherwise, you will have to buy them one day ahead. Scrub the clams with a stiff brush and soak them in salted cool water for about 3 hours. Then wash each clam separately under cold running water. Discard any that are broken or open. Shuck the clams and reserve the juice. Refrigerate.

WINE SUGGESTIONS

Serve any good California Cabernet Sauvignon, such as Domaine Michel, Arrowood, or Jordan throughout the meal.

SAVORY BROILED LITTLENECK CLAMS

6 Servings

36 littleneck clams

5 tablespoons fresh lemon juice

4 large garlic cloves, minced

¼ cup minced shallots

2 celery stalks, including leaves, finely chopped

3 tablespoons finely chopped parsley

1 carrot, minced

6 tablespoons olive oil

⅔ cup fresh breadcrumbs

salt and pepper

1. Preheat broiler. Set the cleaned clams on a broiling tray. Sprinkle with lemon juice.

2. Combine all remaining ingredients, including any reserved clam juice, and toss lightly. Top each clam with some of this mixture. Broil until lightly browned, about 3 to 5 minutes. Serve right away.

Spareribs With Baked Onions

PASTA WITH GINGER AND GARLIC

6 Servings

½ cup olive oil

½ cup finely diced carrot

1 tablespoon finely chopped garlic

2 tablespoons finely chopped fresh ginger

2 tablespoons finely chopped scallions

1 teaspoon dried oregano

salt

¼ to ½ teaspoon dried red pepper flakes

½ cup dry vermouth

1 cup water

1 pound pasta, such as vermicelli, spaghettini, or spaghetti

¼ cup butter

freshly grated Parmesan cheese

1. Bring a large pot of water to boil for the pasta. Meanwhile, heat the oil in a large skillet and sauté the carrot for 3 minutes, stirring a couple of times. Add the garlic, ginger, scallion, oregano, salt, pepper flakes, and vermouth and cook about 5 minutes.

2. Add 1 cup water and bring to boil. Lower the heat and simmer 8 to 10 minutes.

3. Cook the pasta in boiling salted water until al dente and return to the pan in which it cooked. Add the butter and stir until pasta is coated. Add to the sauce in the skillet and toss gently for 2 minutes. Serve with Parmesan on the side or on top of the pasta.

"BARBECUED" SPARERIBS

These ribs may be spit-roasted rather than baked. Thread the spit over every other rib and secure with prongs. Roast 6 inches above the heat source for about 50 minutes, basting every 5 to 10 minutes to keep the ribs from drying out. If the ribs are spit-roasted, it's especially important to remove excess fat to avoid flareups.

6 Servings

¼ cup vegetable oil

2 medium onions, finely chopped

2 garlic cloves, minced

1 can (16 ounces) tomatoes, with liquid, chopped

1 cup canned tomato puree

¼ cup honey

2 tablespoons dry mustard

2 tablespoons red wine vinegar

½ teaspoon red pepper flakes

salt

5 pounds spareribs, trimmed of fat

1. Heat the oil in a large skillet. Add the onions and cook until soft, about 4 minutes; do not brown. Add the garlic and cook a minute longer. Add the tomatoes and liquid, tomato puree, honey, dry mustard, vinegar, pepper flakes, and salt and bring to boil. Lower the heat and simmer until sauce thickly coats a spoon.

2. Place the ribs on a rack, fat side up, in one or more large roasting pans. Baste both sides with the sauce. Bake until browned and crisped, about 1 hour, basting with the sauce every 10 minutes or so. Let stand for 5 minutes before cutting and serving.

CAROLINE'S BAKED ONIONS WITH BALSAMIC VINEGAR

Caroline Rennolds Milbank, author of *Couture: The Great Designers*, a handsome book detailing the evolution of American fashion design, cooked these at a dinner for her father. I was there that evening and found them simply delicious. The onions go perfectly with the spareribs.

6 Servings

12 small to medium white onions, peeled

2 tablespoons olive oil

2 tablespoons balsamic vinegar

salt and pepper

Preheat oven to 350°F. Arrange the onions on a sheet of heavy-duty foil large enough to form a packet around them. Sprinkle with the oil, vinegar, and salt and pepper. Enclose the onions in the foil, sealing the edges tightly. Bake 1 hour without opening the packet. Serve hot.

HAZELNUT CHEESECAKE

If refrigerated, this cheesecake will keep for six or seven days.

12 Servings
CRUST

1 ½ cups finely ground vanilla wafer crumbs

¾ cup husked, toasted, and ground hazelnuts

2 tablespoons sugar

2 tablespoons butter, melted

1. In a bowl, combine the crumbs, hazelnuts, sugar, and butter and blend thoroughly. Pat the mixture into the bottom and sides of an 8-inch springform pan. Refrigerate to firm crust, about 30 minutes.

2. Preheat oven to 300°F. Bake the crust for 15 minutes. Cool thoroughly.

FILLING

3 packages (8 ounces each) cream cheese, at room temperature

1 cup plus 2 tablespoons sugar

3 eggs, lightly beaten

3 tablespoons crème de cacao

1 pint sour cream

1 whole hazelnut

1. Preheat oven to 350°F. In the large bowl of an electric mixer, beat cream cheese at low speed until smooth. Beat in 1 cup sugar a little at a time. Add the eggs and crème de cacao and beat until blended, stopping once to scrape down sides of bowl. Pour the mixture into the cooled crust and bake until set, 45 to 50 minutes. Cool slightly (do not turn off oven).

2. In a small bowl, combine the sour cream and 2 tablespoons sugar and blend well. With the aid of a rubber spatula, spread the mixture over the cheesecake to within ½ inch of the edge. Bake 5 minutes.

3. Preheat the broiler. Run the cake under the broiler, watching carefully, until the top is lightly browned, about 1 to 2 minutes. Let cool. Refrigerate for 5 hours or overnight. Remove the sides of the springform pan and place the single hazelnut in the center of the cheesecake before serving.

Hazelnut Cheesecake

Independence Day in the United States celebrates the Continental Congress' adoption of the Declaration of Independence on July 4, 1776. It is a legal holiday in every state. Picnics, cookouts, barbecues, lawn events, and parties of every description are planned all over the country. Meals are planned not just for the day but for the weekend.

In America, beef has always meant hearty eating. Grazing cattle make up an American portrait. The robust flavor and firm texture of beef satisfy like no other food, and this, perhaps, is why the hamburger is an all-American favorite that's perfect for the Fourth of July celebration cookout. Other classic American images include fields of corn, tomato, and zucchini plants, and rows of strawberries, grown in countless backyard gardens. These foods, now inseparable from American cuisine, make up the holiday menu.

Fourth of July

MENU FOR 8

BURGERS WITH SHALLOT SAUCE

GRILLED BREAD SLICES

ZUCCHINI PUDDING

GRILLED FRESH CORN WITH
BASIL BUTTER

ESCAROLE AND TOMATO SALAD
WITH PARMESAN SHAVINGS

RED AND BLUE BERRIES WITH
WHITE WINE SABAYON

Burger, Corn, and Zucchini

FOOD PREPARATION

This simple meal can be prepared on the day it is to be served. But there are a few things one can do ahead.

1 day ahead:
- Make shallot sauce
- Rinse and dry escarole and refrigerate in plastic bags. Make salad dressing.
- Make white wine sabayon; cover and refrigerate
- Rinse, sort, and drain berries; cover and refrigerate

WINE/BEVERAGE SUGGESTIONS

Serve Arrowood Vineyards, Jordan, or Beaulieu Vineyards Cabernet Sauvignon, or beer.

BURGERS WITH SHALLOT SAUCE

8 Servings

3 pounds ground chuck or sirloin

¼ pound prosciutto or 2 ounces Virginia or Smithfield ham, very thinly sliced

pepper

3 tablespoons light soy sauce

butter (optional; for skillet cooking)

Shallot Sauce (see below)

1. Prepare barbecue or preheat broiler (or see step 2 if you prefer to cook the burgers in a skillet). Place the ground meat in a large mixing bowl. Cut the prosciutto or ham into ½-inch squares (have the meat chilled for easiest cutting). Add to the beef. Season liberally with pepper. Mix lightly with your hands; do not pack the meat. Divide the mixture into 8 pieces and shape lightly into patties. Sprinkle both sides with soy sauce.

2. Grill or broil the burgers 4 to 5 minutes per side. Alternatively, these may be cooked in a skillet. Heat 2 tablespoons butter and sear 4 burgers on both sides over high heat. Transfer to a serving platter and sear the remaining burgers, adding a little more butter if needed.

3. Pour the shallot sauce over and serve.

SHALLOT SAUCE
Makes about ¾ cup

¼ cup butter

2 tablespoons minced fresh thyme

2 shallots, minced

2 tablespoons balsamic vinegar

¼ cup brandy (optional)

¼ cup olive oil

salt and pepper

1. In a skillet, melt the butter. Add the thyme and shallots and cook 1 minute.

2. Whisk in the vinegar, brandy, and oil and bring to boil. Lower heat and simmer 3 minutes. Season with salt and pepper to taste. Serve warm or at room temperature.

GRILLED BREAD SLICES

A slice is especially delicious under a hamburger. If you prefer, serve in a napkin-lined basket.

8 Servings

8 to 16 large slices Italian country-style or sourdough bread

olive oil

3 large garlic cloves, halved

Grill or broil the bread slices on each side just until golden. Brush lightly with olive oil. Rub one side of each slice with the cut side of a garlic clove.

ZUCCHINI PUDDING

8 Servings

4 medium zucchini

1 tablespoon salt

1 jalapeño pepper, seeded and finely chopped

¼ cup chopped fresh basil

3 eggs (room temperature), beaten

¼ cup all-purpose flour

2 tablespoons butter, melted

2 cups half-and-half or light cream

1. Wash the zucchini and trim off the ends; do not peel. Shred on the large holes of a grater or in a food processor. (If the zucchini have large, tough seeds, remove them first.) Place the zucchini in a colander and sprinkle with the salt. Toss and let drain 30 minutes.

2. Preheat oven to 325°F. Press down on the zucchini to remove as much liquid as possible. Transfer to a bowl. Add the jalapeño and basil. Stir in the eggs, then the flour. Add the butter and half-and-half or cream.

3. Pour the mixture into a buttered 1½-quart glass or ceramic baking dish. Place this dish in a larger pan and add hot water to come halfway up the sides of the baking dish.

4. Bake for 1 hour. Serve hot.

GRILLED FRESH CORN WITH BASIL BUTTER

Grilled corn—there's nothing like it, the fresher the better. Fresh corn can also be baked, boiled, or microwaved; see right for specifics. You may use other herbs or a combination of them, and try sprinkling some lemon juice on the corn after it is cooked.

8 Servings

8 ears fresh corn, husked

softened butter

¼ cup finely chopped basil

salt and pepper

1. Prepare barbecue or preheat oven to 350°F. Place 2 ears of corn on each of 4 heavy-duty foil sheets large enough to envelop them securely.

Escarole and Tomato Salad

2. Spread 1 tablespoon butter on each ear of corn, covering all sides. Sprinkle evenly with the basil and salt and pepper. Add a few drops of water to each packet and wrap securely.

3. Place the corn packets on the grill for about 10 minutes, turning the packets 3 times so that each side faces the heat for about 2½ minutes. Or to cook in the oven, wrap each ear as above and bake for 25 minutes. Serve with additional butter and salt and pepper.

TO MICROWAVE

Prepare the corn as above but wrap ears individually in plastic instead of foil. Cook 4 ears at a time on High (100%) power for 12 to 16 minutes. Let stand, covered, for 3 minutes. If using frozen corn, cook on High (100%) power for 10 to 12 minutes. Let stand, covered, 3 minutes.

TO BOIL

Bring water to boil in a large pot. Add 1 tablespoon salt and the corn. Cook 7 minutes. Drain corn and pat dry. Add butter, basil, and salt and pepper.

ESCAROLE AND TOMATO SALAD WITH PARMESAN SHAVINGS

Make the Parmesan shavings using the large holes of a grater.

8 Servings

2 heads fresh escarole or curly endive

*4 ripe large tomatoes or
6 ripe plum tomatoes*

½ cup vinaigrette (see page 193)

salt and pepper (optional)

½ cup shaved Parmesan cheese

1. Remove the outer leaves of the escarole and endive; use only the centers, which are white, yellowish, and very pale green. Rinse under cool water, dry well, and tear into pieces. Place in a salad bowl or store in a plastic bag in the refrigerator until ready to use.

2. Blanch the tomatoes for 10 seconds in boiling water. Remove with a slotted spoon and plunge into cold water. Peel and slice into thin wedges. Add to the salad bowl with the greens.

3. Pour the dressing over the salad. Add salt and pepper if needed. Toss to coat leaves. Add the Parmesan shavings and toss lightly before serving.

RED AND BLUE BERRIES WITH WHITE WINE SABAYON

8 Servings

8 egg yolks

1⅓ cups dry white wine

⅔ cup sugar

1⅓ cups heavy cream, whipped

*4 pints mixed fresh strawberries,
raspberries, and blueberries*

1. Combine egg yolks, wine, and sugar in a nonaluminum bowl and whisk over simmering water until foamy, warm to the touch, and considerably increased in volume. Remove from over water and cool over a bowl of ice.

2. Fold the whipped cream into the cooled sabayon. Cover with plastic wrap and refrigerate for up to 24 hours.

3. Serve the sabayon in an attractive white dish set in the center of a larger white dish or platter. Arrange the berries around the sabayon and have the diners help themselves.

Red and Blue Berries for July 4th

Peter J. McGuire, the tenth child of an impoverished Irish-American family, started it all. Born in New York City in 1852, Peter went to work at the age of 11 when his father joined the Union Army. He worked long hours in various factories and was known to irritate his employers as he pleaded for an eight-hour work day.

Later, as president of the United Brotherhood of Carpenters and Joiners of America, McGuire argued that special honor should be given to the industrial spirit of the country—"the great vital force of the nation," as he called it. He proposed that the holiday be observed on the first Monday in September because it would assure good weather, and also because the date filled a vacuum between the fourth of July and Thanksgiving. And so in September 1882, New York held its first Labor Day celebration. A parade of 10,000 people marched, carrying colorful placards reading "All men are born equal"; "Agitate, educate, and organize"; and "The true remedy is organization and ballot." There were programmed speakers, dancing, and fireworks. The idea caught on; the first Labor Day had been a booming success. It was made a legal and national holiday by Congress on June 28, 1894.

Initially, the main activities were labor union parades, speeches by labor leaders, meetings with union organizers, and placards made by union sympathizers. But by the turn of the century, more emphasis was given to celebrating the holiday as a day of enjoyment and relaxation—to be spent with family and friends on porches, in backyards, or at the beaches. Today Americans think of Labor Day as the end of summer, the opening of school, and the time for more serious work in shop and office. Labor Day has become an integral part of the American way of life. Best of all, it reflects a degree of confidence and optimism in all segments of society that few countries can equal.

Labor Day

MENU FOR 12

CURRIED WALNUTS

MEDITERRANEAN VEGETABLE
TERRINE

HERB-SCENTED BUTTERFLIED
LEG OF LAMB

RAGOUT OF FOUR BEANS WITH
TOMATO PERSILLADE

BLUEBERRY SHERBET WITH
MELON BALL SPEARS

ZOE AND SOPHIE JEAN'S ITALIAN
MERINGUES

Curried Walnuts

FOOD PREPARATION

2 or more days ahead:
- Roast walnuts and freeze
- Make sherbet and meringues

1 day ahead:
- Prepare vegetable terrine
- Marinate lamb

Serving day:
- Make bean ragout
- Broil or grill lamb

The lamb is just about the perfect food for a large group. Because the leg is butterflied, some parts are thin and others are thick—so the cooked leg presents various levels of doneness, from fairly well done to medium to rare cuts. A wonderful trick is to undercook it in the broiler or on the grill and then finish it in a preheated 200°F oven for 20 to 30 minutes, so you can join family and friends at the table.

WINE SUGGESTIONS

Start with an aperitif: a Provençal white; then, a Château de Pressoc Grand Cru (St.-Emilion) with the lamb.

CURRIED WALNUTS

Make these ahead and freeze them—they are even tasty frozen.

Makes 4 cups

¼ cup butter

4 teaspoons curry powder

2 teaspoons salt

1 teaspoon cayenne pepper or several dashes Tabasco or other hot pepper sauce

4 cups walnut halves

1. Melt butter in a large skillet. Add the curry and heat until the butter begins to bubble; do not burn.

2. Add all remaining ingredients and stir-fry for several minutes until the walnuts begin to color. Drain on paper towels. Store airtight at room temperature, or freeze for longer storage.

3. Alternatively, these may be roasted. Preheat oven to 350°F. Melt the butter in a shallow roasting pan in the preheating oven. Add the curry powder and roast for a minute or two, stirring the curry into the butter. Add all remaining ingredients and toss well. Roast until the walnuts take on some color, 8 to 10 minutes.

MEDITERRANEAN VEGETABLE TERRINE

This wonderful dish can be refrigerated for several days. If you plan to do this, it is best to use a glass or ceramic terrine; a metal one will darken the collard greens. Swiss chard may be substituted for the collards.

12 Servings

16 to 20 medium to large collard greens (1 large bunch)

2 small eggplants (about 1½ pounds total)

salt

4 small zucchini

½ to ¾ cup vegetable oil

2 large onions, chopped

3 garlic cloves, minced

2 cups peeled, seeded, and diced fresh tomatoes or drained plum tomatoes (28-ounce can)

2 tablespoons chopped fresh basil or 1 teaspoon dried

2 tablespoons chopped parsley

1 teaspoon fennel seeds

pepper

2 cups fresh bread cubes or purchased croutons

4 red bell peppers, roasted, seeded, and peeled, or 1 jar (12 ounces) roasted peppers

3 eggs

½ cup milk

vinaigrette (see page 193)

1. Wash the collard greens, leaving them whole but cutting off the stems. Steam for 4 minutes; the leaves will turn bright green and become pliable. Pat dry and set aside.

2. Wash and dry the eggplants. Cut off the ends but do not peel. Cut the eggplants lengthwise into thin slices and place in a colander. Sprinkle generously with salt and let drain for 30 minutes.

3. Wash and dry zucchini. Trim the ends but do not peel. Cut lengthwise into thin slices. Add to the eggplant, salt a little more, and allow to drain. Pat the eggplant and zucchini slices dry and set aside.

4. Heat 3 tablespoons oil in a large skillet. Sauté the eggplant and zucchini until lightly browned, adding more oil as needed. Drain on paper towels.

5. Add a little more oil to the skillet as needed and sauté the onions until translucent, about 4 minutes. Add the garlic and cook 1 minute. Add the tomatoes, basil, parsley, fennel, salt, and pepper and cook until nearly all the liquid evaporates, about 10 minutes. Remove from heat.

6. Line a buttered 2-quart (13 × 5 × 3½-inch) terrine or loaf pan with the collard greens, overlapping the leaves and allowing enough overhang to completely encase the filling. Begin the filling by layering some bread cubes in the bottom. Add a layer of zucchini and eggplant and press in some bread cubes. Top with a layer of roasted peppers. Next layer in some of the tomato mixture, again pressing in some bread cubes. Repeat the layers until all the filling ingredients are used, filling in the corners of the pan with bread cubes.

7. Preheat oven to 375°F. Beat the eggs and milk in a bowl. Make knife slits in the layered vegetables to help absorb the egg mixture. Slowly and carefully pour the egg mixture over the mold. Overlap the collard leaves on top and enclose completely. Cover with a double layer of foil and secure it around the edge of the terrine. Place the terrine in a larger pan and add enough water to come halfway up the sides of the terrine. Bake for 1½ hours. Let cool 15 minutes, then turn out. Serve the terrine warm, at room temperature, or cold with the vinaigrette.

Lamb With Herbs

HERB-SCENTED BUTTERFLIED LEG OF LAMB

12 Servings

1 leg of lamb (6 to 8 pounds), butterflied

1 cup olive oil

¼ cup soy sauce

4 garlic cloves, halved

2 tablespoons each Oriental sesame oil, balsamic vinegar, and chopped fresh or preserved ginger

2 tablespoons each chopped fresh rosemary, oregano, and thyme, or 1 teaspoon each dried

2 teaspoons pepper

1. Ask your butcher to butterfly the leg of lamb and to remove as much fat as he can, including the thin silvery membrane that envelops the leg. At home, wipe the leg with damp paper towels and remove any additional fat.

2. Combine all remaining ingredients in a food processor and blend until the herbs and garlic are minced. Place the lamb in a nonaluminum roasting pan and pour the marinade over. Turn to coat all sides. Cover with plastic wrap and refrigerate overnight or, if you have time, for 2 nights, turning occasionally. Remove from the refrigerator 1 hour before cooking.

3. This may be either broiled or grilled. If broiling, preheat the broiler and set the rack 5 to 6 inches below the heat source. Broil about 15 minutes per side, basting frequently with marinade. If grilling, cook the lamb on an oiled grid about 5 inches over the coals for 12 to 14 minutes on each side, basting frequently. Let stand for about 10 minutes, then cut across the grain in thin slices to serve.

RAGOUT OF FOUR BEANS WITH TOMATO PERSILLADE

To serve, spread thinly on both sides of grilled lamb slices.

12 Servings

¼ cup olive oil

2 garlic cloves, halved

1 cup canned black beans, rinsed and drained

1 cup canned Great Northern beans, rinsed and drained

1 cup canned pink or red beans, rinsed and drained

1 cup frozen or canned lima beans, thawed or rinsed and drained (if using frozen, precook for half the time the package directs before adding to recipe)

1 cup coarsely chopped fresh or canned tomatoes

¼ cup dry sherry

2 cups chicken or vegetable stock or broth

3 small dried chilies

½ cup chopped parsley, preferably flat-leaf

salt and pepper

1. In a large skillet or saucepan, heat the oil and sauté the garlic until light brown, pressing with the tines of a fork to help release some of the flavor. When the garlic has browned, discard it.

2. Add the beans and tomatoes and sauté 5 minutes, stirring occasionally. Add the sherry, stock, and chilies and bring to boil. Lower heat and simmer until the beans are heated through, about 5 minutes; do not overcook.

3. Remove from heat and discard the chilies. Add the parsley and toss. Adjust seasoning with salt and pepper.

BLUEBERRY SHERBET WITH MELON BALL SPEARS

This can be done ahead. To make enough for 12 people, you may have to process the sherbet in two batches, as many home ice cream makers accommodate just a quart at a time.

12 Servings

3 cups water

2¼ cups sugar

3 pints blueberries, picked over, rinsed, and drained

⅓ cup fresh lemon juice

Melon Ball Spears (see below)

12 mint sprigs (garnish)

1. In a saucepan, combine the water and sugar and bring to boil. Lower heat and simmer, stirring frequently, until the sugar is dissolved. Transfer to a nonaluminum bowl and set over ice water to chill for 1 hour, stirring occasionally.

2. Meanwhile, put the blueberries through a food mill in batches. Add the puree to the cooled syrup. Stir in the lemon juice. Cover with plastic and refrigerate for several hours.

3. Freeze in an ice cream maker according to manufacturer's instructions. Freeze until ready to serve.

4. Place a scoop of sherbet on each plate and lay a melon ball spear alongside. Garnish with mint sprig.

MELON BALL SPEARS
Makes 12

48 melon balls (from cantaloupe, honeydew, and/or other melon of your choice)

¼ cup kirsch or other clear eau-de-vie

36 fresh blueberries

Marinate the melon balls in the eau-de-vie for at least 1 hour. Drain. Thread on 12 long bamboo skewers, alternating melon and blueberries, using 4 melon balls and 3 blueberries on each.

ZOE AND SOPHIE JEAN'S ITALIAN MERINGUES

Makes 24

1½ cups blanched slivered almonds (about ½ pound)

¾ cup confectioner's sugar

¼ cup sugar

2 egg whites, room temperature

pinch of salt

¼ teaspoon almond extract

1 cup pine nuts

1. Preheat oven to 350°F. Spread the almonds on a baking sheet and toast in the oven, stirring several times, until lightly browned, about 10 minutes. Cool. Grind finely in a food processor.

2. Butter and flour a large cookie sheet. Combine the sugars in a bowl and mix well. Beat the egg whites with the salt until frothy. Add the sugars a tablespoon at a time and beat until stiff. Blend in the almond extract and ground almonds.

3. By heaping tablespoons, drop the meringues about 1 inch apart onto the prepared cookie sheet. Sprinkle the top of each meringue with pine nuts.

4. Bake at 350°F until lightly browned, about 15 minutes. Cool on a rack. Store in an airtight container up to a week, or freeze for longer storage.

Sherbet, Melon Balls, and Meringues

Halloween can be a thrilling celebration for children. Ducking for apples, lighting pumpkin faces, and dressing up to look monstrous were all indispensable when I was a child. These days, such activities are brought to life again by the younger generation, which seems not to have changed all that much.

I remember our grandmother filling her enormous white porcelain bread baking pan with water and apples and setting it in the center of her kitchen for our apple-bobbing event. Of course we never realized that we were observing an old Roman custom of honoring Pomona, Roman goddess of the orchards.

Grandma would create a competitive atmosphere as all 21 of her grandchildren vied for best pumpkin design. It was a sight to see pumpkins carved with jagged teeth, lopsided mouths, and triangular noses, lit with candles. Little did we know that we were following an ancient British practice for warding off evil spirits. We also competed for the most terrifying costume—without being aware of the old custom that said if you dressed horribly enough and went waltzing around with the spirits all night long, they would think you were one of them and do you no harm.

On with our ugly masks (King Kong was my favorite), a rap on every door, and "trick or treat" was the warning slogan of the evening. If we weren't happy with the treat, bang went an old sock filled with white flour against a door, person, or auto—or perhaps all three. In retrospect, it was harmless fun, and each Halloween that approaches is still filled with nostalgia for the gay times we had on Halloween night. I gave up the flour-filled sock a long time ago, but I still enjoy a Halloween evening at home with family and friends, and here is what I shall offer in a King Kong mask.

13

Halloween

SUPPER MENU FOR 8

MUMBO, JUMBO, HERE COMES
THE GUMBO: SHRIMP AND
CRABMEAT GUMBO

BOIL, BOIL, AND DOUBLE BOIL
THE WILD RICE: LOUISIANA WILD
PECAN RICE

BISCUITS ROLLED WITH A WITCH'S
BROOM HANDLE: BUTTERMILK
BISCUITS

THE WITCH'S GREENS: SALAD WITH
APPLE CIDER VINAIGRETTE

SPOOKY ALMOND-FACED
TEMPTATION: MOLDED ALMOND
PUMPKIN CUSTARD

BEWARE, THE DEVIL WILL GET YOU
IN THE END: CAFE DIABLE

Mumbo Gumbo With Biscuits

FOOD PREPARATION

1 week ahead:
 • Bake biscuits and freeze

1 day ahead:
 • Make gumbo but do not add shrimp
  or crabmeat until just before serving
 • Prepare custard

Serving day:
 • Make rice, salad, and coffee
 • Complete gumbo
 • Preheat biscuits

WINE SUGGESTION

Serve Bonny Doon Le Sophiste (the only
wine whose bottle comes formally dressed
in a top hat)

SHRIMP AND CRABMEAT GUMBO

8 Servings

*1 ½ quarts fish stock (see page 193) or
3 cups clam juice and 3 cups chicken
stock or low-salt broth*

3 large onions, chopped

1 large green bell pepper, chopped

*2 cups canned plum tomatoes with
juice, chopped*

¼ pound cooked ham, diced

*2 packages (10 ounces each)
frozen sliced okra*

6 garlic cloves, minced

1 tablespoon paprika

2 teaspoons dried thyme

1 teaspoon saffron threads

*1 to 2 teaspoons Tabasco or other
hot pepper sauce*

*2 ½ pounds uncooked shrimp, peeled
and deveined*

1 pound lump crabmeat, picked over

salt and pepper

2 tablespoons filé powder

*Louisiana Wild Pecan Rice
(see following recipe)*

1. Place the stock in a large saucepan and
add the onions, green pepper,
tomatoes, and ham. Bring to boil, then
lower heat. Cover partially and
simmer for 10 minutes.

2. Add the okra (unthawed), garlic,
paprika, thyme, saffron, and 1
teaspoon hot sauce. Return to boil,
lower heat and simmer 10 minutes
longer. Taste for hot sauce, adding
more if desired.

3. Add the shrimp, cover, and cook until
they turn pink, about 5 minutes. Add
the crabmeat and cook until heated
through. Adjust seasoning with salt
and pepper. Remove from heat and
add the filé powder. Stir thoroughly
but do not cook further after filé
powder has been added.

4. Serve in bowls, adding 2 rounded
spoonfuls of rice to the center of each
serving.

LOUISIANA WILD PECAN RICE

8 Servings

1 ½ cups (8 ounces) wild rice

¼ cup butter

2 tablespoons finely diced carrot

2 tablespoons thinly sliced celery

3 cups chicken stock or broth

¼ pound mushrooms, chopped

½ cup finely sliced scallions

1 cup pecan halves

salt and pepper

1. Run cold water through the wild rice
in a colander until the water runs
clear. Set aside.

2. In a saucepan, heat 2 tablespoons
butter and sauté the carrot and celery
for 10 minutes, stirring frequently. Stir
in the rice and cook uncovered for 3
minutes, stirring to coat the rice.

3. Add the stock and bring to boil.
Lower heat, cover, and simmer until
the rice is tender, about 40 minutes,
checking to be sure the pan is not dry.
(If it is, add spoonfuls of stock; if there
is too much liquid, uncover and cook it
off.) Do not overcook.

4. While the rice is cooking, melt the
remaining butter in a skillet. Add the
mushrooms and scallions and sauté for
5 minutes. Add the pecans and cook 3
minutes more. Add to the rice, tossing
with a fork. Adjust seasoning with salt
and pepper.

BUTTERMILK BISCUITS

These biscuits freeze well and may be reheated in foil.

Makes 12 to 16

2 cups all-purpose flour

1 teaspoon salt

4 teaspoons baking powder

2 tablespoons solid vegetable shortening, melted

¾ to 1 cup buttermilk

1. Place the flour in a large bowl and make a well in the center. Add the salt, baking powder, shortening, and ¾ cup buttermilk, a little at a time, adding more buttermilk if the mixture is dry. Mix with a wooden spoon. Alternatively, blend the dry ingredients in a food processor for 2 seconds. With the machine running, add the shortening and ¾ cup plus 2 tablespoons buttermilk through the feed tube and process just until the dough starts to cling together; do not overmix. Turn out onto a floured work surface and knead only until a dough is formed.

2. Preheat oven to 425°F. Roll out the dough to a thickness of half an inch. Cut out biscuits with a 2½-inch round cutter, cutting as close to one another as you can. Arrange on a buttered baking sheet. Press dough trimmings together and cut additional biscuits.

3. Bake until the biscuits are lightly browned, about 10 to 15 minutes. Serve hot.

SALAD WITH APPLE CIDER VINAIGRETTE

8 Servings

6 heads Bibb or 3 heads Boston lettuce, rinsed and dried

½ orange or yellow bell pepper, cut into ¼-inch squares

4 teaspoons apple cider vinegar

1 teaspoon Dijon-style mustard

6 tablespoons vegetable oil

1 garlic clove, minced

salt and pepper

1. Combine lettuce and bell pepper in a large bowl.

2. Combine vinegar and mustard in a small bowl. Slowly add oil, whisking until mixture emulsifies. Stir in garlic and salt and pepper. Pour over lettuce, toss, and serve.

The Witch's Greens

MOLDED ALMOND PUMPKIN CUSTARD

If you'd like to flambé this, warm ½ cup rum, spoon it around the outer edge of the custard, and light it with a match. But be careful! The Devil will be right there watching.

8 Servings

1½ cups sugar

2 cups half-and-half or light cream

1 cup milk

2 cups canned pumpkin

½ cup rum

1 teaspoon almond extract

1 teaspoon salt

3 pinches freshly grated nutmeg

6 eggs

½ cup slivered almonds, toasted

1 cup heavy cream, whipped

1. In a small saucepan over low heat, melt 1 cup sugar until smooth and amber in color. Immediately pour into a 9- or 10-inch deep pie dish or quiche pan. Quickly rotate the dish to cover the bottom and sides with the caramel.

2. In another saucepan, bring the half-and-half or cream and milk to boil. Add the remaining ½ cup sugar, the pumpkin, rum, almond extract, salt, and nutmeg and blend well. Remove from heat.

3. Preheat oven to 375°F. In a bowl, beat the eggs until well blended. Add ½ cup of the pumpkin mixture and combine thoroughly. Transfer this to the remaining pumpkin mixture and beat well. Pour into the caramel-coated baking dish. Set this dish in a larger pan and add water to come to about halfway up the custard dish.

4. Bake until the custard is set and a knife inserted in the center comes out clean, about 1 hour. Cool for 15 minutes. Turn out onto a serving platter and chill.

5. Arrange the slivered almonds on the custard to make a face.

6. Serve with whipped cream on the side or piped through a pastry bag.

CAFE DIABLE

8 Servings

2 orange zest strips, 1 x 3 inches each

8 whole cloves

¼ cup sugar

2 4-inch cinnamon sticks, broken in half

2 lemon slices, seeded

¾ cup cognac

4 cups strong, freshly brewed coffee

1. Stick each orange zest piece with 4 cloves and set aside.

2. In a shallow, heavy saucepan, mix the sugar and cinnamon and place over low heat until the sugar melts and turns golden; be careful not to scorch. Add the orange zest, lemon slices, and cognac and heat through. Spoon up some of the cognac with a long-handled spoon, hold a match to it, and lower the spoon into the pan, flaming the remaining cognac.

3. Slowly pour in the hot coffee. When the flames subside, strain into a coffeepot. Serve in demitasse cups.

Spooky Almond-Faced Custard

Throughout recorded history, "harvest home" has always called for a celebration to honor the gods who fostered the crops. In the New World, the first autumn holiday of feasting and thanksgiving took place in 1621, when the governor of the colony "sent 4 men on fowling . . . so that we might . . . rejoice together after we have gathered the fruit of our labors." Ninety Native American guests joined the Pilgrims for the three-day feast. By the goodness of God, said one of the colonists, no one was wanting, and everyone was invited to partake of the plenty. This may be the best summation of the spirit of Thanksgiving, then and now.

The Pilgrims faced starvation in the summer of 1623. There had been a long, dismal winter followed by a severe drought. The governor of the colony ordered a day of fasting and prayer. Finally, small clouds appeared in the sky, and the long rain saved the crops. The colonists celebrated a day of thanksgiving on November 23 that year to show their gratitude to God. This second observance, say some historians, was the real birth of Thanksgiving as we know it today.

Though schools and churches all over the country reenact the first Thanksgiving every year, for most people the real focus of the holiday is their own family feast. Relatives fly cross-country and across continents to be with their loved ones on this special day. Each household has at least one or two specialties of home-cooked food it couldn't possibly do without.

I've tried Thanksgiving dinner without turkey—but for my family and friends, it didn't seem like Thanksgiving. I believe the predictable turkey is essential, but there are lots of ways to make the meal interesting by experimenting with the dressing, first course, vegetables, and desserts. There's room for innovation as well as tradition on the Thanksgiving menu.

Thanksgiving

DINNER MENU FOR 10

ROASTED VEGETABLES WITH
VINAIGRETTE

GRATIN OF SCALLOPS

ROAST TURKEY WITH GIBLET GRAVY

SWEET PEPPER STUFFING IN A
CHARLOTTE MOLD

WHITE AND YELLOW CORN
CUSTARD

SWEET POTATOES WITH HONEY,
GINGER, AND ORANGE MARMALADE

CRANBERRY AND GRAPEFRUIT
COMPOTE

FRESH PINEAPPLE CHUTNEY

CHOCOLATE PECAN PIE WITH
MAPLE BOURBON SAUCE

PEAR TART WITH ALMOND CREAM

Gratin of Scallops

FOOD PREPARATION

This celebration dinner may seem formidable, but it can be prepared more easily if cooked in stages. The roasted vegetables with vinaigrette are meant to be an hors d'oeuvre; cook early in the day, reheat a little, and serve before dinner with aperitifs. If you wish to simplify this meal, use the roasted vegetables in place of the sweet pepper stuffing, choose between the pineapple chutney and cranberry compote, and make just one dessert.

2 days ahead:
· Prepare potatoes, cranberry compote, pineapple chutney (may be made weeks ahead), and maple bourbon sauce

1 day ahead:
· Prepare the scallops to step 4; cover and refrigerate
· Make gravy (add turkey drippings the next day, before reheating)
· Make sweet pepper stuffing
· Bake pecan pie and/or pear tart

Serving day:
· Roast turkey; reheat gravy and stuffing
· Reheat roasted vegetables and sweet potatoes
· Make corn custard
· Finish scallops by adding crumb topping and baking

WINE SUGGESTIONS

As an aperitif, serve Piper Sonoma Blanc de Noirs. Serve Kenwood Vineyards Sauvignon Blanc with the scallops and Adelsheim Willamette Valley Oregon Pinot Noir with the turkey.

ROASTED VEGETABLES WITH VINAIGRETTE

This is baked like a crustless vegetable pizza. Cut into wedges and serve on small plates, with a tablespoon or two of the sauce on the side. Accompany the vegetables with crusty French bread.

10 Servings

2 medium eggplants (about 1 ½ to 2 pounds), ends trimmed

3 zucchini (each 1 x 6 inches), ends trimmed

salt

½ cup olive oil

2 medium onions, thinly sliced

2 red or yellow bell peppers, seeded and very thinly sliced

4 garlic cloves, minced

1 ½ cups fresh or canned tomatoes, seeded, drained, and cut into thin strips

⅔ cup vegetable, chicken, or beef stock or broth

2 tablespoons chopped fresh basil or 1 teaspoon dried

2 tablespoons chopped fresh thyme or 1 teaspoon dried

pepper

vinaigrette (see page 193)

1. Cut the eggplants and zucchini into ¼-inch slices and set in a colander. Sprinkle with salt and let drain 30 minutes.

2. Pat the eggplant and zucchini dry. Brush the eggplant slices lightly with some of the oil. Heat 3 tablespoons oil in a skillet and sauté the onions and bell peppers until soft. Add the garlic and cook 1 minute longer.

3. Liberally brush the bottom of a 14-inch-diameter pizza pan with oil. Arrange the eggplant slices in an overlapping pattern to cover the bottom. Arrange the zucchini in the same way on top of the eggplant. Sprinkle with the onion mixture and tomatoes. Sprinkle evenly with the stock, then with the herbs and any remaining oil. Season with salt and pepper.

4. Preheat oven to 350°F. Bake the vegetables until the eggplant is tender, about 50 to 60 minutes. Let cool for 10 minutes. Slice into wedges like a pizza and serve with a tablespoon or two of vinaigrette.

GRATIN OF SCALLOPS

10 Servings

2 pounds bay scallops

½ cup dry white wine

½ cup clam juice

juice of 1 lemon

2 small onions, finely chopped

½ teaspoon fennel seeds

*3 tablespoons cornstarch dissolved
in ⅓ cup water*

¾ cup heavy cream

⅓ cup chopped parsley

¾ cup fresh breadcrumbs

5 tablespoons butter

*4 slices bacon, cooked until
crisp, crumbled*

1. Rinse the scallops in cool water; drain.

2. Combine the wine, clam juice, onions, and fennel seeds in a large non-aluminum skillet and bring to boil. Add the scallops, lower the heat, and simmer until barely opaque, about 6 to 8 minutes. Drain, reserving the liquid. Divide the scallops and onions among 10 buttered scallop shells or ramekins.

3. Add the cornstarch mixture and cream to the reserved liquid and bring to boil. Spoon over scallops.

4. Preheat oven to 450°F. Mix the parsley and breadcrumbs and sprinkle over the scallops. Top with ½ tablespoon butter and some bacon bits. Arrange the shells or ramekins on a rimmed baking sheet. Bake until heated through and bubbling, about 10 minutes. Serve hot.

Roast Turkey With Condiments

ROAST TURKEY WITH GIBLET GRAVY

The dressing for the turkey, Sweet Pepper Stuffing in a Charlotte Mold, is cooked separately—which makes it crispier and easier to serve than a stuffing that's cooked in the bird.

10 Servings

1 16-pound turkey, giblets reserved

juice of 2 lemons

6 tablespoons butter, softened

salt and pepper

Giblet Gravy (see next page)

1. Preheat oven to 325°F. Rinse the turkey in cool water, inside and out. Wipe with a paper towel. Rub the turkey with lemon juice inside and out, and then do the same with the butter, salt, and pepper.

2. Place the bird on a rack in a roasting pan. Roast until a thermometer inserted in the thickest part of the thigh reads 170° to 175°F, about 5 hours, basting every 30 minutes or so with pan drippings. The turkey is done when the drumstick moves up and down easily and the juices run clear when the thigh joint is pierced with a fork.

3. Transfer the turkey to a warm platter, cover loosely with foil, and let rest 20 minutes for easier carving. Pour off all but 3 tablespoons of the drippings from the roasting pan for the gravy.

GIBLET GRAVY
Makes about 1 ½ cups

reserved turkey giblets

1 small to medium onion, quartered

*3 sprigs fresh tarragon or
1 teaspoon dried*

salt

3 cups water

2 parsley sprigs

*3 tablespoons reserved turkey
drippings*

1 cup brown sauce (see page 192)

¼ cup brandy or cognac

pepper

1. In a saucepan, combine the giblets, onion, tarragon, 1½ teaspoons salt, and the water. Bring to boil, skimming the surface as necessary.

2. Add the parsley, reduce heat, and simmer until the giblets are cooked, about 30 to 35 minutes. Strain. Chop the giblets into tiny pieces and reserve. Return the broth to the saucepan.

3. Add the turkey drippings. Scrape up the browned bits in the roasting pan and add to the broth. Boil the broth over high heat until reduced by half.

4. Add the brown sauce, giblets, and brandy and return to boil. Reduce heat and simmer for 5 minutes. Season with salt (if needed) and pepper. Keep the gravy warm until ready to serve. Pass it separately with the turkey.

SWEET PEPPER STUFFING IN A CHARLOTTE MOLD

This is a combination of bread, tomatoes, roasted peppers, and herbs, bound together with a little egg and baked in a mold. If you don't have a 2-quart charlotte mold, use a baking container that is similar in size and form.

10 Servings

8 large red and yellow bell peppers or 2 jars roasted peppers (12 ounces each)

¼ cup balsamic vinegar

⅓ cup dried currants

¾ cup olive oil

¼ cup butter, melted

2 medium onions, finely chopped

4 garlic cloves, minced

2 cups drained canned plum tomatoes, seeded and coarsely chopped

3 tablespoons chopped fresh oregano or 2 teaspoons dried

salt and pepper

16 slices firm white bread

2 eggs, lightly beaten

parsley sprigs and red and yellow bell pepper slices (garnish)

Sweet Pepper Mold

1. Preheat broiler. Broil the peppers on a rimmed baking sheet, turning until they are blackened on all sides, about 10 minutes. Place in a paper bag and let stand 15 minutes. Core the peppers and wipe away seeds; peel. Chop coarsely and set aside.

2. In a nonaluminum saucepan, combine the vinegar and currants and bring to boil. Remove from heat and stand 15 minutes.

3. Combine the oil and butter. Heat ¼ cup of the mixture in a large skillet and sauté the onions for 5 minutes. Add the garlic and sauté for 2 minutes. Add the currants, vinegar, and roasted peppers and cook for 5 minutes. Add the tomato, oregano, salt, and pepper and cook for 5 minutes longer. Remove from heat.

4. Brush the inside of a 2-quart charlotte mold with some of the oil mixture. Lightly brush 12 slices of bread on both sides with the mixture. Cut off and reserve the crusts. Cut bread slices in half. Arrange several pieces of bread in the bottom of the mold, slightly overlapping and trimming as necessary to fit (reserve trimmings). Line the sides of the mold with the remaining half slices, overlapping.

5. Preheat oven to 350°F. Coarsely chop all the remaining bread, crusts, and trimmings. Place in a mixing bowl. Add any remaining oil mixture. Add the pepper mixture and eggs and toss lightly but thoroughly. Pour into the bread-lined mold.

6. Bake until the filling is set and the bread lining is browned, about 50 to 60 minutes. Let cool 5 to 10 minutes, then run a knife carefully around the edge of the mold to loosen. Turn the stuffing out onto a platter. Garnish with parsley sprigs and slices of red and yellow pepper. Serve hot or at room temperature. This may be assembled a day ahead and kept covered in the refrigerator. Bring to room temperature before baking.

WHITE AND YELLOW CORN CUSTARD

10 Servings

1 cup white corn kernels

1 cup yellow corn kernels

3 eggs, room temperature

¼ cup all-purpose flour

salt and white pepper

3 tablespoons butter, melted and cooled

2 cups half-and-half or light cream

1. If using fresh corn, cook 3 or 4 ears of each color. Drain and scrape enough kernels to make 1 cup of each. Alternatively, use thawed frozen or canned corn.

2. In a large bowl, beat the eggs until foamy. Add the corn, flour, salt and pepper, butter, and half-and-half or cream and blend well.

3. Preheat oven to 350°F. Liberally butter a 1½-quart baking dish. Pour in corn mixture. Set in a larger pan. Pour hot water into the pan to reach 1 inch below the rim of the smaller dish.

4. Bake until the custard is set and a knife inserted in the center comes out nearly clean, about 1 hour. Serve within 15 minutes.

SWEET POTATOES WITH HONEY, GINGER, AND ORANGE MARMALADE

10 Servings

10 large sweet potatoes or yams (about 5 pounds)

¾ cup (12 tablespoons) butter

⅓ cup firmly packed dark brown sugar

¼ cup honey

¼ cup orange marmalade

¼ cup dark rum

2 tablespoons minced candied ginger

salt and pepper

1. Preheat oven to 375°F. Bake sweet potatoes until tender, about 1½ hours. Let cool until they can be handled. Peel and slice.

2. Place the sweet potatoes in a large mixing bowl. Add 9 tablespoons butter, the brown sugar, honey, marmalade, rum, ginger, and salt and pepper and mix well, or puree in batches in a food processor. This can be done several days ahead; cover and refrigerate the mixture. Bring to room temperature before baking.

3. Preheat oven to 350°F. Fill a baking dish with sweet potato filling. Dot with the remaining butter. Bake until heated through, about 20 to 30 minutes. Serve hot.

CRANBERRY AND GRAPEFRUIT COMPOTE

This is an easy and delicious way to cook whole cranberries. The compote may be made one or more days ahead and refrigerated.

Makes 2 to 3 cups

1 12-ounce bag fresh cranberries

butter

2 fresh grapefruit

1 cup sugar

¼ cup dry white wine (optional)

1. Preheat oven to 350°F. Rinse, sort, and drain the cranberries. Liberally butter a pizza pan about 14 inches in diameter. Scatter the cranberries in the pan.

2. Peel the grapefruit and discard the pith and seeds. Chop coarsely, catching the juice as best you can. Sprinkle fruit and juice over the cranberries in the pan.

3. Sprinkle the sugar and wine over the fruit. Cover tightly with foil. Bake until the berries have popped, 45 minutes to 1 hour. Transfer to a serving dish. Cover and refrigerate until ready to serve.

FRESH PINEAPPLE CHUTNEY

Makes about 4 pints

1 fresh pineapple, skin and core removed

½ cup minced peeled fresh ginger

¼ cup minced lemon zest

3 cups firmly packed light brown sugar

3 cups cider vinegar

2 cups dates, pitted and chopped

1 cup dried currants

1 teaspoon dried red pepper flakes

½ teaspoon ground allspice

1 teaspoon salt

1. Cut the pineapple into ⅔-inch cubes; there should be about 4 cups.

2. Combine all ingredients in a heavy nonaluminum saucepan and bring to boil. Lower heat slightly and boil until the chutney has thickened, about 1 hour. Transfer to sterilized jars and store in refrigerator.

Pear Tart and Chocolate Pecan Pie

CHOCOLATE PECAN PIE WITH MAPLE BOURBON SAUCE

10 Servings

½ cup butter

3 ounces unsweetened chocolate

4 eggs

3 tablespoons white corn syrup

1½ cups sugar

1 teaspoon vanilla extract

pinch of salt

1 cup pecan pieces

1 unbaked 9-inch pie shell

Maple Bourbon Sauce (see below)

1. Melt the butter and chocolate in the top of a double boiler over simmering water. Cool slightly.

2. Preheat oven to 350°F. Beat the eggs in a large mixing bowl until thick and pale. Add the corn syrup, sugar, vanilla, and salt and mix well. Stir in the pecans and the chocolate mixture.

3. Pour the mixture into the pie shell and bake until the filling is set, 25 to 30 minutes. Do not overbake; the top should be crusty but the inside soft. Let cool. Serve with sauce on the side.

MAPLE BOURBON SAUCE

Spoon a tablespoon or two on the plate next to each slice of chocolate pecan pie. Or use this sauce in many other ways: spoon some over vanilla ice cream, trickle it over lemon, white, or orange cakes, or spoon it onto dessert soufflés at serving time.

Makes about 1¾ cups

1 cup half-and-half or light cream

1 tablespoon sugar

3 egg yolks, room temperature

¼ cup pure maple syrup

¼ cup bourbon

1. Heat the half-and-half or cream and sugar in a small saucepan over low heat, stirring constantly, until the sugar is dissolved. Immediately remove from heat.

2. Beat the egg yolks in a bowl and slowly beat in the cream mixture. Return to the saucepan and cook over low heat until thick, about 2 minutes, stirring constantly; do not boil.

3. Transfer the sauce to a bowl and stir in the maple syrup and bourbon. Cover with plastic wrap and refrigerate until ready to use.

PEAR TART WITH ALMOND CREAM

10 Servings

pâte brisée for 10-inch tart pan (see page 193)

6 Bosc or Bartlett pears

juice of 1 lemon

¼ cup dry white wine

⅓ cup sugar

¼ teaspoon cinnamon

freshly grated nutmeg

2 tablespoons butter

ALMOND CREAM

1 egg

1 egg yolk

½ cup sugar

¼ cup all-purpose flour

1 cup milk, scalded

⅓ cup ground blanched almonds

3 tablespoons butter

½ teaspoon vanilla extract

¼ teaspoon almond extract

2 tablespoons jam or marmalade, if needed to glaze

1. Fit the pastry into a 10-inch tart pan with removable bottom and bake according to the directions on page 193.

2. Preheat oven to 350°F. Peel, core, and halve the pears. Immediately rub lemon juice all over them and place cut side down in a baking dish. Sprinkle the wine, sugar, cinnamon, and nutmeg over the pears. Dot with butter. Bake on the center rack until the pears are tender, about 20 minutes (test by inserting the point of a small, sharp knife into several pears; it should slide in and out easily). Let the pears cool in the pan liquid.

3. For the almond cream, beat the egg and yolk. Add the sugar and beat until the mixture forms a ribbon when the beaters are lifted. Sift in the flour and blend well. Blend in the hot milk. Transfer to a nonaluminum saucepan and bring just to boil, then lower heat and cook until thickened, about 2 minutes. Immediately remove from heat. Fold in the ground almonds, butter, vanilla, and almond extract. Transfer to a small bowl and lay a buttered round of waxed paper on top of the cream. Refrigerate until well chilled.

4. To assemble the tart, spread the almond cream on the bottom of the baked tart shell. Drain the pear halves, reserving the liquid, and arrange the pears cut side down on top of the cream, pointing the stem ends to the center. Transfer the pear liquid to a small saucepan and boil until syrupy; if there is not enough liquid, melt 2 tablespoons jam or marmalade and spoon over the pears. Chill the tart for at least 1 hour. This may be made a day ahead.

anukkah celebrates the victory by religious Jews, led by a family descended from priests, who turned to guerrilla warfare to defeat Antiochus III and his Syrian armies. The Jews managed to reclaim the Temple of Jerusalem, rid it of idols, and rededicate it to God. In celebration, they lit the lamps of the Temple menorah and miraculously, a small portion of oil, only enough to burn for one day, burned for all eight days of the festival. Every year Hanukkah is celebrated for eight days to commemorate the rededication of the Temple.

Because of the miracle of the oil, Jews everywhere include oil as an ingredient in their holiday cooking. In central Europe the quintessential Hanukkah food is fried potato pancakes, or *latkes;* Jews in Spain, Greece, and North Africa serve fried doughnuts called *sufganiyot.*

Annie Nadler is from Fes in Morocco, and Jewish Moroccan cuisine is probably the most sophisticated in all of North Africa. This is the way her parents and grandparents cooked. Years ago these dishes required hours of preparation, but Annie has adapted them to modern cooking styles—for example, she prepares quick-cooking couscous in a saucepan rather than using the classic and somewhat cumbersome *couscoussière.*

Hanukkah

DINNER MENU FOR 10

Cooked Salad (*Tchatchouka*)

Chickpea and Onion Soup

Couscous Royale

Tajine of Chicken, Almonds,
and Prunes

Aniseed Fritters (*Mekroud*)

Chickpea and Onion Soup

FOOD PREPARATION

1 day ahead:
- Prepare cooked salad; refrigerate
- Make soup
- Make fritters

Serving day:
- Fry pastries
- Bring cooked salad to room temperature
- Make couscous
- Make chicken tajine

WINE SUGGESTIONS

Serve a North African Gris de Boulaouane rosé, or if you keep kosher, a California kosher wine such as Hagafen Johannisberg Riesling or Gan Eden Fumé Blanc.

COOKED SALAD
(*TCHATCHOUKA*)

An unusual cooked salad. To stretch the quantity, add another can of tomatoes, well drained.

10 Servings

1 pound mixed red and green bell peppers

2 pounds fresh tomatoes or 1 can (28 ounces) whole tomatoes

¼ cup vegetable oil

3 garlic cloves, minced

½ teaspoon paprika

¼ teaspoon sugar

pinch of cayenne pepper

salt

1. Broil or grill the peppers on all sides until they blacken. Place in a brown paper bag, close the bag, and let stand until the peppers are cooled. Remove the skins, stems, and seeds and cut peppers in strips.

2. If using fresh tomatoes, bring a saucepan of water to boil and blanch the tomatoes for about 2 minutes. Remove cores and skins and cut in half crosswise. Squeeze the halves to dislodge the seeds. Cut the tomatoes into thin strips. If using canned, drain liquid and rinse in running water to remove seeds; chop coarsely.

3. In a large skillet, heat the oil and sauté the garlic for just a few seconds. Add the peppers, canned or fresh tomatoes, paprika, sugar, cayenne, and salt and cook over medium heat, stirring several times, until the liquid from the tomatoes has mostly evaporated. Remove from heat and let cool. Serve at room temperature.

CHICKPEA AND ONION SOUP

10 Servings

1 pound dried chickpeas or 2 cans (16 ounces each) garbanzos

1 teaspoon baking soda

1 pound peeled pumpkin, cut into small cubes

2 large onions, coarsely chopped

½ teaspoon ground coriander

½ teaspoon saffron

2½ quarts chicken stock or broth

salt and pepper to taste

1 tablespoon finely chopped fresh coriander

1. If using dried chickpeas, soak them overnight in cool water. The next day, boil the peas in fresh water with the baking soda until tender. Drain and run under cold water. Remove the skins by rubbing the peas between the hands. Rinse two more times under cold running water. Place the peas in a large soup pot. If using canned garbanzos, drain and rinse under cold water several times and place them in a large soup pot.

2. Add the pumpkin, onions, ground coriander, and saffron. Add enough chicken stock to cover the vegetables. Cover and bring to boil; cook until the vegetables are tender, about 40 minutes.

3. Pass the mixture through a food mill and return to the pot. Thin with more chicken stock or water to achieve the consistency of pea soup. Add salt and pepper to taste and garnish with chopped fresh coriander. Serve hot.

COUSCOUS ROYALE

Most of the couscous sold in this country is precooked; it can be prepared simply by adding it to boiling water and letting it stand for about 5 minutes.

10 Servings

FOR THE VEGETABLES

3 turnips

3 carrots

1 small butternut squash

3 small zucchini

2 medium or 1 large onion, thinly sliced

3 tablespoons vegetable oil

1 small beef marrow bone, about 2 x 3 inches

1 teaspoon turmeric

salt and pepper

½ cup water

½ teaspoon cinnamon

1 tablespoon sugar

1. Peel or scrape the turnips, carrots, and squash; slice them and the zucchini. Set aside.

2. Sauté the onions in the oil until golden. Transfer to a baking dish large enough to hold all the vegetables. Set the marrow bone in the middle of the dish. Layer the vegetables over the onions.

3. Preheat oven to 350°F. Stir the turmeric and salt and pepper into the water. Pour over the vegetables. Cover and bake 45 minutes. Uncover, sprinkle with cinnamon and sugar, and continue cooking another 30 minutes. Keep warm.

Couscous Royale

FOR THE RAISIN-NUT MIXTURE

1 tablespoon margarine

¼ pound raisins

¼ pound sliced almonds

1 teaspoon sugar

¼ cup chicken stock or broth

Melt the margarine in a skillet. Add the raisins and almonds and sauté 3 to 4 minutes. Add the sugar and sauté a few minutes longer, stirring constantly. Add the stock and cook until the liquid evaporates. Keep warm until ready to assemble the couscous.

FOR THE COUSCOUS

3 cups chicken stock or broth

1 pound quick-cooking couscous (about 3 cups)

¼ cup margarine

1 tablespoon sugar

1 teaspoon cinnamon

1. Bring the stock to boil and pour over the couscous. Cover immediately and let the couscous absorb the broth for 20 minutes. Warm in a preheated 300°F oven for 10 minutes.

2. Toss with the margarine lightly but thoroughly to fluff the couscous. Form it into a pyramidal mound on a large platter. Top the pyramid with the raisin-nut mixture. Spoon the vegetable mixture all around the base of the pyramid.

3. Sift the sugar and cinnamon over all and serve at once.

TAJINE OF CHICKEN, ALMONDS, AND PRUNES

10 Servings

1 pound dried pitted prunes

*1 teaspoon saffron threads or
½ teaspoon turmeric*

⅓ cup vegetable oil

1½ whole chickens, cut into 12 pieces

2 large onions, finely chopped

¼ cup ground almonds

salt and pepper

*1 tablespoon finely chopped
candied ginger*

1 cinnamon stick

*2 tablespoons finely chopped fresh
coriander or parsley*

1. Put the prunes and saffron or turmeric in a glass bowl and barely cover with water. Let stand 1 hour or longer. Drain well, reserving the liquid. Set aside.

2. In a large skillet heat half the oil and sauté half the chicken pieces on both sides until lightly browned. Drain on paper towels. Repeat with the remaining oil and chicken pieces.

3. In the oil remaining in the skillet, sauté the onions for about 5 minutes or until golden. Add the almonds, salt, and pepper. Set aside.

4. Transfer the cooked onion mixture to a baking dish large enough to hold the chicken pieces. Place the chicken on top of the onion mixture. Add the prunes and the reserved liquid, the ginger, the cinnamon stick, and salt and pepper.

5. Cover with foil and bake in a preheated 325°F oven for 1 hour or until the chicken is tender. Remove the cover and cook for another 10 minutes. Before serving, sprinkle with freshly chopped coriander or parsley.

Celebrating Hanukkah

ANISEED FRITTERS
(*MEKROUD*)

This pastry is very popular in Fes, Morocco.

Makes about 24

1 envelope dry yeast

1¼ cups warm water

4 cups all-purpose flour

1 tablespoon sugar

1 teaspoon salt

1 teaspoon aniseed

vegetable oil for deep-frying

honey or preserves

1. Sprinkle the yeast over ¼ cup warm water. Set aside for 5 minutes.

2. Place the flour in a large bowl. Add the sugar, salt, aniseed, yeast mixture, and remaining water and mix until a dough is formed. Turn out onto a lightly floured surface and knead until smooth and elastic. Cut the dough in half and form two rounds. Cover with a clean towel and let rise in a warm area until doubled, about 1 hour.

3. Flatten each round with a rolling pin to 1-inch thickness. Cut each round into about twelve 2- to 3-inch diamonds and separate them. Cover and let rise a second time until doubled, about 1 hour.

4. Heat the oil to 375°F in a deep pan. Fry the pieces on both sides until golden. Drain on paper towels. Transfer to a platter and serve warm with honey or preserves.

Tajine of Chicken, Almonds, and Prunes

Filled with joy and nostalgia, Christmas is a glorious holiday. It reminds us of a time when we were happy and carefree, when there was love and kindness, and Santa brought us just what we wanted. Christmas is among the few celebrations that carry us back in time. It has always been a celebration of family, bringing everyone together to feast and celebrate.

I remember the orange and a few other goodies that I always found in the sock I hung on my grandparents' mantel. Sometimes there was a dime, some walnuts, and a few inexpensive candies, too. In fact, most of the items in the sock were of the ten-cent-store variety, but there was always an orange. The custom dates back to the days of St. Nicholas, who was said to have come to New York with the first boatload of Dutch settlers on Christmas Day. (A church in his honor was one of the first buildings erected in the new colony, and he was named its patron saint.) The oranges represented gifts of gold he gave to three poor sisters. According to the legend, the first orange was thrown through an open window and two others were tossed down the chimney because there was no other way to get them into the house. One landed on the hearth. The other bounced into a stocking that had just been hung by the fire to dry—and thus our custom of hanging Christmas stockings was born.

Christmas Eve was the highpoint of the holiday season as I was growing up, for no other event during the year brought my family closer together. On Christmas Eve I still prepare fish the way my grandparents did.

16

Christmas Eve

MENU FOR 8

Fish Soup for Christmas Eve

Thin Spaghetti with White
Clam Sauce

Large Shrimp Sauteed with
Christmas Confetti

Fresh Sea Scallops with
Mediterranean Marinara Sauce

Calamari at Christmastime

Cod with Tiny Pasta Shells

John Imperiale's Eel with White
Wine, Brandy, and Thyme

Sister Bea's Italian Christmas
Bow Pastries

Fresh Fruit/Cheeses

Fish Soup

FOOD PREPARATION

This food was easy to prepare in our home because grandmother and an aunt helped with the cooking. If this traditional menu is too much, select what you like and cook that.

3 days ahead:
  · Make Christmas pastry bows

2 days ahead:
  · Make white clam sauce
  · Make calamari
  · Soak codfish

1 day ahead:
  · Prepare shrimp for cooking
  · Make marinara sauce
  · Prepare eel dish

Serving day:
  · Make fish soup
  · Brew espresso
  · Cook pastas and dress; cook shrimp and scallops, broil eel, reheat other dishes

WINE/BEVERAGE SUGGESTIONS

Serve Brut Spumante for cocktails. Throughout the meal, serve Pinot Grigio Santa Margherita *or* Vernaccia di San Gimignano; with pastry, serve Moscato d'Asti. Complete the meal with Espresso and Sambuca.

FISH SOUP FOR CHRISTMAS EVE

8 Servings

½ pound mussels, cleaned and debearded

½ pound small littleneck clams

¼ cup dry white wine

8 cups fish stock, warmed (see page 193)

1 tablespoon olive oil

1 garlic clove, minced

1 ½ teaspoons saffron threads

½ teaspoon dried thyme

½ teaspoon fennel seed

1 small chili pepper, chopped

1 tablespoon cornstarch

1 pound fish fillets (flounder, sole, striped bass, etc.), cut into 2-inch pieces

1 cup cooked lobster meat, cut into 1-inch pieces

1 tablespoon Pernod or anise liqueur

1. In a saucepan, combine the mussels, clams, wine, and 1 cup stock. Cover and steam the shellfish for 10 to 15 minutes; discard any mussels or clams that refuse to open in that time. Set aside the opened shellfish.

2. In a small skillet, heat the oil and add the garlic, saffron, thyme, fennel seed, and chili pepper. Cook for 2 minutes and set aside.

3. Whisk the cornstarch into ½ cup of the warm stock in a large saucepan. Add the remaining stock and bring to boil. Add the fish fillets and simmer for about

5 minutes or just until the fish is opaque; do not overcook. Add the oil and seasoning mixture, lobster, and Pernod.

4. Divide the mussels and clams among 8 large soup bowls or place in a large tureen. Ladle in the soup and serve hot.

THIN SPAGHETTI WITH WHITE CLAM SAUCE

I use *fedelini* pasta for this; it is thinner than vermicelli but not quite as thin as angel hair (cappellini). Any thin spaghetti may be used. To save time, find clams that have been prepacked and cleaned. If they are unavailable, try chopped canned clams, which I have used successfully on many occasions.

8 Servings

5 dozen littleneck clams or 3 cans (7 ½ ounces each) minced clams

2 large garlic cloves, minced

½ cup olive oil

¼ cup butter or margarine

1 carrot, peeled and finely chopped

½ cup thinly sliced scallions

1 cup clam juice

1 cup dry white wine

pinch of red pepper flakes

salt

1 pound thin spaghetti

¼ cup finely chopped parsley

1. If using whole clams, scrub thoroughly with a wire brush and rinse several times, then soak in cool water for about 30 minutes to remove sand.

2. Place the cleaned clams in a heavy covered saucepan with half the garlic and half the olive oil. Steam over medium heat until the clams open, about 10 to 15 minutes, discarding any that do not open. Shell the clams, reserving all juices. Coarsely chop the clams and set aside.

3. Bring a large pot of water to boil for the pasta. Meanwhile, in a large skillet, heat the remaining oil with the butter. Add the carrot and sauté for 5 minutes. Add the scallions and remaining garlic and cook for 2 to 3 minutes or until lightly colored.

4. Add the reserved clam juice (from the fresh or canned variety), the additional 1 cup clam juice, wine, and red pepper flakes. Bring to boil, then simmer for 10 minutes to cook off the wine. Season to taste with salt and more red pepper if you wish.

5. If using canned minced clams, heat all the oil and butter in a large skillet. Add the carrot and sauté for 5 minutes. Add the scallions and garlic and cook for 2 to 3 minutes. Add the clam juice, wine, and red pepper flakes. Bring to boil; then simmer for 10 minutes.

6. Add salt to the pasta cooking water and cook the pasta until al dente. Drain and add to the large skillet. Toss thoroughly. Add the clams and parsley and cook for 2 minutes. Toss again and serve. If your skillet is not large enough to hold the pasta and sauce, return the cooked pasta to the pot in which it cooked, add the sauce, toss over medium heat, and serve.

LARGE SHRIMP SAUTEED WITH CHRISTMAS CONFETTI

This is simple to prepare once the shrimp have been cleaned.

8 Servings

3 pounds large shrimp

½ cup olive oil

1 red bell pepper, seeded and cut into ¼-inch cubes

3 garlic cloves, minced

salt and pepper

½ cup finely chopped flat-leaf parsley

1. Shell and devein the shrimp and rinse thoroughly in cold water. Pat dry with paper towels and set aside.

2. In a large skillet, heat 2 tablespoons of the oil and sauté the red pepper until lightly colored. Transfer to a small bowl.

3. In the same skillet, heat the remaining oil and sauté the shrimp over high heat until they turn pink, about 5 minutes, tossing in the garlic during the last minute. Season liberally with salt and pepper. Transfer the cooked shrimp to a large platter. Add the red pepper and sprinkle with parsley.

FRESH SEA SCALLOPS WITH MEDITERRANEAN MARINARA SAUCE

8 Servings

2 pounds fresh whole sea scallops

juice of 1 lemon

6 tablespoons olive oil

1 large onion, finely chopped

2 garlic cloves, minced

2 cups canned plum tomatoes, put through a food mill

¼ cup chopped fresh basil or 1 teaspoon dried

8 fennel seeds

1 tablespoon sugar

salt and pepper

1. Rinse the scallops in cold water and drain. Place in a glass bowl, add the lemon juice, and toss. Let stand at room temperature for about 20 minutes.

2. In a large skillet, heat 4 tablespoons of the oil and sauté the onion until softened and lightly colored. Add the garlic and cook 1 minute. Add the tomatoes, half the fresh basil or all of the dried, the fennel, sugar, and salt and pepper. Bring the sauce to boil, lower the heat, and simmer for 5 minutes. Remove from heat.

3. Drain the scallops and pat dry.

4. In another skillet, heat the remaining 2 tablespoons oil. Add the scallops and sauté until opaque, 3 to 5 minutes; do not overcook or they will toughen. Add to the warm tomato sauce and bring just to boil, then immediately remove from heat. Sprinkle with the remaining fresh basil and serve.

Calamari, Pasta, and Shrimp

CALAMARI AT CHRISTMASTIME

Most fish stores now sell whole squid that have been cleaned and are ready for filling. They even come frozen in packages.

8 Servings

STUFFED SQUID

1 tablespoon olive oil

1 tablespoon butter

2 pounds fresh or frozen whole squid, about 8 medium or 12 small

½ cup finely chopped onion

¼ cup dry white wine

1 cup fresh breadcrumbs

1 tablespoon grated orange zest

⅓ cup raisins

1 tablespoon grated Parmesan cheese

1 large egg, lightly beaten

salt and pepper

SAUCE

2 tablespoons olive oil

2 tablespoons butter

½ cup finely chopped onion

1 garlic clove, minced

2 cups canned plum tomatoes, put through a food mill (reserve 2 or 3 whole tomatoes; cut into pieces and add to the pureed tomatoes)

¾ cup dry white wine

½ teaspoon dried oregano

pinch of red pepper flakes

salt and pepper

2 tablespoons finely chopped flat-leaf parsley

FOR THE SQUID

1. In a skillet, heat the oil and butter. Cut off the tentacles from the squid and chop them. Add the onion and chopped tentacles to the skillet and sauté until lightly browned. Transfer to a mixing bowl.

2. Add the wine to the skillet and boil over high heat until reduced by half. With a rubber spatula, scrape the liquid into the mixing bowl. Add the breadcrumbs, orange zest, raisins, cheese, egg, and salt and pepper to taste and mix well. The stuffing should be fairly dry; if it is too dry, add a tablespoon more of white wine.

3. Stuff the squid a little more than half full to allow room for expansion. Secure the opening with a toothpick or sew loosely with white thread.

FOR THE SAUCE

1. In a skillet, heat 1 tablespoon each of the oil and butter until bubbling. Add the stuffed squid and cook over low heat until whitish and almost translucent. Transfer to a dish and set aside.

2. In a large covered saucepan, heat the remaining oil and butter. Sauté the onion until pale yellow, about 4 minutes. Add the garlic and cook 1 minute, stirring. Add the tomatoes, wine, oregano, pepper flakes, and salt and pepper. Cook uncovered over high heat for 5 minutes, stirring frequently.

3. Add the squid to the pan (in a single layer, if possible), cover, and simmer over low heat for 30 minutes. Sprinkle with chopped parsley and serve.

Christmas Pastries

COD WITH TINY PASTA SHELLS

8 Servings

1 pound salted dried codfish

2½ cups milk

1 garlic clove, peeled and halved

¼ cup olive oil

2 tablespoons butter

pepper

1 cup half-and-half or light cream

1 pound tiny pasta shells

1. Soak the codfish in cool water for 24 hours, changing water frequently.

2. Preheat oven to 350°F. Drain the fish and place in a covered baking dish. Add the milk and garlic, cover, and bake 30 minutes.

3. Drain and discard milk; reserve garlic. Remove bones and skin from fish. Puree the cod with the garlic, adding oil and butter a little at a time. Season liberally with pepper. Add half-and-half or cream and process just to blend.

4. Cook the pasta and drain well. Add the sauce and toss, seasoning with more black pepper.

John Imperiale's Eel with White Wine, Brandy, and Thyme

Eel must be freshly killed and skinned at once. Your fishmonger will do this for you. Conger eel, also known as sea eel, is common along the Atlantic coast.

8 Servings

8 pieces of eel, each about 2 inches long

juice of 1½ lemons

1 cup semidry white wine

3 tablespoons brandy

1 tablespoon chopped fresh thyme or 1 teaspoon dried

¼ cup olive oil

salt and pepper

2 tablespoons chopped fresh basil or 1 tablespoon dried

½ teaspoon paprika

1. Rinse and dry the eel and place in a glass or ceramic dish in one layer.

2. Combine lemon juice, wine, brandy, thyme, half the olive oil, and salt and pepper; mix and pour over fish. Refrigerate 2 hours or overnight. Bring to room temperature before broiling.

3. Preheat broiler. Split each eel piece lengthwise and pat the basil between the halves. Broil 10 to 15 minutes, turning several times and basting with remaining olive oil and paprika. (Eel is done when it turns white and a wooden skewer can be inserted with no resistance.) Serve immediately.

Sister Bea's Italian Christmas Bow Pastries

Since these keep well for up to two weeks in a cool place, it's a good idea to make the whole recipe and have the pastries on hand for family and friends during the holiday season.

Makes about 100

7 cups all-purpose flour

1 teaspoon salt

2 teaspoons baking powder

12 eggs, beaten

3 tablespoons vegetable oil

6 cups vegetable oil (for deep-frying)

honey and/or confectioner's sugar

1. In a large bowl, combine 6 cups flour with the salt and baking powder. Make a well in the center of the mixture. Add the eggs and 3 tablespoons oil to the well and mix thoroughly.

2. Turn the dough out onto a floured work surface and knead until very smooth and elastic, about 20 minutes, adding as much of the reserved 1 cup flour as necessary. Cover with a kitchen towel and let the dough rest for 15 minutes.

TO SHAPE THE PASTRIES

1. If you have a pasta machine, first shape the dough to resemble a loaf about 17 inches long and 3 inches wide. Cut the loaf into 1-inch slices and flour lightly. Flatten the pieces with a rolling pin and then put each piece twice through the rollers of the pasta machine. Change the dial setting to narrow the opening; pass the dough strips through four or five more times, or until the dough is less than ⅛ inch thick.

2. Arrange the dough strips on floured waxed paper. Cut each strip cross-wise, diagonally, into 1½-inch-wide pieces, using a zigzag-edge ravioli cutter if available; each pastry should be approximately 1½ by 5 inches.

Pinch each strip together in the center with the thumb and index finger to give the pastries a bow shape.

3. If you don't have a pasta machine, divide the dough into 8 parts. Roll each part into a circle less than ⅛ inch thick. Cut the circle into strips about 4 to 5 inches wide with a ravioli cutter, then slice again into 1½-inch widths. Pinch each center to make bows.

TO FRY THE PASTRIES

1. For fastest results, use a roasting pan that will fit over two burners on your stovetop; failing this, use a large skillet. Half-fill the pan with oil. Do not use pans deeper than 2½ inches; the extra depth simply is not necessary and will waste oil.

2. Heat the oil until hot but not smoking. Test for the right temperature by adding a tiny piece of dough to the oil; if it rises to the top, the oil is hot enough.

3. Drop the pastries into the hot oil one at a time, leaving some space in between. Fry until golden on one side, about 1 minute; use a wooden spoon and fork to turn each pastry and cook the other side. Keep to an assembly-line rhythm: by the time you've put the eighth or tenth pastry into the oil, the first will be ready to come out, and so on.

4. Transfer the cooked pastries to paper toweling and cool. Arrange on a platter or store in a covered box. They will keep in a cool place for about two weeks.

5. To serve, stack the pastries in layers and sprinkle with honey in thin lines resembling angel's hair, or sprinkle with confectioner's sugar.

Though it is difficult to believe today, the New England Puritans of the 17th century disliked Christmas, probably because it reminded them of the Anglican Tories who had persecuted them. In 1640 a law was passed in Massachusetts declaring that Christmas, Easter, and Whitsuntide were not to be observed by merrymaking or the like, under penalty of 5 shillings for every offense. In 1643, pastry, plum cakes, and "sinful dalliance" were held in abomination by the Puritan court of New Haven. Though the Massachusetts anti-Christmas law was repealed in 1681, December 25 remained a workday.

It was not until 1791, when the separation of Church and State were assured by a Constitutional amendment, that members of the Puritan churches began to soften their opposition to Christmas because it no longer seemed that the Church of England dominated politics. But we should not ignore the influence of the new Irish Catholic and German Protestant immigrants, who were determined to celebrate Christmas.

From about 1840 on, Christmas became popular in the New England states. Newspapers and magazines advertised holiday food and decorations, and some historians claim that the commercialization of Christmas began in New England. Look at the Christmas card, for example: Louis Prang, the father of American Christmas cards, popularized them in the Boston area and dominated the printing of Christmas cards for the rest of the century.

Today, Boston's Christmas festivities would draw sneers from the graves of the Puritans. The city sparkles with thousands of festive lights, strings itself in miles of green garlands, and displays a life-size crèche for public viewing.

Christmas in New England

DINNER MENU FOR 12

CRABMEAT CANAPES

LIGHT VEGETABLE CREAM SOUP
WITH PASTRY STARS

ROAST TURKEY WITH SUGARED
GRAPES AND GIBLET GRAVY

CHESTNUT STUFFING WITH
SCALLIONS AND TARRAGON

MARION CLEVELAND'S CRANBERRY
AND LEMON COMPOTE
WITH GRAND MARNIER

BUTTERED BRUSSELS SPROUTS
WITH A HINT OF CURRY

SUGARED PLUM TOMATOES

YEAST ROLLS

SALAD OF THREE GREENS WITH
OIL AND VINEGAR

STILTON CHEESE

MAPLE MACADAMIA PIE

FRESH FRUIT

MENU

The Christmas Table

FOOD PREPARATION

3 days ahead:
- Bake yeast rolls and freeze
- Make cranberry and lemon compote

2 days ahead:
- Prepare soup
- Make sugared grapes

1 day ahead:
- Make chestnut stuffing and gravy
- Prepare salad greens
- Bake pie
- Assemble crabmeat mixture

Serving day:
- Roast turkey
- Make pastry stars for the soup
- Cook brussels sprouts, plum tomatoes; heat soup, rolls, and crabmeat; whip cream for pie

WINE SUGGESTIONS

Wines for this American dinner should have an Eastern accent. A small sherry glass of Madeira, the wine most popular during Colonial times, accompanies the soup; you might even want to pour a little from your glass into the soup to reaffirm a tradition.

Serve Blandy Rainwater Madeira with the soup, Bedell Cellars North Fork Long Island Merlot and Millbrook Hudson River Valley Chardonnay with the dinner, and Taylor 10-year-old Tawny Port with the cheese.

CRABMEAT CANAPES

Instead of broiling the canapés, you may want to serve the warmed crabmeat mixture in a chafing dish, accompanied by bread and crackers.

12 Servings

6 ounces cream cheese, room temperature

½ pound crabmeat

1 tablespoon mayonnaise

½ teaspoon Worcestershire sauce

salt and white pepper

36 bread or cracker rounds

paprika

1. Beat the cream cheese with an electric mixer until soft and fluffy. With a rubber spatula or wooden spoon, fold in the crabmeat, mayonnaise, Worcestershire sauce, and salt and pepper. Store in refrigerator; bring to cool room temperature before serving.

2. Preheat the broiler. Spread the crabmeat mixture onto the bread rounds and arrange on a broiler pan. Sprinkle lightly with paprika. Broil the canapés 4 inches below the heat source for several minutes or until hot and bubbling. Serve right away.

LIGHT VEGETABLE CREAM SOUP WITH PASTRY STARS

12 Servings

4 large or 8 small leeks, washed and cut into ½-inch-thick slices

6 cups cooked vegetables (combine as many as you can: broccoli, carrots, celery, peas, zucchini, etc.)

½ cup butter

¼ cup all-purpose flour

6 cups chicken stock or broth

1 tablespoon sugar

2 tablespoons chopped fresh tarragon or 2 teaspoons dried

1 cup half-and-half or light cream

¼ cup dry sherry

salt and pepper

Pastry Stars (see next page)

1. In a large saucepan, sauté leeks and cooked vegetables in melted butter for about 10 minutes. Sprinkle flour over the vegetables, stir well, and cook 4 minutes longer.

2. Add the stock, sugar, and tarragon, stirring constantly. Bring to boil, then lower heat, cover, and cook 15 minutes.

3. Puree the mixture in batches in a processor or food mill. Return to the saucepan and add the half-and-half or cream, sherry, and salt and pepper. Bring just to the boiling point but do not let the soup boil. Thin with a little more stock if you wish. (Soup can be made ahead and refrigerated up to 3 days. Reheat before serving.)

4. Pour the soup into 5-inch bowls. (If the bowls are a different size, adjust the size of the pastry stars accordingly.) Top each with a pastry star. Serve immediately.

PASTRY STARS

Frozen puff pastry is available in the supermarket. Each 17 ½-ounce (489 g) package contains two sheets, about 10 inches square.

Makes 12

2 sheets frozen puff pastry, thawed

1 egg

1 tablespoon half-and-half or light cream

½ cup grated Parmesan cheese

paprika

1. Lay the pastry sheets flat on a lightly floured surface. Whip the egg and half-and-half or cream together and brush lightly over both sheets. To make stars to fit 5-inch bowls, cut a 3 × 10-inch strip of pastry off one edge of each sheet. With a sharp knife or plain ravioli cutter, cut the remainder of the pastry sheet into 18 strips, about one-half inch wide and 7 inches long. Cut the 3 × 10-piece into 6 more strips of the same size. You will need 24 of the 7 × one-half-inch strips; there will be a little waste.

2. Cut the second pastry sheet in half to make two 5 × 10-inch pieces, then cut them crosswise into 5 × one-half-inch strips. You will need 24; there will be some pastry left over.

3. Arrange two of the longer strips on a cookie sheet to make a cross. Lay two of the shorter strips between the longer strips to form a second cross at a 45-degree angle to the first. (In other words, the long strips point north, south, east, and west; the short strips point northeast, southwest, northwest, and southeast.) Repeat to make 12 stars. Press lightly in the center of each star to help the strips stick together.

4. Preheat oven to 400°F. Sprinkle Parmesan over the strips. Dust with a little paprika. Bake until lightly browned, about 10 minutes.

Vegetable Cream Soup With Pastry Star. (If using bowls larger than 5 inches in diameter, place star directly in soup bowl just before serving. Otherwise, set star on top of bowl as in recipe.)

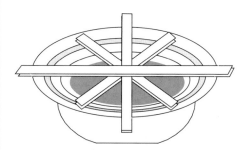

ROAST TURKEY WITH SUGARED GRAPES AND GIBLET GRAVY

This turkey is roasted without a stuffing and decorated with sugared grapes. The stuffing is baked in a separate dish, making it crispier and easier to serve. Both are served with special giblet gravy.

12 Servings

TURKEY

1 14- to 16-pound turkey, giblets reserved

juice of 2 lemons

6 tablespoons butter, softened

salt and pepper

1. Rinse the turkey inside and out, or clean with damp paper towels. Rub the inside and out with the lemon juice, then with butter. Season lightly with salt and pepper.

2. Preheat oven to 325°F. Place the bird on a rack in a roasting pan and roast about 5 hours, or until a thermometer inserted in the thickest part of the thigh reads 170°F to 175°F, basting every 30 minutes with pan drippings. When done, the drumstick will move up and down easily and juices will run clear when the thigh is pricked.

3. Transfer the turkey to a warm platter, cover loosely with foil, and let rest 20 minutes for easier carving.

4. Drain off fat from the drippings, leaving 3 tablespoons of the drippings in the roasting pan to make the gravy.

GRAVY
Makes about 2 ¾ cups

reserved turkey giblets

1 small to medium onion, quartered

1 ½ teaspoons salt

pepper

3 cups water

3 sprigs fresh tarragon or 1 teaspoon dried

2 parsley sprigs

3 tablespoons turkey drippings

1 cup brown sauce (see page 192)

¼ cup cognac or brandy

1. Combine the giblets, onion, salt, pepper, and water in a saucepan and bring to boil, skimming any froth that rises to the surface.

2. Add the tarragon and parsley. Lower heat and simmer until the giblets are cooked, about 30 to 35 minutes. Strain. Chop the giblets into tiny pieces and reserve. Return the broth to the saucepan.

3. Add the pan drippings. Scrape up the browned bits in the roasting pan and add them too. Over high heat, boil the mixture until reduced by half.

4. Add the brown sauce, reserved giblets, and cognac and bring to boil. Lower heat and simmer for 5 minutes. Add salt and pepper, if needed. Keep warm until ready to serve. Pass the gravy separately in a sauceboat.

SUGARED GRAPES
Makes 6 small clusters

6 small clusters of grapes

2 egg whites, beaten until frothy

½ cup sugar

1. Dip grape clusters into the egg whites, coating completely. Pour the sugar into a wide saucer and press the grapes lightly into it.

2. Arrange the grape clusters around the turkey just before serving. The sugared grapes may be made a day or two ahead and refrigerated until needed.

Maple Macadamia Pie

CHESTNUT STUFFING WITH SCALLIONS AND TARRAGON

12 Servings

3 cups chopped roasted fresh or peeled canned chestnuts (if canned, you will need 20 ounces drained or 31 ounces undrained)

1½ cups thinly sliced scallions

1 cup diced celery

½ to ¾ cup butter

2 tablespoons chopped fresh tarragon or 1 teaspoon dried

1 tablespoon salt

1½ teaspoons freshly ground pepper

1 tablespoon poultry seasoning

1 cup chopped parsley

8 cups freshly made soft French or Italian breadcrumbs or store-bought packaged stuffing

1. To roast fresh chestnuts, first wash them, then cut slits in both sides of each nut. Preheat oven to 475°F. Place the chestnuts in a shallow pan and bake 15 minutes. Shell the nuts and peel off the skins. Place in a saucepan, cover with boiling salted water, and cook, covered, until tender, 15 to 20 minutes. Drain and set aside.

2. Sauté the scallions and celery in ½ cup butter just until soft. Add the tarragon, salt, pepper, poultry seasoning, parsley, and chestnuts and sauté 2 to 3 minutes.

3. Place the crumbs in a large bowl. With a rubber spatula, add the chestnut mixture to the crumbs and toss lightly but well, adding more melted butter to make the mixture moist but not soggy. Adjust seasoning. Transfer to a lightly buttered 2-quart baking dish. Bake until stuffing is crisp on top, 50 to 60 minutes, basting occasionally with juices from the turkey roasting pan. Serve hot.

MARION CLEVELAND'S CRANBERRY AND LEMON COMPOTE WITH GRAND MARNIER

12 Servings

2 bags (12 ounces each) cranberries, rinsed and sorted

2 tablespoons finely chopped lemon zest

juice of 2 lemons

1 cup sugar

¼ cup Grand Marnier

Preheat oven to 325°F. Lightly butter a large, shallow baking pan. Scatter the cranberries in it. Sprinkle with the lemon zest and juice, then with the sugar and liqueur. Cover tightly with foil and bake until the berries have popped and the sugar has melted, about 45 minutes. Transfer to a serving dish and serve warm, at room temperature, or chilled.

BUTTERED BRUSSELS SPROUTS WITH A HINT OF CURRY

Brussels sprouts are available all winter. They may be sold in pints or quarts, or by the pound as they are at the Waterfront Market in Key West, Florida. I prefer to choose the ones I want from an open bin. If you must use frozen sprouts, cook them according to package directions.

12 Servings

2 quarts fresh brussels sprouts

¼ cup butter

1 teaspoon curry powder

salt and pepper

1. Trim the outer leaves of the sprouts and cut off the lower part of the stem with a sharp knife. Cut a cross in the stem end. Soak the sprouts in cool salted water at least 30 minutes before cooking. Drain.

2. Place 1 quart sprouts in a 10-inch microwave-safe pie dish. Add 2 tablespoons water, cover with plastic wrap, and cook on High 10 minutes. Cook the second quart in the same way. If you do not have a microwave, cook the sprouts, covered, in a small amount of boiling salted water for 10 to 15 minutes or until just tender; do not overcook. Drain well.

3. In a large skillet, melt 2 tablespoons butter. Add ½ teaspoon curry powder and stir well for 10 seconds. Add 1 quart cooked brussels sprouts and stir well to coat. Season with salt and pepper. Toss again and transfer to a large serving bowl. Repeat this procedure for the second quart and serve.

SUGARED PLUM TOMATOES

12 Servings

6 cups peeled, seeded fresh tomatoes, halved, or drained canned plum tomatoes, seeded but kept whole

½ cup firmly packed brown sugar

2 tablespoons finely chopped preserved ginger

2 garlic cloves, minced

salt and pepper

Preheat oven to 375°F. Place the tomatoes in a baking pan and sprinkle with the sugar, ginger, and garlic. Bake until the tomatoes are heated through and the sugar is melted, about 20 to 30 minutes. Season with salt and pepper. Serve hot.

Yeast Rolls

These rolls should be served piping hot with butter. They freeze exceptionally well.

Makes 40 to 50

½ cup sugar

1 teaspoon salt

1 cup milk, scalded

¼ cup butter, melted

¼ cup vegetable shortening, melted

6 cups all-purpose flour

2 eggs

2½ envelopes dry yeast dissolved in ⅔ cup lukewarm water

butter or shortening

1. In a large bowl, combine the sugar and salt. Add the milk, butter, and shortening and combine well.

2. Add 2 cups flour, 1 cup at a time, and stir with a wooden spoon. Blend in eggs one at a time.

3. Add the yeast mixture and the remaining 4 cups flour, ½ cup at a time.

4. Turn the dough out onto a floured work surface and knead until smooth and elastic, about 10 minutes, adding more flour if dough is sticky.

5. Warm a large, deep bowl and grease it. Place the dough in the bowl and cover with a towel. Let rise in a warm place until doubled.

6. Turn the dough out onto a lightly floured work surface and cut in half. Set one half aside, covered. Roll the other half into a circle about ½ inch thick. Using a 2½-inch biscuit cutter, cut out circles as close to one another as possible. Remove the trimmings, roll into a ball, and set under the towel with remaining dough.

7. With a knife, mark a straight line across each dough circle, without cutting all the way through. Fold in half on the scored line and make a thumb impression in the curved edge. Arrange the rolls on a greased baking sheet, spacing 1 inch apart. Cover with a towel and let rise in a warm place 1 hour. Repeat with the remaining dough and trimmings.

8. Preheat oven to 400°F. Bake the rolls about 15 minutes or until browned. Serve warm. To make the rolls ahead, cool, wrap tightly in foil, and freeze. Thaw, then heat (still wrapped) in a 450°F oven for 15 minutes.

Salad of Three Greens with Oil and Vinegar

I like to serve this accompanied by a wedge of Stilton cheese, passed separately.

12 Servings

3 large heads of lettuce and/or other greens (choose among romaine, Boston, Bibb, curly endive, watercress, and so on)

¼ cup white wine vinegar

1 teaspoon sugar (optional)

salt and pepper

¾ cup olive oil

1. Sort over the lettuce leaves, rinse well, and dry. Place in one or more plastic bags and refrigerate until ready to use. (This may be done a day ahead.)

2. In a small bowl, stir together the vinegar, sugar, and salt and pepper. Whisk in the oil a little at a time. (The dressing may be made a day ahead and refrigerated; bring to room temperature before using.) Dress the greens just before serving.

Maple Macadamia Pie

Makes one 9-inch pie; double for 12 servings

1 cup macadamia nuts, halved

1 unbaked 9-inch pie shell (see page 193)

1 cup shredded coconut

3 eggs, room temperature

¼ cup sugar

1 cup pure maple syrup

6 tablespoons butter, melted and cooled

¼ teaspoon salt

1 cup heavy cream, whipped

1. Preheat oven to 400°F. Arrange the halved macadamias in one layer over the bottom of the pie shell, covering as much of the pastry as you can. Sprinkle the coconut over the macadamias.

2. Beat the eggs in a large bowl. Add the sugar, maple syrup, melted butter, and salt and mix well. Pour into the pie shell.

3. Bake the pie for 15 minutes. Lower the heat to 350°F and bake until the filling is set and a knife inserted in the center comes out clean, 20 to 25 minutes longer. Cover the top with foil if it browns too quickly. The filling will rise substantially, but it will fall to the level of the pie dish as it cools.

4. Serve the pie lukewarm with a dollop of whipped cream.

Crabmeat Canapés

The southern states' first colonial cuisine was English, but it didn't take long for other cultures to make a lasting impact on southern kitchens. Before the end of the 17th century, French refugees fleeing Huguenot persecution moved to South Carolina and Florida; many Rhinelanders settled in those areas not much later. Nevertheless, many consider the slaves to have been the real southern cooks. Instinctively changing and improving recipes given them by the plantation mistresses, slave cooks often substituted local ingredients for foreign imports—and isn't this, after all, what's done today by a league of young culinary celebrities all over the country?

There were, and are, bounties of black walnuts, pecans, and hickory nuts used in stuffings, dressings, salads, compotes, preserves, breads, cakes, and pies. There were, and are, wild berries and fruits, and beautiful ears of corn. The corn fattened the pigs and made the hams taste better; it was ground into flour or meal for muffins, breads, and puddings. It was and still is customary to make cornbread, then crumble it to make a stuffing for pork, ham, and fowl.

Most of the South shares culinary roots; perhaps this has to do with the limitless supply of vegetables and fruits, river fish, and game, pork products, and seafood brought up from the Gulf. But I think it's because Southerners make good eating the main point of every meal.

Christmas in the South

DINNER MENU FOR 8

COLD SHRIMP WITH GINGER

WILD MUSHROOM SOUP WITH
THYME

CROWN ROAST OF PORK WITH
GARLIC, MINT, AND LEMON

BAKED CORNBREAD-PECAN STUFFING

SAVORY COLLARD GREENS

CORN CUSTARD

BRANDIED FIGS

MIXED GREENS WITH JEFFERSON
DRESSING

DIANA BUCHANAN'S BUTTERMILK
BISCUITS

PRALINE MERINGUE PIE

POACHED PEARS WITH RASPBERRIES

BOURBON BALLS

Wild Mushroom Soup

FOOD PREPARATION

1 month ahead:
- Make brandied figs

1 week ahead:
- Make bourbon balls

2 to 3 days ahead:
- Prepare shrimp with ginger, mushroom soup, and cornbread
- Bake biscuits and freeze
- Poach pears

1 day ahead:
- Bake pie
- Make salad dressing

Serving day:
- Roast pork and dressing
- Make corn custard
- Heat soup
- Dress salad

WINE SUGGESTIONS

Serve Mumm's Cuvée Napa Blanc de Noirs before the meal. Then serve Sercial Madeira with the soup, Arrowood Vineyards Cabernet Sauvignon with the pork, and Bonny Doon Framboise with the desserts.

COLD SHRIMP WITH GINGER

8 Servings

2 pounds large shrimp (16 to 18 count per pound), shelled and deveined

2 lemons, sliced as thinly as possible, seeded

1 onion, sliced as thinly as possible and separated into rings

1 ½-inch piece fresh ginger, peeled and sliced as thinly as possible

⅓ cup chopped parsley

2 cups cider vinegar

2 tablespoons pickling spice

2 teaspoons salt

1 teaspoon dry mustard

½ cup olive oil

½ cup vegetable oil

1. Bring a large pot of salted water to boil. Add the shrimp and cook until they turn pink, about 3 to 4 minutes; do not overcook or they will toughen. Drain and dry the shrimp well. Place in a large glass bowl.

2. Add the lemon slices, onion, ginger, and parsley and toss lightly.

3. In a nonaluminum saucepan, combine the vinegar, pickling spice, salt, and dry mustard and bring to boil, stirring to dissolve the mustard and salt. Add the hot liquid and the oils to the shrimp mixture and toss well to coat. Top with a plate to keep the shrimp immersed. Cover tightly with plastic wrap and refrigerate at least overnight or up to 3 days. Serve as an hors d'oeuvre by spooning 3 or 4 shrimp, with some of the sauce, onto individual plates.

WILD MUSHROOM SOUP WITH THYME

8 Servings

1 pound white mushrooms

¾ pound shiitake or chanterelle mushrooms

juice of 2 lemons

¼ cup butter

4 scallions, thinly sliced, including tender green parts

2 large sprigs fresh thyme (leaves only) or ½ teaspoon dried

salt and pepper

4 cups half-and-half or light cream

3 cups chicken stock or broth

2 teaspoons cornstarch dissolved in 2 tablespoons water

1. Wipe the mushrooms clean. Place in a bowl and sprinkle them with lemon juice. Toss well. Remove enough mushrooms to make about ½ cup very thin slices; reserve for garnish. Coarsely chop the remaining mushrooms in a food processor.

2. In a large saucepan, melt the butter and cook the scallions until they become limp. Add the chopped mushrooms and the thyme and cook until most of the liquid disappears, about 12 to 15 minutes. Add the salt and pepper, half-and-half or cream, and stock, and bring to boil. Lower the heat and simmer for 15 minutes.

3. Add the cornstarch mixture and simmer 15 minutes longer, stirring frequently. Serve in individual soup bowls, garnished with several slices of fresh mushroom.

Cold Shrimp With Ginger

CROWN ROAST OF PORK WITH GARLIC, MINT, AND LEMON

Add a white paper frill to the end of each chop bone before serving.

8 to 10 Servings

6 tablespoons butter

2 garlic cloves, minced

1 tablespoon finely chopped fresh thyme or 1 teaspoon dried

1 teaspoon dried mint

1 teaspoon grated lemon zest

1 teaspoon each salt and pepper

1 crown roast of pork made of 18 to 20 chops (about 7 to 8 pounds)

1. Preheat oven to 350°F. Combine 4 tablespoons butter with the garlic, thyme, mint, lemon zest, and salt and pepper in a small bowl to make a paste. Rub the paste all over the crown roast. Wrap foil over the end of each bone to prevent blackening. Arrange the meat in a roasting pan.

2. Roast in the center of the oven for about 2½ hours or until a thermometer inserted in the thickest part reads 160°F to 170°F. Carefully transfer the roast to a serving platter and let rest for about 10 minutes before serving.

BAKED CORNBREAD-PECAN STUFFING

Makes about 8 cups

2 tablespoons butter

1 cup thinly sliced celery

1 cup finely chopped scallions or onion

½ cup finely chopped red bell pepper

1 8-inch-square Cornbread (see below), crumbled

1 cup coarsely chopped pecans

½ cup chopped parsley

1 large or 2 small eggs, lightly beaten

1½ teaspoons poultry seasoning

salt and pepper

½ cup milk, or more

1. Preheat oven to 350°F. In a skillet, melt the butter. Add the celery, scallions, and red pepper and cook until softened, about 4 minutes. Transfer to a large bowl.

2. Add the crumbled cornbread and all remaining ingredients, using enough milk to make a moist stuffing. Toss lightly but well. Transfer to a buttered 2-quart baking dish. Bake 1 hour, covering the top with foil if it browns too quickly.

CORNBREAD
Makes one 8-inch pan

1 cup all-purpose flour

1 cup yellow cornmeal

4 teaspoons baking powder

2 teaspoons sugar

½ teaspoon salt

1 egg, lightly beaten

1 cup milk

¼ cup butter, melted

1. Preheat oven to 425°F. In a large bowl, combine the flour, cornmeal, baking powder, sugar, and salt. Add the egg, milk, and melted butter and stir just until the dry ingredients are moistened.

2. Spread the batter in a buttered 8-inch square pan and bake until the cornbread is golden and the sides are coming away from the sides of the pan, about 20 to 25 minutes. Cool on a rack before crumbling.

SAVORY COLLARD GREENS

This may also be prepared with mustard greens or fresh young turnip greens.

8 Servings

4 pounds fresh collard greens

¼ cup olive oil

2 large onions, coarsely chopped

4 garlic cloves, minced

1 cup chicken stock or broth

2 tablespoons fresh lime juice

salt and pepper

1. Snip away the stem of each collard leaf and cut away any discolored or blemished parts. Tear the leaves into smaller pieces and rinse in several changes of cool water. Drain but do not spin dry; the leaves should have some drops of water on them.

2. Over medium heat, heat the oil in a large saucepan. Add the onions and sauté until golden, 7 to 10 minutes. Add the garlic and cook 1 minute longer.

3. Add the collard greens, cover, and cook over high heat for 5 minutes or until they begin to wilt. Add the stock and continue to cook over medium heat, covered, until the greens are tender; this may take up to 45 minutes. Add the lime juice and salt and pepper and toss well.

CORN CUSTARD

8 Servings

2 cups fresh or thawed frozen corn kernels

3 eggs, room temperature

¼ cup all-purpose flour

salt and white pepper

3 tablespoons butter, melted

2 cups half-and-half or light cream

1. If using fresh corn, drop 6 to 8 ears of corn into boiling salted water and cook 7 minutes. Drain and rinse under cool water. Cut or scrape the kernels to make 2 cups. If using frozen corn kernels, thaw according to package directions.

2. Preheat oven to 350°F. Beat the eggs until well blended. Add the corn and mix well. Add the flour and salt and pepper and mix well. Stir in the melted butter and half-and-half or cream.

3. Liberally butter a 1½-quart baking dish and pour the corn mixture into it. Set it in a larger pan and add hot water to the larger pan to reach 1 inch below the top of the custard dish.

4. Bake until the custard is set and a knife inserted in the center comes out fairly clean and dry, about 1 hour. Serve hot.

BRANDIED FIGS

These should be made when fresh figs are available and should be allowed to stand for about a month. They are a perfect complement to meat and fowl alike.

Makes two 1-quart or four 1-pint jars

5 pounds sugar

2 cups water

12 whole cloves

4 cinnamon sticks

1 lemon, very thinly sliced, seeded

2 tablespoons finely chopped preserved or grated fresh ginger

24 large fresh figs

½ cup brandy

1. Have 4 pint-size or 2 quart-size jars washed, sterilized, and ready to be filled.

2. In a large saucepan, combine the sugar, water, cloves, cinnamon, lemon, and ginger. Cook over low heat until the sugar is dissolved, about 10 minutes.

3. Carefully add the figs (they bruise easily) and simmer until the figs become translucent, about 45 minutes.

4. Transfer the figs to the jars with a slotted spoon, dividing equally. Also apportion the cloves, cinnamon sticks, lemon slices, and ginger among the jars. Pour an equal amount of brandy into each jar and top up the jars with the syrup. Cover and seal the jars. Let them stand 1 month or longer before serving.

MIXED GREENS WITH JEFFERSON DRESSING

Rinse and dry enough salad greens for eight portions. Use two or three of the following: bibb lettuce, romaine, curly endive hearts, leaf lettuce, limestone, mâche, arugula, watercress. Store in a plastic bag in the refrigerator until ready to use. Just before serving time, pour the dressing over the greens a little at a time, being sure not to overdress the salad. A general rule is that the more delicate the lettuce, the less dressing is needed.

8 Servings; makes 1 cup dressing

1 garlic clove, minced

½ teaspoon salt

½ teaspoon white pepper

⅓ cup tarragon wine vinegar

⅓ cup olive oil

⅓ cup sesame oil

1. In a bowl, mash the garlic with the salt and pepper. Whisk in the vinegar a little at a time, then gradually whisk in the oils until the dressing is well combined and smooth.

2. This can be made well ahead and refrigerated in a covered jar. Bring to room temperature before using.

DIANA BUCHANAN'S BUTTERMILK BISCUITS

Makes 12 to 16; can be doubled

2 cups all-purpose flour

1 teaspoon salt

4 teaspoons baking powder

2 tablespoons vegetable shortening, melted

¾ to 1 cup buttermilk

1. Preheat oven to 425°F. Place the flour in a large bowl and make a well in the center. Add the salt, baking powder, shortening, and ¾ cup buttermilk to the well.

2. Mix all the ingredients with a wooden spoon. When thoroughly combined, turn the mixture out onto a lightly floured work surface and knead just until a dough is formed. Roll out ½ inch thick right away. Cut out biscuits with a 2½-inch round cutter as close to one another as possible. Arrange on a buttered baking sheet.

3. Bake until biscuits are lightly browned, about 10 to 15 minutes. Serve right away, or freeze; wrap the biscuits in foil to reheat.

PRALINE MERINGUE PIE

8 Servings
PIE SHELL

4 egg whites, room temperature

pinch of cream of tartar

pinch of salt

¾ cup sugar

¼ teaspoon vanilla extract

vegetable oil

1. Beat the egg whites until frothy. Add the cream of tartar and salt and beat until soft peaks form. Beat in sugar a tablespoon at a time until the whites form shiny, firm peaks. Blend in vanilla.

2. Preheat oven to 200°F. Generously oil a 9- or 10-inch glass pie plate, being sure to oil the top of the rim. With a rubber spatula, scrape the meringue into the pie plate. Mound the meringue in the center; then, beginning at the center of the mound, push the meringue to the outer edge of the pie plate in sweeping motions to create a free-form, swirled meringue crust.

3. Bake in center of oven for 2 hours; the meringue should look dry, lightly cracked, and a light beige color. Cool on a rack before filling.

FILLING

4 egg yolks, room temperature

½ cup sugar

1 tablespoon fresh lemon juice

3 tablespoons bourbon

1 cup heavy cream, whipped

Praline Powder (see next page)

2 tablespoons unflavored gelatin

3 tablespoons cold water

1. Combine the yolks and sugar in the top of a double boiler, mixing well with a small wire whisk. Heat the yolk mixture over simmering water until thickened to the consistency of soft custard, about 10 minutes, stirring constantly. The egg must not be allowed to curdle; if you think the yolks are cooking too quickly, either lower the heat or lift the top pan off the simmering water for a few seconds. Cook until mixture thickens to a soft custard.

2. Remove the top pan and set into a bowl of ice cubes. Add the lemon juice and bourbon and mix well. When cooled, transfer to a large bowl. Fold in the whipped cream and praline powder.

3. Sprinkle the gelatin over the water in a measuring cup and let stand 5 minutes. Set the cup in a pan of simmering water and stir until the gelatin dissolves. Fold into the filling mixture.

4. Fill the meringue shell and refrigerate the pie for about 3 hours.

Praline Meringue Pie

PRALINE POWDER

1 cup sugar

1 cup chopped pecans

pinch of salt

1. Butter a baking sheet.

2. In a skillet, caramelize the sugar over low heat until it turns light brown. Stir in the pecans. Immediately pour this mixture onto the prepared baking sheet. Let cool and harden. Break the praline in pieces and pulverize it in a blender or processor.

POACHED PEARS WITH RASPBERRIES

8 Servings

8 ripe pears

juice of 1 lemon

1 bottle (750 ml) white wine

1 vanilla bean, split in half

⅓ cup sugar

cinnamon

2 cups fresh raspberries

1. Peel the pears; halve lengthwise and core. Place lemon juice in a bowl and, as each pear is prepared, toss the halves lightly in the juice to coat.

2. Combine the wine, vanilla bean, and sugar in a large nonaluminum saucepan and bring to boil. Reduce heat, add the pears, and poach at a very gentle simmer until tender, 15 to 20 minutes.

3. Serve in a bowl with a little of the poaching syrup or arrange two halves on each of 8 plates. Sprinkle lightly with cinnamon. Accompany the pears with raspberries.

BOURBON BALLS

Makes 4 to 5 dozen

3 cups (about 60) crushed vanilla wafers

1 cup finely chopped pecans

1½ cups sugar

8 ounces semisweet chocolate, melted and cooled

½ cup bourbon

¼ cup light corn syrup

1. Combine the crushed wafers, pecans, and ⅔ cup sugar in a large bowl. Add the chocolate, bourbon, and corn syrup and mix with a wooden spoon until blended.

2. Place the remaining sugar on a plate and set it near the bowl. Roll a tablespoon of the mixture into a ball about 1 inch in diameter. Roll in sugar. Repeat with the remaining mixture.

3. Dampen a white paper napkin or towel with bourbon and use it to line the bottom of a candy tin or cake box. Set the balls close to one another on the towel. Continue layering as needed, separating the layers with bourbon-dampened towels. Cover tightly. Let the bourbon balls stand at room temperature for a few days before serving. They will last for several weeks.

In the southwestern United States a variety of feasts and celebrations, including dances, punctuate the Christmas holiday period. The spectacle of Christmas in Santa Fe, New Mexico, confirms the fact that the first Americans have added a wonderful flavor to Christmas. Beside the ancient Indian ceremonies, those of Spanish descent honor the Virgin of Guadalupe, a Mexican saint, patroness of the Americas, whose feast day opens the Christmas season; it commemorates the appearance of the Virgin to an Indian convert near Mexico City in 1531. The Indian Matachine dancers in a procession are well known in Albuquerque, New Mexico, along with the mariachis (Mexican brass bands) who play music for the Christmas Mass. At Tortugas, three miles south of Las Cruces, a three-day celebration begins at nightfall on December 10. The Matachine dancers perform all night, after a statue of the Virgin has been moved from its chapel to the pueblo's ceremonial house. Maracas, violins, tom-toms, and traditional chants are all part of this scene. As the sun rises, a candlelit procession begins as the Virgin's image is returned to the chapel.

A striking sight in Santa Fe—and throughout New Mexico—is the *farolitos:* candles, set into a layer of sand, are placed in brown paper bags and then used to outline roofs, balconies, and walkways. Here, too, the lights flicker back as far as the 16th century, when we read that the Indians on Christmas Eve set "many luminarias [bonfires] on the patios of churches and even on some of the flat roofs of the houses . . . the whole impression is that of a brightly lit sky."

Christmas in the Southwest

DINNER MENU FOR 8

CHARRED PEPPERS AND ONIONS
IN ANCHO CHILI OIL

WHITE CORN SOUP WITH
CHRISTMAS CONFETTI

GAME HENS BARBECUED WITH
SOUTHWEST SAUCE

HOT BELL PEPPER CHUTNEY

PUREE OF GARBANZOS SPRINKLED
WITH TOASTED PINE NUTS

FRESH ORANGE SLICES WITH
LEMON AND SCALLIONS

AVOCADO WITH LIME JUICE

CREME BRULEE WITH MERINGUE

Charred Peppers

FOOD PREPARATION

2 weeks ahead:
- Make chutney

1 week ahead:
- Prepare charred peppers and onions

5 to 6 days ahead:
- Make sauce for game hens

1 day ahead:
- Cook white corn soup; refrigerate
- Prepare garbanzo puree

Serving day:
- Toast or grill bread for charred pepper appetizer
- Cook game hens
- Prepare orange salad
- Assemble avocado salad
- Make crème brûlée
- Garnish white corn soup

WINE SUGGESTIONS

Serve Domaine Chandon Brut before the meal and Calera Central Coast Chardonnay and Ridge Vineyards Geyserville Zinfandel throughout the dinner.

CHARRED PEPPERS AND ONIONS IN ANCHO CHILI OIL

These may be made one week ahead and stored in a covered container or wide-mouth jar. To serve them as an hors d'oeuvre or appetizer, place them in a bowl and surround with toasted pita pieces, strips of dry toast, crackers, or grilled slices of French or Italian bread. Add some herb-scented olives to the bowl for taste and color.

8 Servings

3 red and 2 yellow bell peppers, roasted (see page 193) and cut into 1-inch strips

1 jalapeño pepper, seeded and minced

1½ pounds red onions (about 3 medium)

¼ cup olive oil

½ large dried ancho chili

2 garlic cloves, halved

salt and pepper

1. Preheat broiler. Place the roasted red and yellow peppers in a shallow glass dish. Sprinkle the jalapeño over and set aside.

2. Cut the onions into slices about ¼ inch thick. Lay them on a baking sheet. Brush with half the olive oil. Broil until cooked through and lightly charred. Add to the peppers and separate the rings with a fork.

3. Soften the ancho chili in 1 cup boiling water in a small bowl for about 15 minutes. Drain and slice thinly.

4. In a small saucepan, heat the remaining olive oil. Add the garlic and cook just until lightly browned, pressing lightly with a fork to extract some of the juices (do not break up the garlic). Add the garlic to the pepper mixture. Add the ancho strips and cook over low heat for 6 to 7 minutes, pressing to extract some of the juices; be careful not to scorch. Add to the peppers. Season with salt and pepper and toss

lightly. Cover with plastic wrap and cool. This can be made ahead and refrigerated; bring to room temperature before serving. If desired, remove garlic just before serving.

WHITE CORN SOUP WITH CHRISTMAS CONFETTI

This may be made ahead, refrigerated, and reheated before serving, adding the garnish at the last minute. Tasting the occasional fennel seed is unexpected and exciting. Do not overdo the confetti—just two or three pieces of red and green will do, and no more than 4 fennel seeds in each soup bowl.

8 Servings

1 tablespoon vegetable oil

¼ pound Spanish chorizo, cut into small pieces

1 medium-size white onion, coarsely chopped

1 small celery heart, thinly sliced

3 cups fresh or thawed frozen white corn kernels

1 teaspoon dried thyme

6 cups chicken stock or broth

2 medium-size boiling potatoes, peeled and cut into small cubes

1 cup heavy cream

salt and white pepper

1 tablespoon each finely chopped red bell pepper and fresh coriander

32 fennel seeds

1. In a skillet, heat the oil and sauté the sausage over low heat. Transfer 2 tablespoons rendered fat to a large saucepan. Discard the remaining fat and sausage meat, or save for another use.

2. Add the onion and celery to the large saucepan, cover, and cook until soft but not browned. Add the corn and thyme and cook, covered, for 2 minutes without browning. Add the stock, cover, and simmer for 30 minutes.

3. Add the potato and cream, cover, and cook another 30 minutes, stirring occasionally.

4. Put the soup through a food mill or a fine strainer; the goal is to achieve a smooth, silky texture. Adjust the seasoning with salt and white pepper. Thin with a bit more chicken stock if necessary.

5. To serve, spoon into individual soup bowls. In the center of each, put a tiny amount of chopped bell pepper and coriander. Sprinkle 4 fennel seeds into each bowl, being sure they are not clustered.

GAME HENS BARBECUED WITH SOUTHWEST SAUCE

The sauce may be made five or six days ahead and refrigerated, lightly covered. Test for chili power—if you think it needs more, add it.

8 Servings

2 tablespoons butter

1 medium onion, chopped

1 garlic clove, minced

1 ½ cups canned plum tomatoes, coarsely chopped

¼ cup ketchup

2 tablespoons each Dijon-style mustard, honey, Worcestershire sauce, and lemon juice

1 tablespoon each brown sugar, ancho chili powder, and paprika

1 teaspoon cayenne pepper or ½ teaspoon red pepper flakes

4 Cornish game hens, about 1 ½ pounds each, halved

1. Heat the butter in a saucepan and sauté the onion until soft. Add the garlic and sauté 1 minute. Add the tomatoes, lower the heat, and simmer 15 minutes.

2. Add all remaining ingredients except game hens and cook over low heat for 15 minutes. Puree the sauce in a food processor or put through a food mill. Cool before using.

3. Rinse the hens and dry them well. Place in a large glass or ceramic container.

4. Liberally brush hens all over with the barbecue sauce. Refrigerate at least 4 hours, preferably overnight. Bring to room temperature before cooking.

5. These hens may be grilled, broiled, or roasted; no matter which method you use, brush with the remaining marinade during cooking. If grilling, be sure to oil the grid first. Grill each side until the juices run clear when pricked with a fork, about 10 to 15 minutes per side. If broiling, preheat the broiler. Place the hens about 5 inches below the heat source and broil on each side until the juices run clear. If roasting, place hens skin side up in a preheated 350°F oven until the juices run clear, about 50 to 60 minutes. Finish off by running under the broiler for a minute or two.

White Corn Soup With Christmas Confetti

HOT BELL PEPPER CHUTNEY

Use red, yellow, or green bell peppers, or any combination. If covered tightly and refrigerated, this will keep for 3 to 4 weeks.

Makes about 1 quart

6 bell peppers, cored, seeded, and cut into ½-inch cubes

3 jalapeño chilies, seeded and minced

1 large onion, cut into ½-inch slices and then into ½-inch pieces

1 ½ cups cider vinegar

1 ½ cups firmly packed brown sugar

2 tablespoons finely chopped candied ginger

salt

Combine all ingredients in a nonaluminum saucepan and bring to boil. Lower the heat and simmer until the liquid thickens to a syrup, about 1½ hours. Cool, then refrigerate.

PUREE OF GARBANZOS SPRINKLED WITH TOASTED PINE NUTS

This delicious puree will remind you of chestnuts. It can be made hours ahead and reheated in the microwave (in a microwave-safe dish covered with plastic) or in the oven (covered with foil).

8 Servings

3 cans (16 ounces each) garbanzos (chickpeas)

3 cups beef broth

2 slices bacon

2 carrots, thinly sliced

1 onion, coarsely chopped

1 herb bundle (2 sprigs each parsley, oregano, and thyme, wrapped and tied in cheesecloth)

¼ cup butter

salt and pepper

½ cup toasted pine nuts

1. Rinse and drain the garbanzos well and place in a large saucepan. Add 2½ cups of the beef broth with the bacon, carrots, onion, and herb bundle and bring to boil. Cover, lower the heat, and simmer for 30 minutes or until the vegetables are cooked. Discard the bacon and herb bundle.

2. Puree the garbanzo mixture in a food processor with the butter and salt and pepper, or run through a food mill. Thin with more beef broth if necessary. Keep warm in a liberally buttered dish in a low oven. Top with toasted pine nuts.

FRESH ORANGE SLICES WITH LEMON AND SCALLIONS

8 Servings

8 oranges, peeled and sliced crosswise

8 scallions, thinly sliced

juice of 2 lemons

3 or 4 drops Tabasco or other hot pepper sauce

salt

1. Combine all ingredients in a bowl and toss lightly but well. Cover with plastic wrap and chill.

2. Arrange the salad on a platter or individual plates and serve.

AVOCADO WITH LIME JUICE

8 Servings

8 lettuce leaves

2 ripe avocados, peeled, seeded, and sliced

2 limes, quartered

On individual plates, arrange a lettuce leaf, some avocado slices, and 1 lime wedge. Pass the salt and a peppermill.

CREME BRULEE WITH MERINGUE

8 Servings

8 eggs, separated, room temperature

⅔ cup plus 2 tablespoons confectioner's sugar

2⅔ cups heavy cream

1 tablespoon instant espresso powder

⅔ cup sugar

1. Beat the egg yolks and half the confectioner's sugar until the mixture forms a ribbon when the beaters are lifted.

2. Preheat oven to 325°F. Combine the cream and espresso powder in a saucepan and heat just to the simmering point; do not boil. Pour the cream slowly into the yolk mixture, beating constantly. Pour into a ceramic, glass, or other nonmetallic 1½- to 2-quart baking dish.

3. Set the baking dish into a larger pan. Fill the larger pan with hot water to a depth of 1 inch from the top of the baking dish. Bake the custard until set, about 1 hour. Let cool.

4. Preheat oven to 350°F. Beat the egg whites until soft and fluffy. Add the sugar 1 tablespoon at a time, beating until peaks form. Spread the meringue over the cooled custard and sift the remaining confectioner's sugar over the top as evenly as you can.

5. Bake until browned, about 10 minutes (but start checking a few minutes earlier). This does not have to be served immediately; it may sit out for an hour or so, or refrigerated for several hours.

Crème Brûlée With Meringue

With godchildren in England, the Virgin Islands, Pennsylvania, Connecticut, Kentucky, Illinois, Florida, and New York, it's evident that I have been to a few baptisms. Baptism is the ceremony by which one is given a name and admitted into the Christian faith. It is a holy and beautiful sacrament; though brief, the ceremony at the baptismal font is filled with meaning.

Baptismal gowns are passed on from generation to generation, and the family, godparents, relatives, and friends often celebrate the event with lunch at a restaurant or at home.

It's simplest to prepare food that can be served lukewarm or at room temperature, and this is what the following menu offers. Almost all of it can be made ahead and pulled together in a matter of minutes.

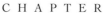
Baptism

LUNCH MENU FOR 12

SPAGHETTINI WITH SHRIMP, SMOKED
SALMON, AND DILL

BAKED CHICKEN BREASTS WITH
BLACK FOREST HAM AND SHALLOTS

CURRIED WILD RICE WITH
CURRANTS

SLICED TOMATOES WITH BASIL
CREAM

HEAVEN CAKE WITH MY SISTER
MARY'S LIQUEUR SAUCE

Chicken, Wild Rice, and Tomatoes

FOOD PREPARATION

1 day ahead:
- Make cake and sauce
- Prepare chicken breasts for baking
- Prepare shrimp

Serving day:
- Bake chicken
- Make rice and tomato dishes
- Prepare pasta

WINE SUGGESTIONS

Serve a German Riesling Kabinett Trocken throughout the meal. Vin santo is a sweet Tuscan wine made from sun-dried grapes. It is the perfect wine for a baptismal toast when serving the dessert.

SPAGHETTINI WITH SHRIMP, SMOKED SALMON, AND DILL

This unusual pasta dish is made with warm pasta and a cool sauce—almost like a pasta salad, but not quite. It's perfectly all right to cook the pasta ahead and serve the dish at room temperature; this will give the flavors a chance to mellow.

12 Servings

½ cup dry white wine

⅓ cup white wine vinegar

1 ¼ cups olive oil

¼ cup finely chopped fresh dill or 2 teaspoons dried

2 teaspoons salt

1 teaspoon pepper

1 ½ pounds shrimp, shelled, deveined, cooked, and halved lengthwise

1 ½ pounds spaghettini

½ pound thinly sliced smoked salmon, cut into julienne

1. Combine all ingredients except the shrimp, pasta, and salmon and mix until well blended. Add the shrimp and marinate at least 30 minutes. If longer, cover and refrigerate, but bring to room temperature before adding to the pasta.

2. Cook the pasta al dente and drain well. Return to the pan in which it cooked and add the salmon and the shrimp sauce. Toss well to coat all the pasta. Serve on a large platter as a first course or a buffet item.

Pasta With Shrimp and Salmon

BAKED CHICKEN BREASTS WITH BLACK FOREST HAM AND SHALLOTS

12 Servings

12 boned, skinned chicken breast halves

juice of 1 lemon

salt and pepper

½ cup butter

½ cup finely chopped shallots

⅓ cup thinly sliced celery

12 medium mushrooms, finely chopped

2¾ cups fresh egg-breadcrumbs

¼ cup finely chopped parsley

12 thin slices Black Forest or other smoked ham

1 ½ cups all-purpose flour

3 eggs, beaten

12 lemon wedges, seeded

1. Place the chicken breasts in a shallow bowl. Add the lemon juice and let stand for 15 minutes.

2. Drain the chicken and pat dry. Place each breast between 2 pieces of waxed paper and pound lightly to flatten. Remove the top sheet of paper and season both sides with salt and pepper.

3. Heat half the butter in a large skillet and sauté the shallots and celery for 5 minutes. Add the mushrooms and cook another 5 minutes, stirring. Remove from heat and stir in ¾ cup of the breadcrumbs and the parsley, reserving 1 tablespoon for garnish. Taste for seasoning.

4. Arrange a piece of ham on each breast and divide the stuffing among them. Beginning with the smaller end, roll up each breast and secure with a wooden skewer running completely through the breast.

5. Preheat oven to 400°F. Roll each breast in flour, then dip in the egg. Coat it completely with the remaining 2 cups breadcrumbs. Spread 2 tablespoons of the remaining butter in a baking pan and arrange the chicken in it. Dot with the remaining 2 tablespoons butter. Bake until the breasts are browned and cooked through, about 40 minutes.

6. To serve, arrange the stuffed breasts on a platter with all skewers pointing in the same direction. Sprinkle with the reserved parsley and accompany with the lemon wedges. Alternatively, remove the skewers, slice the breasts ½ inch thick and overlap the slices on the platter.

CURRIED WILD RICE WITH CURRANTS

12 Servings

5 tablespoons butter

1 large onion, finely chopped

1½ green bell peppers, seeded and finely chopped

¾ cup dried currants

1½ cups wild rice

1 teaspoon curry powder

6 cups chicken stock or low-salt broth

salt and pepper

1. Melt the butter in a 4-quart saucepan and sauté the onion, green pepper, and currants until the onion softens, about 5 minutes.

2. Add the wild rice, curry powder, and chicken stock and bring to boil. Lower heat, cover, and simmer until the rice is tender, about 50 minutes. Uncover, toss lightly with a fork, and cook a little longer to boil off any liquid remaining in the pan. Adjust the seasoning with salt and pepper.

SLICED TOMATOES WITH BASIL CREAM

12 Servings

6 ripe large tomatoes or 12 ripe plum tomatoes

¾ cup heavy cream

salt and pepper

½ cup finely chopped fresh basil or 2 tablespoons dried

1. Blanch the tomatoes in boiling water for 10 seconds. Lift out with a slotted spoon and immediately place in a bowl of cold water. Peel the tomatoes and slice as thinly as you can. Arrange on a large platter.

2. Pour the cream over all. Salt and pepper liberally and sprinkle with the basil.

HEAVEN CAKE WITH MY SISTER MARY'S LIQUEUR SAUCE

This is an angel food cake with a sauce devised by a good cook in our family, my sister Mary.

12 Servings

1 cup all-purpose flour

1¼ cups sugar

8 egg whites

½ teaspoon cream of tartar

½ teaspoon salt

½ teaspoon almond extract

Liqueur Sauce (see right)

1. Preheat oven to 375°F. Sift flour and 1 cup sugar into a large bowl.

2. Beat the egg whites until foamy. Add cream of tartar and beat 30 seconds. Add salt and almond extract. Beat in the remaining sugar a tablespoon at a time. Fold into flour mixture.

3. Transfer mixture to ungreased 9-inch tube pan. Bake until cake springs back when lightly pressed, about 30 minutes. Invert the pan on a rack or over the neck of a bottle and let cake cool, then remove from pan. Serve with sauce.

LIQUEUR SAUCE
Makes 2 to 3 cups

4 egg yolks

½ cup sugar

1 cup milk, scalded

½ teaspoon salt

¼ cup liqueur, such as Grand Marnier, kirsch or Cointreau

1 cup heavy cream, whipped

1. Combine yolks and sugar in the top of a double boiler and whisk over simmering water until thickened.

2. Add milk and salt and whisk until the consistency of light cream. Remove from over water.

3. Add liqueur. Let cool somewhat, then refrigerate.

4. Fold in whipped cream just before serving.

Heaven Cake With Mary's Sauce

Glorious spring! What does one say, what can one do, at the beautiful and lonely sight of the first crocus parting its way through the frozen earth. Tulips white, yellow, pink, lavender, red, and purple, highlighted against the Botticelli-blue sky. And then the first shoots of new spring vegetables in a garden that has been asleep all winter. The city dweller will see piles of asparagus at the greengrocer's and none of us seems to tire of eating this wonderful vegetable. Spring onions, the young dandelion and small spears of arugula, tiny radishes alongside morning glories, tastes and sights as stimulating as any in nature tell us that winter has left and another cycle has begun. What a wondrous time of year to be born.

ASTROLOGICAL SIGNS

ARIES, the Ram: March 21–April 19

TAURUS, the Bull: April 20–May 20

GEMINI, the Twins: May 21–June 21

BIRTHSTONES AND FLOWERS

March: Aquamarine, jonquil

April: Diamond, sweet pea

May: Emerald, lily of the valley

Springtime Birthday

LUNCH MENU FOR 8

KIR ROYALES

FRESH ASPARAGUS

GRILLED ROSEMARY LAMB CHOPS

RICOTTA AND PASTA CUSTARD

ARUGULA SALAD WITH SHERRY
VINAIGRETTE

FENNEL BRIOCHE LOAVES

YELLOW SILK CAKE WITH
SNOW-WHITE FROSTING

Kir Royales

FOOD PREPARATION

1 day ahead:
  • Marinate lamb
  • Bake fennel brioche loaves
  • Make cake and icing

Serving day:
  • Prepare asparagus and custard
  • Grill lamb chops
  • Make salad and vinaigrette

WINE SUGGESTIONS

Start with Kir Royales. This delightful and festive drink is one of the easiest to make. Ice the champagne and have a bottle of cassis ready. The pale pink tint in the champagne glass is festive in itself. Throughout the rest of the meal, sip champagne.

KIR ROYALES

8 Servings
2 teaspoons crème de cassis
2 bottles chilled champagne

Place ¼ teaspoon cassis into each of 8 champagne glasses and fill ⅔ full with ice-cold champagne. Serve right away.

FRESH ASPARAGUS

The microwave is great for cooking asparagus. Here's how.

8 Servings
1½ to 2 pounds fresh asparagus
¼ to ½ cup butter, melted
juice of 2 lemons
8 large red radishes, thinly sliced
salt and pepper

1. If the asparagus have thick stalks, it is best to peel the lower half of the stalk with a vegetable peeler. Snap off the bottoms of the stalks where they break naturally. Soak the remaining stalks in cold salted water for 10 minutes. Drain.

2. Arrange the asparagus in a microwave-safe container (do not add any water), cover with plastic wrap, and cook on High until crisp-tender, 5 to 6 minutes. Carefully remove the plastic.

3. Arrange the cooked asparagus on individual plates and drizzle with the butter and lemon juice. Garnish with the radish slices and sprinkle with salt and pepper.

GRILLED ROSEMARY LAMB CHOPS

8 Servings
8 lamb rib chops, 1½ inches thick
2 garlic cloves, minced
2 tablespoons finely chopped fresh rosemary or 2 teaspoons dried, crushed
⅓ cup olive oil
salt and pepper

1. Trim the chops of most of the fat; with a sharp paring knife, make shallow slashes into the edges of the meat where the fat was removed to prevent curling. Arrange the chops in one layer in a large glass dish.

2. Combine all the remaining ingredients in a small bowl and mix well. Brush both sides of the chops with the mixture. Refrigerate for several hours or overnight.

3. Prepare the barbecue grill or preheat broiler. Cook the chops about 4 to 5 inches from the heat source on both sides until the centers are pink, about 10 minutes. Serve hot.

RICOTTA AND PASTA CUSTARD

8 Servings

1½ cups ricotta cheese

3 eggs, beaten

½ cup thinly sliced scallions, including green part

1½ cups milk

¼ teaspoon Tabasco or other hot pepper sauce

1½ teaspoons salt

3 nests (about 6 ounces) fresh angel hair pasta

3 tablespoons butter

coarsely ground black pepper

1 sprig fresh rosemary or 1 trimmed scallion (garnish)

1. Combine the ricotta, eggs, scallions, milk, hot sauce, and salt in a bowl and mix well. Set aside.

2. Preheat oven to 350°F. Cook the pasta in boiling salted water until al dente. (Fresh pasta cooks much faster than dried; this should not take more than 2 to 3 minutes.) Drain well and return to the pot in which it cooked. Add 2 tablespoons of the butter and toss to coat. Transfer the pasta to a liberally buttered 1½-quart baking dish.

3. Spread the ricotta mixture on top of the cooked pasta. Season with pepper and dot with the remaining 1 tablespoon butter.

4. Bake for 75 minutes. Let the custard cool for at least 15 minutes. Loosen the edges with a small knife and unmold. Serve hot or warm. Garnish the top with the rosemary sprig or scallion and serve.

ARUGULA SALAD WITH SHERRY VINAIGRETTE

8 Servings

2 bunches arugula (long stems removed), washed thoroughly and dried

¾ cup olive or vegetable oil

¼ cup dry sherry

1 teaspoon sugar

1 teaspoon Dijon-style mustard

salt and pepper

1. Refrigerate arugula in a plastic bag until ready to use.

2. Combine remaining ingredients until well blended. Use right away or refrigerate in a tightly covered jar. Just before serving, pour half the dressing over the greens and toss well. Add more dressing to taste.

Grilled Lamb Chop With Asparagus and Custard

FENNEL BRIOCHE LOAVES

A buttery-rich celebration bread.

Makes 2 loaves

4 to 5 cups all-purpose flour

½ cup sugar

¼ cup nonfat dry milk

2 envelopes rapid-rise yeast

1 tablespoon salt

1 cup water, about 125°F

2 tablespoons Pernod (optional)

2 teaspoons fennel seeds

*1 cup unsalted butter,
room temperature*

3 large eggs

2 egg yolks

1. In a medium bowl, combine 2 cups of the flour, the sugar, dry milk, yeast, and salt.

2. In large bowl, combine the water, Pernod, and fennel seeds. Blend in the flour mixture. Gradually add the softened butter, beating with an electric mixer until the dough is shiny and smooth.

3. Add the eggs and yolks one at a time, beating well after each addition.

4. Add as much of the remaining flour, ½ cup at a time, as is needed to make a smooth, elastic dough. Cover and let rise for about 1 hour or until the dough has doubled in volume.

5. Punch the dough down, cover, and refrigerate until well chilled, about 3 hours, or up to 2 days.

6. Punch the dough down and cut in half. Flatten each piece into a rectangle, then roll into a cylinder with tapering ends. Fit each piece of dough into a buttered 8 × 4-inch loaf pan, folding the ends under. Let rise until doubled in volume, about 1½ hours.

7. Preheat oven to 400°F. Bake the loaves on the center rack for 15 minutes. Reduce heat to 350°F and bake until the bread is golden and sounds hollow when tapped, about 20 more minutes. Let cool for a few minutes, then turn out onto a rack to cool completely before slicing.

YELLOW SILK CAKE WITH SNOW-WHITE FROSTING

8 to 10 Servings

2 eggs, separated

1½ cups sugar

2¼ cups sifted cake flour

1 tablespoon baking powder

½ teaspoon salt

⅓ cup vegetable oil

1 cup milk

1 teaspoon vanilla extract

Snow-White Frosting (see right)

1. Preheat oven to 350°F. Grease and flour two 9-inch round cake pans.

2. Beat egg whites until frothy. Add ½ cup sugar a tablespoon at a time, beating until stiff.

3. Sift the remaining sugar, flour, baking powder, and salt into another bowl. Add the oil, half the milk, and the vanilla. Beat at high speed of an electric mixer for 2 minutes.

4. Add the egg yolks and remaining milk and beat 1 minute longer. Fold in whites. Spread batter in prepared pans and bake 30 to 35 minutes or until tops spring back when lightly pressed with a finger.

5. Let layers cool in pans for 10 minutes then turn out onto racks to cool completely. Spread frosting between layers and over top and sides of cake.

SNOW-WHITE FROSTING
Makes 4 to 5 cups

2 egg whites

1½ cups sugar

¼ teaspoon salt

⅓ cup water

2 teaspoons light corn syrup

1 teaspoon vanilla extract

1. In the top of a double boiler, combine the egg whites, sugar, salt, water, and corn syrup; whisk until thoroughly mixed, about 1 minute. Place over boiling water and beat at high speed of a hand mixer until stiff peaks form, about 6 to 8 minutes. Transfer to a clean, cool bowl.

2. Add vanilla and beat until the frosting is thick enough to spread, about 1 minute. Use immediately.

Yellow Silk Cake With Snow-White Frosting

Shelling fresh green peas, putting them in a pot with a little butter and water and cooking them to a peak of sweetness is proof positive of the arrival of summer.

Summer also means food that has been cooked and allowed to cool to room temperature. And it means cooking ahead and refrigerating such dishes as ice-cold soups. This summertime birthday menu is virtually all do-ahead; only the shrimp must be cooked just before serving, but it's easy to prepare and can be put on the coals or in the broiler at the last minute. It isn't necessary to whisk the rosemary chicken from the oven to the buffet table; in fact, let it sit for an hour for easier carving and best flavor. And make the pasta dish ahead; it is delicious at room temperature.

ASTROLOGICAL SIGNS

CANCER, the Crab: June 22–July 22

LEO, the Lion: July 23–August 22

VIRGO, the Virgin: August 23–September 22

BIRTHSTONES AND FLOWERS

June: Pearl/moonstone, rose

July: Ruby, larkspur

August: Peridot, gladiolus

Summer Birthday

BUFFET MENU FOR 8

ICED SUMMER-WHITE GAZPACHO

ROASTED ROSEMARY CHICKEN

GRILLED SHRIMP, SCALLOPS,
AND PEPPERS WITH GINGER
BUTTER SAUCE

PASTA WITH GREEN PEAS,
SCALLIONS, AND CURRIED WALNUTS

BIBB LETTUCE WITH SILKY BLUE
CHEESE DRESSING

KIRBY CUCUMBERS IN MINT
AND ICE

CHOCOLATE PECAN BIRTHDAY CAKE

Summertime Buffet

FOOD PREPARATION

1 day ahead:
- Make birthday cake
- Make gazpacho
- Prepare lettuce and make salad dressing
- Prepare cucumbers

Serving day:
- Roast chicken
- Grill shrimp
- Make pasta
- Dress salad

WINE SUGGESTIONS

Serve a California sparkling wine or French champagne throughout.

ICED SUMMER-WHITE GAZPACHO

This is a good soup for a summertime buffet because it can be made ahead and kept in the refrigerator. It should be served in an attractive punchbowl or a ceramic soup tureen. The soup can be part of the buffet table or can stand on a different table and be served as a first course. Skip the formal soup plates; instead, use oversize stemmed water goblets, coffee mugs, or small clear beer glasses with soup spoons.

8 Servings

2 5-inch sections of homemade white, French, or Italian bread

10 ounces blanched almonds

3 garlic cloves

2 teaspoons salt

6 cups ice water

⅔ cup olive oil

¼ cup tarragon vinegar

2 cups seedless white grapes, halved lengthwise

1 ½ cups diced cucumber

½ cup thinly sliced white radishes

⅓ cup thinly sliced scallions

white pepper

2 tablespoons toasted slivered almonds (garnish)

1. Soak the bread in cool tap water in a large bowl and squeeze dry. Set aside.

2. Combine the almonds, garlic and salt in the processor and grind but do not puree. Add the bread and 2 cups of the ice water and process until blended. Transfer to a large bowl and blend in the remaining 4 cups ice water, olive oil, and vinegar. Return to the processor in batches and blend well.

3. Transfer the soup to a large ceramic or glass bowl, adding the grapes, cucumber, radishes, and scallions. Check for seasoning, adding some white pepper. Cover and chill overnight. Garnish with a few toasted almond slivers at serving time.

ROASTED ROSEMARY CHICKEN

8 Servings

2 whole chickens, 3½ pounds each

2 tablespoons olive oil

12 small rosemary sprigs

6 garlic cloves, thinly sliced

salt and pepper

1. Preheat oven to 500°F. Rinse the chickens and pat dry. Cut off any extra fat. Rub the oil all over the outside of the chickens.

2. Insert some rosemary and garlic under the skin around the breasts and legs of each chicken and inside the cavities; do not break the skin.

3. Liberally salt and pepper the chickens inside and out.

4. Arrange the chickens breast side up in a baking pan and roast 20 minutes. Reduce heat to 450°F and bake 40 minutes longer; the meat should be moist and the skin crisp. Serve warm or at room temperature.

Grilled Shrimp With Ginger Sauce

GRILLED SHRIMP, SCALLOPS, AND PEPPERS WITH GINGER BUTTER SAUCE

Prepare these ahead up to the point of skewering them. Refrigerate until 10 minutes or so before cooking time. They are easy to broil or grill.

8 Servings

24 large shrimp, peeled and deveined

16 sea scallops

1 red bell pepper

1 yellow bell pepper

*10 tablespoons butter,
2 tablespoons melted*

2 tablespoons vegetable oil

salt and pepper

4 scallions, thinly sliced

3 tablespoons white wine vinegar

1 tablespoon grated fresh ginger

3 tablespoons heavy cream

1. Rinse and dry the shrimp and scallops. Stem and seed the peppers and cut into 1¼-inch squares. Coat the shrimp, scallops, and peppers with 2 tablespoons melted butter and the oil. Season with salt and pepper. Toss and set aside.

2. In a small saucepan, sauté the scallions in 1 tablespoon butter for 2 minutes. Add the vinegar and ginger and boil until the vinegar is reduced by half. Add the cream and boil until reduced by half. Add the remaining butter. When melted, remove from heat and keep warm.

3. Prepare barbecue or preheat broiler. Alternate the shrimp, scallops, and peppers on 8 thin skewers. Grill on an oiled grid or broil several minutes per side until the shrimp are pink and the scallops opaque. Arrange on a serving platter and pour the sauce over. Serve right away.

PASTA WITH GREEN PEAS, SCALLIONS, AND CURRIED WALNUTS

This is a great summertime dish if you can pick fresh peas, scallions, and tarragon from your garden. It is especially delicious made with freshly made fettuccine or other egg noodles.

8 Servings (as a buffet item)

2 cups fresh or frozen green peas

3 tablespoons butter

½ cup dry vermouth

½ cup chopped fresh scallions, including tender green parts

2 tablespoons finely chopped fresh tarragon or 1 teaspoon dried

½ cup chicken stock or broth

salt and freshly ground black pepper

½ pound pasta

1 teaspoon curry powder

½ cup coarsely chopped walnuts

1. Bring a large saucepan of water to boil for the pasta.

2. If using fresh peas, bring 2 cups water to boil, add peas, cook 3 minutes and drain. If using frozen, thaw and drain.

3. Heat 2 tablespoons butter in a large skillet. Add the vermouth and scallions and cook until the scallions soften and the vermouth thickens and deglazes the pan, about 10 minutes.

4. Add the peas, tarragon, chicken stock, and salt and pepper and boil over high heat for 2 minutes. Turn heat as low as you can to keep sauce warm.

5. Cook the pasta and drain. (If using fresh pasta, remember that it cooks considerably faster than dried.) Turn the pasta into the sauce and toss over high heat to blend. Transfer to serving bowl or platter.

6. In a small skillet, heat the remaining 1 tablespoon butter. Add the curry powder and cook 1 minute, stirring. Add the walnuts and toss well to coat. Sprinkle over the pasta and serve.

Pasta With Peas, Scallions, and Walnuts

BIBB LETTUCE WITH SILKY BLUE CHEESE DRESSING

Make the dressing ahead; it will keep in the refrigerator for about 10 days. Use what you need and refrigerate the remainder in a tightly covered jar.

Makes about 2 cups

*2 to 4 heads Bibb lettuce
(about 8 cups after cleaning)*

1 cup light mayonnaise

½ cup plain low-fat yogurt

*2 tablespoons white wine vinegar
or tarragon vinegar*

freshly ground pepper

*1 cup crumbled blue cheese
(4 to 6 ounces)*

3 tablespoons thinly sliced scallions

1. Separate and wash the lettuce leaves; if not using right away, store in a plastic bag in the refrigerator.

2. Combine the mayonnaise and yogurt in a bowl and mix until smooth. Add the vinegar and a liberal sprinkling of pepper. Blend in the blue cheese and scallions. Do not overmix; the dressing should be textured and a bit lumpy.

KIRBY CUCUMBERS IN MINT AND ICE

This is one time you don't have to drain and dry a vegetable!

8 Servings

6 nicely shaped small Kirby cucumbers

1 tablespoon salt

6 large mint sprigs, 3 whole and 3 finely chopped

2 cups ice cubes

1. Slice off the ends of the cucumbers and remove almost all of the skin with a vegetable peeler. Run the tines of a fork up and down the full length of the cucumbers. Cut in eighths lengthwise.

2. In a serving dish wide enough to hold the cucumber lengths, combine them with the salt, mint, and ice cubes. Refrigerate for 1 hour or longer to crisp and scent the cucumbers.

3. Serve just as they are.

Chocolate Pecan Cake

CHOCOLATE PECAN BIRTHDAY CAKE

This can be made the day before the celebration. If refrigerated, remove from the refrigerator two to three hours before serving.

8 Servings

1 cup cake flour

½ cup unsweetened cocoa powder

1 cup minced pecans

1 cup sugar

¾ cup milk

¾ cup butter, softened

2 eggs, lightly beaten

2½ teaspoons baking powder

1 teaspoon vanilla extract

1. Preheat oven to 375°F. Butter and flour a 9-inch round cake pan.

2. Sift the flour and cocoa into a mixing bowl. Add all remaining ingredients and mix just until smooth. Transfer to the prepared cake pan and bake until the edges are browned and pull away from the sides of the pan, about 35 minutes.

3. When the cake is cool, apply the icing and decoration.

ICING AND DECORATION

½ cup butter, cut into small pieces

½ pound milk chocolate, preferably imported, cut into small pieces

3 tablespoons butter

3 ounces semisweet or bittersweet chocolate

12 nicely shaped pecan halves

1. In the top of a double boiler, combine ½ cup butter and the milk chocolate. Measure 1 cup water into the bottom pan, bring to boil and remove from heat. Set the top pan over the bottom pan and stir the butter and chocolate until smooth and melted. Spread over the top and sides of the cake.

2. Combine 3 tablespoons butter and the semisweet chocolate in the top of a double boiler over simmering water and stir until melted and smooth. Dip in each pecan half to coat one end. Let cool on waxed paper.

3. Make a cone of waxed or parchment paper and fill it ⅓ full with the remaining semisweet chocolate mixture. Fold the wide end of the paper cone to give more control in writing. Cut the writing point of the cone into a small hole. Test the size of the hole on a small piece of paper.

4. Working quickly, write birthday wishes on the cake with the chocolate mixture. Set the pecan halves around the edge of the cake.

Summer winds down and autumn brings its colors—chrysanthemums, asters, and beautiful dahlias; bright red tomatoes, brilliant orange pumpkins, green winter squash. All make up the palette of the harvest. Old-fashioned kitchens become beehives of activity as pears are turned into preserves, jalapeños into jellies, cabbages into kraut, and cucumbers into pickles.

At the first whiff of cool air I recollect the gathering of the grapes and the barrels of red and amber juice that flowed from my father's and grandfather's winepresses. The grapes were not on vines, for we lived in a big city; instead, they were boxed and came off a truck that backed toward the basement doors, the entrance to my father's home winery in an old mid-Manhattan apartment building. Fire-brigade fashion, my brothers and I passed the boxes along. Autumn winemaking was a real event in our family. So was the tomato canning; the women were busy putting up fresh tomatoes in hundreds of jars, and they also made tomato paste and puree.

It has always seemed to me that people who have birthdays at this time are fortunate—for with the nip in the air comes a keener appetite.

ASTROLOGICAL SIGNS

LIBRA, the Scales: September 23–October 23

SCORPIO, the Scorpion: October 24–November 21

SAGITTARIUS, the Archer: November 22– December 21

BIRTHSTONES AND FLOWERS

September: Sapphire, aster

October: Opal/tourmaline, calendula

November: Topaz, chrysanthemum

Autumn Birthday

MENU FOR 6

BASIL TOMATO TART

BROCHETTES OF BEEF WITH
LEMON AND THYME *OR*
FISH FILLETS BAKED IN
BROWN PAPER

FALL SQUASH WITH MINT AND
HONEY

FLUFFY WHITE BIRTHDAY CAKE
WITH AUTUMN LEAVES

Basil Tomato Tart

FOOD PREPARATION

This is an easy meal to prepare, but there are two things you may wish to do the day before:

· Make birthday cake
· Make pastry for tomato tart

WINE SUGGESTIONS

Serve pink champagne or Blanc de Noirs throughout.

BASIL TOMATO TART

This delicious tart must be made with fresh, ripe tomatoes; anemic pink ones will not work here.

8 to 10 Servings
PASTRY

1 ¾ cups all-purpose flour

pinch of salt

1 tablespoon sugar

¾ cup chilled butter, cut into ¼-inch pieces

¼ cup ice water

1. Combine the flour, salt, and sugar in the bowl of a food processor and blend 2 seconds. With the machine running, add the butter through the feed tube and process until the mixture resembles coarse crumbs. Add the water through the feed tube and mix just until the dough begins to cling together.

2. Transfer the dough to floured waxed paper and press into a ball, then flatten into a disc. Wrap and refrigerate for 1 hour.

3. Using as little flour as possible, roll out the pastry into a 12-inch circle. Fit into a 10-inch tart pan with removable bottom, trimming any overhang even with the edges of the pan. Cover and refrigerate or freeze until ready to use.

FILLING

½ cup Dijon-style mustard

1 pound mozzarella, thinly sliced

8 to 10 ripe tomatoes, thinly sliced

2 tablespoons chopped fresh basil or 1 teaspoon dried

2 tablespoons chopped fresh oregano or 1 teaspoon dried

2 tablespoons minced garlic

2 tablespoons olive oil

salt and pepper

whole basil leaves (garnish)

1. Spread the mustard over the bottom of the unbaked tart shell. Overlap the mozzarella slices over the mustard.

2. Preheat oven to 400°F. Overlap tomato slices on the mozzarella to make one layer; sprinkle with some of the herbs, garlic, oil, and salt and pepper. Repeat with the remaining tomatoes, herbs, garlic, oil, and seasonings.

3. Place the tart on a baking sheet and bake until the pastry edge is browned and the filling is bubbling, 50 to 60 minutes. Let cool for about 10 minutes and serve hot. Garnish the center of the tart with 2 or 3 whole basil leaves before serving.

BROCHETTES OF BEEF WITH LEMON AND THYME

This beef filet *en brochette* can be cooked on a charcoal grill or under the broiler.

6 Servings

2 pounds filet mignon, cut into 1½-inch cubes

¼ cup olive oil

½ cup butter, melted

2 tablespoons chopped fresh thyme or 1 teaspoon dried

1 tablespoon Dijon-style mustard

¼ teaspoon hot pepper flakes

salt and black pepper

juice of 2 lemons

1. Thread the beef cubes on 3 long skewers, about 6 to 8 pieces per skewer.

2. Combine the oil, half the butter, the thyme, mustard, and pepper flakes and mix well. Brush this mixture on all sides of the beef. Season with salt and pepper.

3. Prepare barbecue or preheat broiler. Grill or broil the brochettes to desired doneness, about 3 to 4 minutes per side, basting with the olive oil mixture.

4. Combine the remaining melted butter with the lemon juice and heat quickly. Pour over the brochettes at serving time.

Beef With Lemon and Thyme

FISH FILLETS BAKED IN BROWN PAPER

A simple approach to the classic technique of cooking fish *en papillote*.

6 Servings

6 fillets of white-fleshed fish (sole, bass, flounder, grouper, etc.), about 2 to 2½ pounds total

12 mushrooms, thinly sliced

juice of 1 lemon

9 tablespoons butter, room temperature

salt and pepper

2 tablespoons dry sherry

1 tablespoon chopped fresh tarragon or 1 teaspoon dried

2 tablespoons chopped fresh chives

6 tablespoons sour cream

6 small brown paper bags, 1-pound size

1 lemon, cut lengthwise into 6 slices, seeded

1. Rinse the fillets in cool water and pat dry. Lay them flat on a work surface. Place the mushrooms in a bowl, add the lemon juice, and toss well.

2. Brush each side of the fillets with softened butter, using about 2 tablespoons total. Season with salt and pepper.

3. In a small skillet, combine 2 tablespoons butter with the sherry, tarragon, and 1 tablespoon chopped chives. Cook over high heat, stirring constantly, until thickened, about 2 minutes. Spoon some of this sauce over each fillet. Add 1 tablespoon sour cream to each fillet. Divide the mushrooms among the fillets. Fold the fillets in half crosswise.

4. Place ½ tablespoon butter on top of each folded fillet. Salt and pepper again and add the remaining chives.

5. Preheat oven to 375°F. Spread the remaining butter over the outside of each paper bag, coating evenly. Using a spatula, place one fillet in each bag. Fold over the opening of each bag twice to seal. Set the bags on a rimmed baking sheet or jelly-roll pan and bake 25 minutes.

6. Bring the paper bags to the table. Cut a cross in each bag with a sharp knife or scissors and fold back the points. Have each diner eat directly from the bag, accompanying the fish with the lemon slices.

Fall Squash with Mint and Honey

Actually, so-called summer squash is used here, yellow or green, but it is widely available during the fall months. This can be assembled hours ahead and baked just before serving; do not add salt until just before baking time.

6 Servings

2 pounds (about 4 cups)
summer squash, sliced

¼ cup butter

½ cup honey

¼ cup chopped fresh mint or
1 tablespoon dried

salt and pepper

1. Trim the ends of the squash and slice the squash as thinly as you can.

2. Preheat oven to 350°F. Layer the squash slices in a buttered 9-inch square glass baking dish, dotting each layer with butter, honey, mint, and salt and pepper. Cover with foil.

3. Bake until the squash is cooked through, about 30 minutes. Serve hot.

Fluffy White Birthday Cake with Autumn Leaves

This is a two-layer white cake with lemon filling and fluffy white frosting. The recipe calls for self-rising flour, but if you prefer you can use all-purpose flour, adding 3½ teaspoons baking powder and 1 teaspoon salt. The cake can be made the day before serving; cover carefully and store at room temperature.

8 to 12 Servings

CAKE

2¼ cups self-rising flour

1⅔ cups sugar

1¼ cups milk

⅔ cup vegetable shortening

1 teaspoon vanilla extract

5 egg whites

1. Grease and flour two 8- or 9-inch round cake pans and set aside.

2. Preheat oven to 350°F. Combine the flour, sugar, milk, shortening, and vanilla in a large mixer bowl and beat 30 seconds at low speed, scraping the sides of the bowl often. Beat at high speed for 2 minutes, scraping the bowl several times. Whip in the egg whites at high speed for 2 minutes more, scraping the sides 2 or 3 times. Pour into the prepared pans.

3. Bake until a wooden pick inserted in the center of one layer comes out clean and the cake springs back when pressed lightly with a fingertip, about 30 to 35 minutes. Let cool on a rack for 10 minutes, then remove the layers from the pans and cool completely.

FILLING
Makes enough for one
8- or 9-inch layer cake

¾ cup sugar

3 tablespoons cornstarch

pinch of salt

¾ cup water

1 teaspoon grated lemon zest

1 tablespoon butter

⅓ cup fresh lemon juice

In a small saucepan, mix the sugar, cornstarch, and salt. Slowly stir in the water. Cook, stirring constantly, until the mixture thickens and starts to boil; boil 1 minute. Immediately remove from heat. Add the lemon zest and butter and stir to melt the butter. Stir in the lemon juice. Let cool, then refrigerate.

FROSTING
**Makes enough for one
8- or 9-inch layer cake**

½ cup sugar

¼ cup light corn syrup

2 tablespoons water

2 egg whites

1 teaspoon vanilla extract

1. In a saucepan, combine the sugar, corn syrup, and water; cover and bring to boil. Uncover and place a candy thermometer into the mixture. Boil rapidly over high heat until the syrup reaches 242°F.

2. While the syrup is cooking, beat the egg whites to stiff peaks. Pour the hot syrup into the egg whites in a thin stream, beating constantly at medium speed. Add the vanilla and beat at high speed until the frosting forms stiff peaks.

AUTUMN LEAVES
Makes 6

3 ounces semisweet chocolate

*6 leathery leaves, such as rose,
gardenia, camellia or ivy
(use 3 large and 3 smaller ones)*

1. Melt the chocolate in the top of a double boiler until smooth. Paint or spread thinly over the bottom, veined side of each leaf. Arrange on waxed paper and place the leaves on a large plate or jelly-roll pan. Refrigerate until the chocolate is firm.

2. Grab the stem ends of the leaves and peel them away from the chocolate.

ASSEMBLY

Place one of the cake layers on a serving plate and spread with the lemon filling. Top with the other layer and frost the cake. Arrange the chocolate leaves at one side of the base of the cake, slightly overlapping.

Fluffy White Birthday Cake With Autumn Leaves

When I was 10 years old, my brothers and sisters gave me a birthday party. At that time, we ranged in age from 6 to 16 and every one of us was a cook. I didn't have to make a culinary contribution that day, but everyone else did, and willingly. There were sliced banana and peanut butter sandwiches on homemade bread; thick French fries with two dips—ketchup and Gulden's mustard; wonderful, warm homemade pizza with slices of Mom's Italian sausage; store-bought vanilla ice cream; a birthday cake from Marquart's German Bakery; and Grandma's coffee, mostly heated milk with about two tablespoons of real coffee. I remember it well. We celebrated in our big kitchen and wonder now if we were the ones who set the trend for kitchen-centered parties.

I often ask why, as kids, we liked to cook so much. Perhaps the smells from Mom's kitchen on cool September days worked up our appetites. Or was it because our father played around in the kitchen with his spareribs and steamed Savoy cabbage preparations? Mom was always making things from scratch, and most of the time we helped her. I remember that one of my tasks was to prick the homemade sausage with a needle as she filled the casings. Everyone pitched in on the sausagemaking in those days.

So here we are, planning another birthday party for a 10-year-old. What shall it be? Pizza, of course. Some things change, but not the craving for pizza by children and adults alike. It might be a good idea to have the children help create this party. We'll make individually designed birthday ice cream pie slices with all kinds of decorations to keep the kids busy and out of trouble. Happy Birthday, Joey! Happy Birthday, Beadie, wherever you may be! And Happy Birthday to you, Kate—oh, you're growing up so fast.

A Child's Birthday

MENU FOR 8

INDIVIDUAL PIZZAS

JOEY'S TAMALE PIE

OUR GANG DESIGNER ICE CREAM
PIE SLICES

HOMEMADE LEMONADE WITH
CHERRIES

A Tasty Pizza

FOOD PREPARATION

1 day ahead:
- Make pizza dough and refrigerate
- Make tomato sauce
- Assemble ice cream pie and freeze

Serving day:
- Bake pizzas
- Make tamale pie
- Mix lemonade

BEVERAGE SUGGESTION

Serve homemade lemonade with cherries.

INDIVIDUAL PIZZAS

Make the sauce first so that it is ready to use.

Makes eight 6-inch pizzas
PIZZA DOUGH

1 ⅓ cups lukewarm water (105° to 115°F)

1 ½ tablespoons honey

1 ½ envelopes dry yeast

¼ cup olive oil

1 teaspoon salt

4 ½ to 5 cups all-purpose flour

1. Mix ⅓ cup of the lukewarm water and ½ tablespoon of the honey in a large bowl. Sprinkle in the yeast, stir well, and set aside until foamy, about 10 minutes. Add the olive oil, salt, remaining 1 tablespoon honey, and remaining water, blending well with a wooden spoon.

2. Stir in about 4 cups flour, ½ cup at a time. Turn the dough out onto a floured work surface and knead until smooth and elastic, adding as much more flour as necessary to keep the dough from sticking. Knead for about 10 minutes total. Cover the dough with a towel or plastic wrap and let rest for 15 minutes.

3. Cut the dough into 8 pieces. Roll each piece into a ball and arrange on 2 greased large cookie sheets. Cover again and let rise until doubled in volume, about 1 hour.

4. Flatten each piece into a 6-inch circle, shaping a slightly raised edge. Transfer the pizzas to baking sheets that have been dusted lightly with cornmeal. Only 2 small pizzas will fit on each normal-size baking sheet, so be sure you have enough of them.

TOMATO SAUCE
Makes about 2½ cups

2 tablespoons olive oil

2 garlic cloves, minced

3 cups canned plum tomatoes with a little of their liquid, or peeled and chopped fresh tomatoes

2 tablespoons chopped fresh basil

1 teaspoon salt

2 teaspoons dried oregano

In a skillet, heat the oil and sauté the garlic for 1 minute. Add the tomatoes, basil, salt, and oregano and simmer for 10 minutes. Set aside.

ASSEMBLY

1 ¼ pounds mozzarella cheese, grated through large holes of grater

3 tablespoons grated Parmesan cheese

½ pound pepperoni, thinly sliced

8 pitted black olives, chopped

2 tablespoons olive oil

1. Preheat oven to 450°F. Spread some tomato sauce on each small pizza with the back of a spoon; do not overdo on the amount of sauce. Add some mozzarella, Parmesan, pepperoni, and a sprinkle of olive pieces. Drizzle with the olive oil.

2. Bake 2 trays at a time until the crust browns and the cheese is bubbling, about 12 to 15 minutes. Serve hot.

JOEY'S TAMALE PIE

The microwave technique given at right is safer for kids than the traditional method of baking. Both give good results.

8 to 10 Servings

1 pound lean ground chuck

¼ pound bulk pork sausage

2 cups stewed tomatoes, drained

1 ½ cups fresh, frozen, or canned corn niblets

1 cup Tomato Sauce (see preceding recipe)

1 small onion, chopped

2 teaspoons chili powder

2 garlic cloves, minced

salt

8 ½ ounces (1 packet) corn muffin mix

1 egg

⅓ cup milk

⅔ cup grated cheddar cheese

additional chili powder

1. In a large skillet, brown the chuck and the sausage meat, breaking it up with a wooden spoon so it cooks evenly. Drain off fat. Add the tomatoes, corn, tomato sauce, onion, 2 teaspoons chili powder, garlic, and salt and cook uncovered for 10 minutes. Transfer to an 8-inch round or square baking dish.

2. Preheat oven to 350°F. Blend the corn muffin mix, egg, and milk in a bowl and spread over the meat. Bake until the top is set, about 30 minutes. Sprinkle with the cheese and a little more chili powder and bake for 4 to 5 minutes to melt the cheese. Serve in wedges.

TO MICROWAVE

1. Mix the chuck, sausage meat, onion, and garlic in an 8-inch microwave-safe round or square dish. Cook on High (100%) for 9 minutes, stirring once or twice to break up the meat. Drain off fat.

2. Add the tomatoes, corn, tomato sauce, chili powder, and salt. Stir well and cook on High for 6 minutes.

3. Combine the muffin mix, egg, and milk and spread over the meat mixture. Cook on Medium-High (70%) for 5 minutes, then on High for 6 minutes or until the top is set. Sprinkle with the cheese and a little more chili powder and cook on High until the cheese melts, 1 to 2 minutes.

Joey's Tamale Pie

OUR GANG DESIGNER ICE CREAM PIE SLICES

This is ice cream in a simple pie crust made with ground nuts, frozen until ready to use, and then decorated by the children with colored creams and toppings. An alternative to colored creams is flavored ice cream toppings served in plastic squeeze bottles.

8 Servings

CRUST

1 cup ground Brazil nuts

2 tablespoons all-purpose flour

¼ cup sugar

¼ teaspoon salt

3 tablespoons butter, melted

Preheat oven to 375°F. Blend all the ingredients in a bowl and press into the bottom and sides of a 9-inch tart pan with removable bottom or a 9-inch glass pie dish. Bake until golden, about 12 minutes. Let cool on a rack. Do not remove the shell from the tart pan.

ASSEMBLY

1 quart vanilla ice cream, softened

1 cup heavy cream, whipped

1 drop each of red, yellow, and blue food coloring

½ cup chocolate sprinkles

½ cup crushed peanuts

8 fireworks sparklers

1. Spread the ice cream into the cooled pie crust and freeze until firm.

2. Divide the whipped cream into 3 bowls. Add a drop of one food coloring to each bowl and blend to make pastel tints. Refrigerate until ready to use.

3. Transfer the whipped creams to 3 decorating or icing bags fitted with different tips. If you don't have icing bags, cut a corner off each of 3 plastic zip-lock bags and insert decorating tips. Cut the pie into 8 wedges and put each on an individual plate. Allow the children to decorate their own with sprinkles, peanuts, and piped whipped cream. When each slice is decorated, insert a sparkler as you would a candle. Light the sparklers—with supervision—and sing "Happy Birthday"!

HOMEMADE LEMONADE WITH CHERRIES

Makes about 2 ½ quarts

juice of 8 lemons, strained

1 cup sugar

2 quarts cold water

ice cubes

8 maraschino cherries

1. Combine first 3 ingredients and stir until sugar is dissolved. Add more lemon juice or sugar to taste.

2. Add ice cubes to 8 tall glasses and fill with the lemonade. Add a cherry and a straw to each glass.

Our Gang Designer Ice Cream Pie Slices

It matters not how strait the gate,
How charged with punishments the scroll,
I am the master of my fate
I am the captain of my soul.

    —from "Invictus," by William Ernest Henley
    (1849–1903)

This was required memorization during senior year at high school, with the express purpose, I'm sure, of emphasizing the important goal we were achieving as graduation time approached. The message in these four lines seems to apply equally well to any stage of one's life, which may explain the stanza's immortality. I recall another four lines that my classroom teacher put on the board for the last school session:

Here was an old owl liv'd in an oak
The more he heard, the less he spoke;
The less he spoke, the more he heard
O, if men were all like that wise bird.

    —*Punch*, vol. 1, xviii, p. 155 (1875)

Most of us had to rent tuxedos for the senior prom and scrounge for dollars to pay for corsages. Parents always offered to do a party before and after the prom, but that was out of the question. There was, however, a gathering at home after formal graduation exercises for family and friends.

So Jimmy or Jenny will be graduating this June. What will you do? Here is a menu for you.

High School Graduation

BUFFET MENU FOR 12

ITALIAN COUNTRYSIDE HERO

BAKED BEANS WITH MAPLE SYRUP

APRICOT-PECAN CRUNCH CAKE

ICE CREAM

Italian Hero

FOOD PREPARATION

This is very easy to prepare. Consider having the graduates make the hero sandwich as they gather to celebrate. The host or hostess can make the cake a day ahead; the beans, too, can be prepared ahead and reheated before serving time. Feel free to add condiments and purchased deli salads, such as cole slaw or potato salad, if you wish.

Table decoration idea: print this menu with the heading "Graduation Party," showing date, time, and location; list the menu items and the names of those in attendance. Roll each sheet like a scroll, tie with a white silk ribbon, and stack them on the buffet table (or place them in a basket on the table).

BEVERAGE SUGGESTIONS

Serve lemonade, iced tea, and sodas.

ITALIAN COUNTRYSIDE HERO

Four loaves of Italian or French bread are used here; they are put together to resemble a single 4-foot-long loaf. The open sandwich is filled heavily with Italian meats, cheese, and condiments. The loaves should be placed on a long, clean board, about 1 inch thick and 10 inches wide; it's easy to find such a piece of wood at your local lumberyard. This board will make the sandwich easy to present and slice.

12 Servings

2 jars (12 ounces each) Kalamata or other black olives, chopped

2 jars (12 ounces each) pimiento-stuffed olives, chopped

1 jar (12 ounces) sweet pickled peppers or roasted red peppers, seeded and chopped

2 medium onions, finely chopped

½ cup finely chopped parsley

2 garlic cloves, minced

2 teaspoons dried oregano

1 cup olive oil

⅓ cup balsamic or red wine vinegar

salt and pepper

4 loaves (each about 14 inches long) Italian or French bread

1 pound thinly sliced provolone cheese

1 pound thinly sliced salami

1 pound thinly sliced mortadella or capocollo

4 large tomatoes, thinly sliced

1 large head romaine lettuce, rinsed, dried, and shredded

1. Combine the olives, peppers, onions, parsley, garlic, oregano, olive oil, vinegar, and salt and pepper in a large bowl and let stand for at least 1 hour or overnight. Drain well, reserving the liquid.

2. Place the 4 loaves of bread on a long board. Cut both ends off the 2 inside loaves and cut off the inside ends of the 2 outside loaves. The loaves should fit together loosely; don't fret if they don't fit exactly. Slice through each loaf horizontally without cutting all the way through. Open as wide as possible and remove the soft bread inside.

3. Brush all cut sides of the bread with the reserved oil mixture. Spread the olive and pepper mixture on each piece of bread. Layer the cheese and meats on the bottom 4 bread halves, letting some meat overhang the bread slightly. Layer the tomatoes and shredded lettuce on the top bread halves. Do not fold the bread closed until ready to cut and serve.

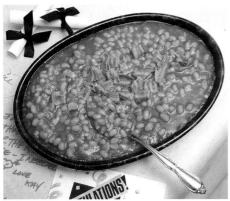

Baked Beans

BAKED BEANS WITH MAPLE SYRUP

12 Servings

4 cans (16 ounces each) baked beans

½ cup pure maple syrup

¼ cup ketchup

1 teaspoon A-1 steak sauce

1 teaspoon Worcestershire sauce

*6 thin bacon slices,
thinly sliced crosswise*

1. Preheat oven to 350°F. Combine all ingredients except the bacon in a 2-quart baking dish and toss well. Sprinkle the bacon bits over.

2. Bake until heated through and bubbling, about 30 minutes. If all the bacon is not crisped, run quickly under the broiler. Serve from the baking dish.

APRICOT-PECAN CRUNCH CAKE

This may be made a day ahead, wrapped in foil, and kept at room temperature.

12 Servings

1 ½ cups all-purpose flour

2 teaspoons baking powder

pinch of salt

6 eggs, separated, room temperature

2 cups sugar

1 tablespoon vanilla extract

*1 pound dried apricots, cut into
¼-inch pieces, dusted with flour*

4 cups chopped pecans

pinch of cream of tartar

confectioner's sugar

1. Sift the flour, baking powder, and salt into a large bowl.

2. In the bowl of an electric mixer, beat the egg yolks with 1½ cups sugar until thick and pale. Add the vanilla and fold in the apricots and pecans.

3. Preheat oven to 325°F. Butter a 12-cup bundt pan. Using clean beaters and a clean bowl, whip the egg whites with the cream of tartar to soft peaks. Beat in the remaining ½ cup sugar a tablespoon at a time until the whites form stiff peaks.

4. Fold the flour mixture and egg whites into the yolk mixture. Pour into the prepared pan and bake until the top is browned and a bit cracked, about 1¼ hours. Let cool for 10 minutes, then turn the cake out onto a rack and cool completely. Dust with confectioner's sugar before serving.

Apricot-Pecan Crunch Cake

Most people love a picnic—perhaps because of the informality, a sense of togetherness, or just because it's an old-fashioned idea. Sure, there's always the curmudgeon who complains of sand in the sandwiches, but such objections are easily overcome by the green of the grass, the shimmer of the sea, the Botticelli blue of the sky, the aroma of hickory-grilled food, the feeling of delicious spontaneity.

Here is a picnic to fit a number of celebratory events, be it a football game on home ground or a welcome for friends who are visiting from afar. A picnic need not take place on the beach or at the river's edge; it can just as well be in your own backyard. One summer evening I moved an old hooked rug onto the lawn and placed some white wicker furniture on it. I added three or four old quilts, one draped over the table, others on the backs of chairs. An oversize summer bouquet in an old copper pot was prominently displayed. Candles in hurricane lamps and good china and sterling with large white damask napkins set off the country scene.

26

Special Picnic Day

PICNIC MENU FOR 12

BLUEPOINT OYSTERS ON
THE HALF SHELL

PICNIC PATE WITH PISTACHIOS

FOUR-BEAN PERSILLADE WITH
SCALLIONS, VINAIGRETTE

WALNUT AND YOGURT BREAD

SUGARED RED CABBAGE WITH
CARAWAY SEEDS

COMPOTE OF PEARS, APRICOTS,
AND PLUMS IN PORT

Four-Bean Persillade

FOOD PREPARATION

1 week ahead:
- Make pâté

2 days ahead:
- Make four-bean persillade, red cabbage, and fruit compote

1 day ahead:
- Bake bread

Serving day:
- Prepare oysters

Note that the fruit compote is best if made two or three days ahead and refrigerated for the flavors to mellow. Use fresh fruit if at all possible, but canned or jarred fruit will work also.

WINE SUGGESTIONS

Serve a Hargrave Long Island Chardonnay with the oysters, and Charles Shaw Napa Gamay throughout the meal.

BLUEPOINT OYSTERS ON THE HALF SHELL

12 Servings

10-pound bag of ice

36 fresh bluepoint oysters

1 cup red wine vinegar

½ cup finely chopped shallots

freshly ground black pepper

1. Place some ice in the bottom of a large pail. Add the oysters and cover with more ice.

2. Combine the vinegar, shallots, and lots of black pepper in a jar. Cover tightly and shake well.

3. Be sure to bring one or two shucking knives to the picnic site. To serve, shuck the oysters and drizzle a scant teaspoon of the vinegar mixture on top.

Picnic Pâté With Pistachios

PICNIC PATE WITH PISTACHIOS

This may be made one week ahead and refrigerated. It can also be wrapped well and frozen for several weeks, but if frozen longer it loses flavor.

12 Servings

1 pound chicken livers, trimmed

½ cup orange juice

1 ounce dried mushrooms

½ cup dry sherry

6 garlic cloves, coarsely chopped

3 eggs

½ cup brandy or cognac

¼ cup heavy cream

1 tablespoon salt

2 teaspoons white pepper

1 teaspoon allspice

1 pound veal, 1 pound pork shoulder, and ¾ pound pork fat (from fresh ham or pork loin), ground together

½ cup all-purpose flour

½ cup shelled pistachios

1 pound sliced bacon

½ cup chopped parsley and 4 bay leaves (garnish)

1. Combine the chicken livers and orange juice in a small bowl. In another small bowl, combine the dried mushrooms and sherry. Let both soak for about 30 minutes.

2. Combine the garlic, eggs, brandy, cream, salt, pepper, and allspice in a bowl and beat lightly.

3. Drain the livers well and add to the egg mixture. Transfer half of this mixture to a food processor and blend until smooth. Repeat with the remainder. Stir in the ground meats. Sift the flour over the meat mixture and mix well. Add the pistachios. Drain the mushrooms and chop finely; add to the meat mixture.

4. Preheat oven to 400°F. Line a 10-inch-diameter, 4-inch-deep soufflé dish with ¾ of the bacon slices. Pour in the pâté mixture to within an inch of the top. Tap the dish firmly on the counter to remove air bubbles. Lay the remaining bacon slices on top of the pâté. Cover with foil. Set the dish in a larger pan and add warm water to come halfway up the pâté dish.

5. Bake for 3 hours, topping up the water bath as necessary and removing the foil for the last 20 minutes of baking.

6. Remove the pâté from the water bath and cover again with foil. Top with a plate. Set a weight, such as a brick or several cans of food, on top of the plate. Refrigerate overnight or at least 8 hours, until the pâté is chilled through.

7. To serve, bring the pâté to cool room temperature. Turn out of the dish and remove the congealed bacon fat. Pat the chopped parsley around the sides of the pâté and add the 4 bay leaves to the top.

FOUR-BEAN PERSILLADE WITH SCALLIONS, VINAIGRETTE

This can be made two days ahead and refrigerated, but it should be served at room temperature for full flavor.

12 Servings

1 can (16 ounces) each black, white, red, and lima beans

1 cup chopped fresh tomatoes

½ cup finely chopped parsley

½ cup thinly sliced scallions

2 garlic cloves, minced

1 tablespoon finely chopped fresh thyme or 1 teaspoon dried

1 cup vinaigrette (see page 193)

1. Place the beans in a colander and rinse under cold water. Drain well and transfer to a large bowl.

2. Add all remaining ingredients and toss well. Cover and refrigerate. Bring to room temperature before serving.

WALNUT AND YOGURT BREAD

Makes two 9 x 5-inch loaves

3½ cups all-purpose flour

2½ cups wholewheat flour

1½ cups chopped walnuts

½ cup wheat germ

⅓ cup sugar

2 teaspoons salt

2 envelopes fast-rising yeast

1½ cups water

¾ cup plain yogurt

¼ cup margarine

1. Set aside 1 cup of the all-purpose flour. Combine the remaining flours, the nuts, wheat germ, sugar, salt, and yeast in a large bowl.

2. In a small saucepan, heat the water, yogurt, and margarine over low heat to about 125°F (hot to the touch). Stir into the dry mixture. Add enough of the reserved flour to make a stiff dough. Turn out onto a lightly floured surface and knead until smooth and elastic, about 10 minutes.

3. Divide the dough in half. Roll each half into a 12 × 8-inch rectangle. Beginning at the short end, roll each rectangle into a loaf and place in 2 greased 9 × 5-inch or 8 × 4-inch loaf pans. Cover and let rise in a warm place until doubled in volume, about 1 hour.

4. Preheat oven to 400°F. Bake the loaves until golden brown, 25 to 30 minutes. Remove from the pans and let cool on racks.

SUGARED RED CABBAGE WITH CARAWAY SEEDS

This may be made two or three days ahead, covered, and refrigerated.

12 Servings

1 medium head red cabbage, cored and sliced as thinly as possible

½ cup vegetable oil

¼ cup red wine vinegar

2 tablespoons firmly packed brown sugar

1 tablespoon caraway seeds

salt and pepper

1. Blanch the cabbage in a large pot of boiling salted water for 3 to 4 minutes. Drain and refresh under cool water. Pat dry with paper towels. Place in a large bowl.

2. Combine the remaining ingredients in a small bowl and whisk until well combined. Pour over the cabbage and toss well. Cover and refrigerate for several hours or up to 3 days.

COMPOTE OF PEARS, APRICOTS, AND PLUMS IN PORT

12 Servings

6 ripe pears

juice of 1 lemon

6 fresh apricots, halved and pitted

6 large red plums, halved and pitted

24 black cherries, halved, stemmed, and pitted

1 bottle (750 ml) port

1. Peel, halve, and core the pears. Coat with the lemon juice to prevent discoloration.

2. Combine all the fruit in a nonaluminum saucepan. Pour in the wine and bring to boil. Lower the heat and simmer until the pears are just tender; do not overcook. (If using canned fruit, drain the fruit, cover with the wine, and bring just to boil, then turn off the heat.) Remove from heat and transfer to a bowl. Cover and refrigerate until ready to serve.

Walnut and Yogurt Bread

Compote of Pears, Apricots, and Plums in Port

Big, old-fashioned weddings are back. Along with engraved invitations, pale blue and outrageous pink floral chintz tablecloths, impressionist bouquets on each table, and overflowing champagne glasses, splendid and spectacular food is expected. June is a favorite month for such goings-on, of course, but so is September—and, for that matter, any month of the year.

Although the wedding itself is the main event under the big tent, there's no reason why the bridal shower shouldn't have its own panache and excitement. In this and the following two menus, it is possible to scale up or down as necessary, depending on the number of people involved.

Invitations have been sent, the wedding gown has been chosen, and the menus have been planned . . . so let's start with the bridal shower.

Bridal Shower

MENU FOR 12

OLD-FASHIONED ROSE PETAL
WHITE WINE PUNCH

SMOKED SALMON FINGER
SANDWICHES WITH BUTTER AND
BLACK PEPPER

CUCUMBER SANDWICHES WITH
CURRIED MAYONNAISE

WATERCRESS SANDWICHES WITH
RASPBERRY VINEGAR MAYONNAISE

PARISIAN "COQUILLES" IN WHITE
WINE SAUCE IN PASTRY SEASHELLS

JULIENNE SPINACH SALAD WITH
TOASTED PINE NUTS AND
LEMON DRESSING

STRAWBERRIES, MERINGUE, AND
RASPBERRY SAUCE

Rose Petal White Wine Punch

FOOD PREPARATION

1 day ahead:
- Assemble sandwiches, cover tightly, and refrigerate
- Bake pastry seashells
- Make meringue cups, strawberry filling, and sauce and keep each separate until ready to serve

Serving day:
- Make punch
- Prepare coquilles
- Make salad

WINE/BEVERAGE SUGGESTIONS

Serve the punch and Grand Chardonnay Ardèche (Louis Latour) throughout the meal.

OLD-FASHIONED ROSE PETAL WHITE WINE PUNCH

Be sure to use rose petals that have not been treated with any pesticides. The petals will perfume the punch, which is more or less a spritzer with a rose scent.

12 Servings
1 cup scented rose petals, any color you wish

2 tablespoons sugar

2 bottles (1 liter each) sparkling water

juice of 2 lemons, strained

2 bottles (750 ml each) chilled white wine

1. Two hours before serving, place all the rose petals except one generous tablespoonful in a large bowl and sprinkle with the sugar. Toss lightly but well. Add 1 bottle sparkling water and the lemon juice. Refrigerate.

2. When ready to serve, strain the mixture into a punchbowl. Add 1 bottle sparkling water, the wine, and the reserved tablespoon of rose petals. Ladle into champagne or other tall glasses.

SMOKED SALMON FINGER SANDWICHES WITH BUTTER AND BLACK PEPPER

Makes 15
2 tablespoons butter, softened

10 very thin slices egg bread

½ pound thinly sliced smoked salmon

freshly ground black pepper

chopped parsley

1. Lightly butter all 10 slices of bread. Lay 5 slices on a work surface and arrange a layer of salmon carefully on top. (If you use just one layer of salmon, there will be some left over.) Pepper liberally and cover with the other 5 slices of bread.

2. With a sharp knife, trim the crusts on all 4 sides. Cut each sandwich twice lengthwise to make 3 fingers. Arrange 3 finger sandwiches on a plate. Top with 3 or more, set in the opposite direction. Continue until 5 layers are made. Sprinkle lightly with parsley. Cover with plastic wrap and refrigerate.

CUCUMBER SANDWICHES WITH CURRIED MAYONNAISE

Makes 15

Curried Mayonnaise (see below)

10 very thin slices egg bread

*1 to 2 cucumbers, peeled in stripes and very thinly sliced
(use a mandoline, if possible)*

Assemble in the same manner as the smoked salmon sandwiches, spreading mayonnaise on all the slices of bread and filling with the cucumber slices. Cover with plastic and refrigerate.

CURRIED MAYONNAISE

All ingredients should be at room temperature.

Makes 1 cup

1 cup prepared mayonnaise

1 ½ teaspoons curry powder

1 tablespoon lemon juice

Combine all ingredients and mix well.

WATERCRESS SANDWICHES WITH RASPBERRY VINEGAR MAYONNAISE

Makes 15

*Raspberry Vinegar Mayonnaise
(see below)*

10 very thin slices egg bread

1 bunch fresh watercress, large stems removed, coarsely chopped

Assemble in the same manner as the smoked salmon sandwiches, spreading mayonnaise on all the slices of bread and filling with the watercress. Cover with plastic and refrigerate.

RASPBERRY VINEGAR MAYONNAISE

All ingredients should be at room temperature.

Makes 1 cup

1 cup prepared mayonnaise

1 tablespoon raspberry vinegar

Combine mayonnaise and vinegar and mix well.

Assorted Finger Sandwiches With Salad

Parisian "Coquilles" in White Wine Sauce in Pastry Seashells

This dish is similar to Coquilles St. Jacques, but it is brought to the table in a large baking dish and spooned into tasty pastry seashells. The shells take a little time to make, but they aren't difficult—and they look sensational. Use either bay or sea scallops. If you use the larger sea scallops, cut them in half against the grain; if you use bay scallops, leave them whole.

12 Servings

3 cups chicken stock or low-salt broth

3 cups dry white wine

6 large shallots, thinly sliced

1 herb bouquet (parsley and tarragon sprigs, celery leaves, and a bay leaf), tied in cheesecloth

3 pounds scallops

1½ pounds mushrooms, thinly sliced

9 tablespoons butter

¾ cup all-purpose flour

1½ cups milk

3 egg yolks

1 to 1½ cups heavy cream

1 tablespoon fresh lemon juice

salt and white pepper

¾ cup grated Gruyère, Emmentaler, or similar Swiss cheese

Pastry Seashells (see right)

1. In a large, wide saucepan, bring the stock, wine, shallots, and herb bouquet to boil. Add the scallops and mushrooms, lower the heat, cover, and simmer just until the scallops are opaque, 6 to 8 minutes. Transfer the scallops and mushrooms to a bowl with a large slotted spoon. Raise the heat and bring the liquid to boil again, uncovered. Boil until reduced to 3 cups. Strain the liquid.

Parisian "Coquilles" With Pastry Seashells

2. Melt the butter in a clean saucepan. Remove from heat and whisk in the flour. Stir in the reduced cooking liquid and the milk. Return the pan to the heat and cook until the mixture is smooth and thick. Remove from heat and whisk in the egg yolks and 1 cup cream. Return to the heat and cook until the sauce coats a spoon, about 2 minutes, stirring constantly; do not boil or the yolks will curdle. If the sauce is too thick, thin with more cream or stock. Stir in the lemon juice and season with salt and pepper.

3. Preheat oven to 375°F. Add the scallops and mushrooms to the sauce and pour into a 2- to 3-quart baking/serving dish that can take a few minutes under the broiler. Top with the cheese. Bake until the sauce bubbles, about 20 minutes. Run under the broiler to brown lightly. At the table, spoon each serving into a pastry seashell.

PASTRY SEASHELLS
Makes 12

1. Make 2 recipes of pâte brisée on page 193. You'll also need 12 large (about 5-inch) seashells to be used as forms; these are widely available at kitchen specialty shops and in many supermarkets.

2. Preheat oven to 375°F. Line the inside of 6 shells with the pastry, as you would to make a pie shell. Place another shell on top of each pastry-filled shell and press together lightly. With a small sharp knife, trim off the excess pastry.

3. Arrange the shell "sandwiches" on a baking sheet and bake 15 minutes. Remove the top shells and bake the crusts uncovered in the base shells until light brown, about 5 more minutes. Let cool on a rack. Repeat to make 6 more shells. These can be made the same day and left out at room temperature, or they may be made well ahead and frozen.

JULIENNE SPINACH SALAD WITH TOASTED PINE NUTS AND LEMON DRESSING

If you cannot get fresh spinach, use other greens such as hearts of escarole, curly endive, or Bibb lettuce.

12 Servings

3 pounds fresh spinach, or other fresh greens to make 12 cups

½ cup olive oil

¼ cup fresh lemon juice

½ cup toasted pine nuts

salt and pepper

1. Rinse the spinach leaves in several changes of cool water and remove the stems. Dry the leaves well. Cut into the thinnest possible julienne strips. Place in plastic bags, tie them closed, and refrigerate until ready to use.

2. Whisk the oil, lemon juice, and salt and pepper. Add as much as you like to the spinach and toss. Sprinkle with the toasted pine nuts, toss again, and serve.

STRAWBERRIES, MERINGUE, AND RASPBERRY SAUCE

12 Servings

Meringue Cups (see below)

Strawberry Filling (see right)

Raspberry Sauce (see right)

Place a meringue cup on each individual plate. Spoon in strawberry filling and top with 2 tablespoons sauce.

MERINGUE CUPS

These can be made a day ahead and stored in airtight containers.

Makes 12

6 egg whites, at room temperature

½ teaspoon cream of tartar

¼ teaspoon salt

1 ½ cups confectioner's sugar

4 ounces slivered almonds, ground

1. Preheat oven to 275°F. Line 2 large baking sheets with parchment paper and draw six 4-inch circles on each sheet.

2. Beat whites with cream of tartar and salt until soft peaks form. Add sugar by tablespoons, beating until the mixture is stiff and shiny. Fold in ground almonds.

3. Swirl the meringue mixture onto the circles on the parchment paper. Make a depression in each circle to form a cup. Bake 1 hour.

STRAWBERRY FILLING
Makes about 6 cups

3 pints strawberries, rinsed, hulled, and sliced

½ cup confectioner's sugar

¼ cup orange liqueur

Combine all ingredients in a bowl and toss well. Cover tightly and refrigerate until ready to use.

RASPBERRY SAUCE
Makes about 1 ½ cups

⅓ cup currant jelly

2 pints raspberries, pureed

1. Melt the jelly in a small saucepan over low heat.

2. Sieve the berry puree into the saucepan. Stir well. Cool and chill.

Strawberries in Meringue Cups

To assure a smooth wedding ceremony, a rehearsal is almost always necessary. It usually takes place the evening before the actual wedding day. It was once considered bad luck for a bride to participate in her own rehearsal, but times have changed and a bride now takes part. At the rehearsal, the minister, priest, or rabbi explains the parts of the ceremony and the role of each member of the wedding party.

Most rehearsals are followed by a dinner to allow members of the two families to get to know each other better. Often, this supper or dinner is hosted by the groom's parents, but any member of the family may host—at home, or in a restaurant. The dinner party should include the bridal party, parents of the bride and groom, and any close relatives who may have traveled a long distance to come to the wedding.

The person giving the dinner should decide its format, location, and menu. Should it be a sit-down dinner? A buffet? In any case, time should provide for a short cocktail period, but don't plan a long evening. Help keep people sober and ready for the big event.

If the groom's father is hosting, he should make the first toast. If the groom's mother is widowed or divorced, she should make the first toast. Other toasts can be made; however, these toasts shouldn't be as formal as they will be on the wedding day and should be kept low-keyed.

When arranging a seating plan, consider seating the bride's mother to the right of the groom's father and the bride's father to the right of the groom's mother. When I gave a rehearsal dinner for my niece, I placed my niece and her husband-to-be side by side in the center of a very long table. Remember, rehearsal dinners should have their own individuality and be an exciting part of the wedding celebration.

Rehearsal Dinner

MENU FOR 12

Orange Blossoms

Bloodlines

Thin Spaghetti with Arugula

Herbed Fish Grilled with
Ginger and Mustard

Watercress and Curly Endive
with Lemon Dressing

Chocolate Almond Cake
with Creme Anglaise

Orange Blossoms

FOOD PREPARATION

This menu is informal and can be expanded easily.

1 day ahead:
- Make dessert and sauce
- Prepare salad greens and make lemon dressing but keep separate
- Make drinks but do not add champagne or fruit until ready to serve

Serving day:
- Marinate and grill or broil fish
- Prepare pasta dish
- Complete drinks
- Dress salad

WINE SUGGESTIONS

Serve Santa Inez Valley Sauvignon Blanc or Washington State Sauvignon with the pasta and fish courses.

ORANGE BLOSSOMS

A nonalcoholic refresher.

Makes 1 Serving

1 cup orange juice

2 tablespoons Sugar Syrup (see below)

1 tablespoon fresh lime juice

1 tablespoon fresh lemon juice

1-inch cube fresh pineapple

1-inch cube fresh apple, rubbed with lemon juice

1. Combine the liquids and pour into a large glass filled with ice cubes.

2. Thread the pineapple and apple on a wooden skewer, dip fruit into the drink to prevent discoloration, and add to the glass for garnish.

SUGAR SYRUP
Makes about ⅔ cup

½ cup water

¼ cup sugar

Combine the water and sugar in a small saucepan and boil until sugar dissolves. Remove from heat and cool before using.

BLOODLINES

Makes 1 Serving

2 tablespoons (1 ounce) Grand Marnier

2 tablespoons (1 ounce) Curaçao

1 tablespoon crème de cassis

iced champagne

Combine the liquors in a 6-ounce glass and top off with chilled champagne. Serve immediately.

THIN SPAGHETTI WITH ARUGULA

This was created by Chef Fernando Spriano of the New York restaurant Orsini's.

12 Servings

1 cup olive oil

3 onions, finely chopped

4 garlic cloves, minced

6 bunches fresh arugula, washed well, drained, and finely chopped

2¼ cups canned tomatoes, put through food mill

2¼ cups chopped peeled, seeded fresh tomatoes

salt and pepper

9 tablespoons butter, cut into 1-tablespoon pieces

1½ pounds thin spaghetti, cooked and drained

grated Parmesan cheese (optional)

1. Heat the olive oil in a saucepan large enough to hold the sauce and pasta and sauté the onions just until they begin to color. Add the garlic and arugula and cook until the greens are tender, about 5 minutes.

2. Add the tomatoes and salt and pepper and cook 7 to 8 minutes. Add the butter and stir to melt. Add the cooked pasta and toss briefly over high heat. Serve with Parmesan if you wish.

HERBED FISH GRILLED WITH GINGER AND MUSTARD

This may be cooked on a gas or charcoal grill and is also good broiled. Be sure to baste often with the marinade.

12 Servings

1½ pounds swordfish steak, about 1¼ inches thick

1½ pounds tuna steak, about 1¼ inches thick

12 sea scallops (about ¾ pound)

12 large shrimp (about ¾ pound), peeled and deveined

3 tablespoons grated fresh ginger

3 tablespoons coarse-grained mustard

¼ cup fresh lemon juice

⅔ cup oil, part vegetable, part olive

⅓ cup finely chopped scallions

3 tablespoons finely chopped fresh coriander

salt and pepper

2 cups mayonnaise

12 lemon wedges

1. Cut the swordfish and tuna into 1¼-inch cubes. Pat all the seafood dry and arrange in one layer in one or more large glass or ceramic dishes.

2. Combine the ginger, mustard, and lemon juice; gradually whisk in the oil. Add the scallions, coriander, and salt and pepper. Pour over the seafood and toss to coat all pieces. Cover and marinate 30 minutes.

3. Prepare the barbecue or preheat grill or broiler. When the fire is almost ready, thread the seafood on 12 skewers, alternating the various kinds. Grill or broil just until the seafood is opaque, about 10 minutes, turning the skewers so all sides are cooked and brushing frequently with the marinade. (If broiling, place skewers 4 to 5 inches below the heat source.)

4. Serve with the mayonnaise and lemon wedges.

Herbed Fish on Skewer With Spaghetti and Arugula

WATERCRESS AND CURLY ENDIVE WITH LEMON DRESSING

The dressing ingredients make about 1 cup; make it at least an hour or two ahead for flavors to blend.

12 Servings

2 bunches watercress

2 hearts curly endive

5 tablespoons frozen lemonade concentrate, thawed

5 tablespoons clear honey

5 tablespoons vegetable oil

1 teaspoon celery seeds

salt and pepper

1. Remove heavy stems from the watercress. Rinse the watercress and endive and spin both dry.

2. To make the dressing, combine the lemonade concentrate, honey, oil, and celery seeds in a bowl. Season with salt and pepper. Mix well, pour over salad greens, and toss.

CHOCOLATE ALMOND CAKE WITH CREME ANGLAISE

12 Servings

10 tablespoons butter

⅔ cup sugar

4 eggs, separated

5 ounces semisweet chocolate, melted

5 ounces almonds (about ½ cup), finely ground

1 tablespoon confectioner's sugar

Crème Anglaise (see below)

1. Preheat oven to 375°F. Butter and flour a 9- or 10-inch springform pan. Cream the butter and ⅓ cup sugar until fluffy. Add egg yolks one at a time, beating until light and fluffy. Fold in the chocolate, blending well, and set aside.

2. In a clean bowl, with clean beaters, beat the whites until foamy. Gradually add the remaining sugar and beat until stiff. Fold into the chocolate mixture and blend until no streaks of white remain. Fold in the nuts.

3. Pour batter in to the prepared pan and bake until a wooden skewer inserted in the center comes out clean, about 30 minutes. Let the cake cool on a rack, then refrigerate until ready to serve.

4. Just before serving, sift the confectioner's sugar over the cake. Remove the side of the springform. Accompany the cake with crème anglaise.

CREME ANGLAISE
Makes about 1 cup

1 cup half-and-half or light cream

2 egg yolks

¼ cup sugar

1 teaspoon vanilla extract

1. Heat the half-and-half or cream just to the boiling point. Set aside.

2. Beat the yolks and sugar until the mixture is pale yellow and forms a ribbon when the beaters are lifted. Mix a little of the warm cream into the yolk mixture, then pour the mixture back into the remaining cream. Stir over medium heat until thickened, about 10 minutes; do not boil. Remove from heat.

3. Add the vanilla and mix well. Transfer to a bowl and cover the surface with waxed paper to prevent a skin from forming. Chill until ready to serve.

Chocolate Almond Cake With Crème Anglaise

Pussy said to the owl, You elegant fowl
How charmingly sweet you sing!
O let us be married, too long we have tarried
But what shall we do for a ring?
They sailed away for a year and a day,
To the land where the Bong-tree grows,
And there in a wood a Piggy-wig stood
With a ring at the end of his nose.

> —from "The Owl and the Pussycat,"
> by Edward Lear (1812–1888)

A Wedding Buffet

MENU FOR 50

LITTLE BASKETS OF CURRIED WALNUTS
(PAGE 58) AND ROSEMARY-ROASTED
PECANS (PAGE 46)

BACON AND WATER CHESTNUT CRUNCH
(PAGE 194)

BELGIAN ENDIVE WITH BRANDIED
GORGONZOLA (PAGE 194)

FISH TABLE:

SHRIMP WITH REMOULADE AND SPICY
TOMATO SAUCE

SMOKED SALMON POTATO SALAD

MEAT TABLE:

SMOKED TURKEY SLICES WITH
CRANBERRY SALSA

GINGER-GLAZED HAM WITH BRANDY

BLUEBERRY AND APRICOT CHUTNEY

CUCUMBER YOGURT RELISH

SALAD TABLE:

CHICKEN PECAN SALAD

AVOCADO, PINK GRAPEFRUIT, AND ORANGE
SALAD WITH LEMON PEPPER DRESSING

ROUND OF RIPE BRIE WITH ASSORTED
CRACKERS

WEDDING CAKE

Shrimp With Remoulade and Tomato Sauce

FOOD PREPARATION

Tightly cover and refrigerate all food except pecans and walnuts (they are frozen). Be sure to bring salad dressings to room temperature before using.

5 days before wedding:
- Curry walnuts, roast pecans, and freeze separately in airtight containers
- Prepare blueberry and apricot chutney
- Prepare cranberry salsa

4 days before wedding:
- Prepare remoulade and spicy tomato sauce
- Order shrimp and turkey but do not pick up until the day before the wedding

3 days before wedding:
- Make smoked salmon potato salad
- Prepare grapefruit and oranges for salad
- Make salad dressings

2 days before wedding:
- Make cucumber yogurt relish
- Make chicken pecan salad
- Chill champagne

1 day before wedding:
- Bake ginger-glazed hams
- Set tables and bar

Wedding day:
- Arrange shrimp bowl, ham, turkey, and salad platters; fill sauce bowls

WINE/BEVERAGE SUGGESTIONS

Serve Chablis Premier Cru Montée de Tonnerre and Robert Mondavi Napa Valley Pinot Noir throughout the buffet. Serve champagne before the meal if you wish, but surely with the wedding cake. Coffee may also be served with the cake.

BUFFET PLANNING AND PRESENTATION

The plan for this buffet is to set three tables each with different offerings. Young people's taste in food today is eclectic; they know a lot, have traveled a lot, and have tasted even more.

Therefore, the buffet consists of a fish table, a table with meats, and one with two elegant salads and a cheese. A wedding buffet for 50 cooked and served at home is a tall order, but it can be done with proper planning and helping hands from family members and friends. (If you don't want to do it all yourself, this menu can also provide ideas for a caterer.)

Since much of the food is prepared ahead and refrigerated, more than one refrigerator is needed, so seek space in someone else's fridge unless you keep an extra one in the basement or garage. You will need a minimum of six large platters, so borrow what you need. Friends and family enjoy helping in this way, for everyone wants to be part of a wedding. Also needed are serving utensils and attractive bowls and containers for relishes and sauces.

Tablecloths and napkins should be special. If you can, use white lace on the buffet tables. Consider a pink or pale green underliner cloth to allow some color to show through the lace. Napkins should be compatible with the tablecloths; for example, use large white damask napkins with white lace cloths. Attractive table arrangements may also be realized with pretty, crisp floral chintzes, but beware they don't clash with the display of food.

Arrangements of white or pink roses, a variety of spring or summer flowers set country-style in baskets, or stylized seasonal bouquets of hydrangeas, zinnias, or marigolds can be striking. In addition to flowers, enrich the buffet tables by adding baskets of seasonal fruit. For example, in June add baskets filled to the brim with fresh, clean, and unhulled strawberries; in September, use baskets overflowing with grapes, and so on.

Although smoked turkey slices are easy to buy and set out, the attractiveness of the platter will be enhanced if it also holds a small whole smoked or baked turkey—about 10 or 12 pounds, ideally carved and offered by a friend or family member. It may be bought already cooked and will also serve as a good backup if more sliced turkey is needed.

If you plan on serving coffee with the wedding cake, arrange cups, saucers, spoons, milk, cream, sugars, and so on on a separate table, away from the main buffet.

Wine and champagne bottles (750 ml) serve six. Conservative estimates of two wine and two champagne servings per person require one case of each to serve 50. However, I suggest that you have on hand a minimum of 1½ cases of champagne and a case each of white and red wines. You will probably also want to stock vodka, scotch, and so on, as not everyone will opt for champagne.

FISH TABLE

SHRIMP WITH REMOULADE AND SPICY TOMATO SAUCE

50 Servings

10 pounds freshly cooked shrimp, peeled, deveined, with tails left on

juice of 6 lemons

lettuce leaves, if needed

Remoulade (see right)

Spicy Tomato Sauce (see right)

1. Combine the shrimp and lemon juice and toss well to coat. Refrigerate, covered, until ready to use.

2. Layer the shrimp in a large glass punchbowl or arrange on lettuce-lined platters. Set out the sauces in attractive bowls to serve as dips, or place small spoons next to each sauce bowl for spooning the sauce onto the shrimp.

REMOULADE
Makes about 5 cups

5 cups mayonnaise

¼ cup plus 1 tablespoon finely chopped chives

¼ cup plus 1 tablespoon Dijon-style mustard

¼ cup plus 1 tablespoon finely chopped gherkins

¼ cup plus 1 tablespoon finely chopped parsley

¼ cup plus 1 tablespoon finely chopped fresh tarragon

3 tablespoons chopped capers

1 tablespoon anchovy paste or 10 canned anchovy fillets, drained and mashed

Combine all ingredients and mix well. Cover and refrigerate until ready to use.

SPICY TOMATO SAUCE
Makes about 7 cups

5 cups bottled chili sauce

1 cup finely chopped onion

1 cup finely chopped celery heart

¼ cup fresh lemon juice

Tabasco or other hot pepper sauce

Combine all ingredients except the hot sauce and mix well. Add the hot sauce a few drops at a time until you reach the desired spiciness. Cover and refrigerate.

SMOKED SALMON POTATO SALAD

50 Servings

12 pounds small red potatoes

1 cup Dijon-style mustard

1 cup sugar

1 cup white wine vinegar

2 cups finely chopped dill or 3 tablespoons dried dillweed

salt and pepper

3 cups vegetable, corn, or peanut oil

1 pound sliced smoked salmon, cut into ½-inch pieces

1. Scrub the potatoes but do not peel. Cover with water in one or more large pots and bring to boil. Lower the heat and simmer until tender. Drain and pat dry. Cut the potatoes into quarters and place in one or more large mixing bowls.

2. Combine the mustard, sugar, vinegar, dill, and salt and pepper in a large bowl and mix well. Whisk in the oil a little at a time until well blended.

3. Pour the sauce over the potatoes and mix gently, being careful not to break up the potatoes. Add the salmon pieces and toss lightly but well. Cover and refrigerate but bring to room temperature before serving.

The Fish Table

MEAT TABLE

SMOKED TURKEY SLICES WITH CRANBERRY SALSA

The cranberry salsa can be made several days ahead, covered, and refrigerated.

Makes 4 to 6 cups

4 cups fresh or thawed frozen cranberries

3 tablespoons grated orange zest

4 large oranges, peeled, membranes removed, coarsely chopped

½ cup finely chopped onion

¼ cup finely chopped candied ginger

2 tablespoons minced fresh coriander

2 tablespoons minced seeded jalapeño pepper

salt

4 pounds thinly sliced smoked turkey

4 scallions, trimmed and quartered lengthwise

1. Chop the cranberries in batches in a food processor; transfer to a large bowl. Add the orange zest. Chop the oranges in the processor and add to the bowl.

2. Add all remaining ingredients except the turkey and scallions and mix well. Let stand at room temperature for 2 hours, or cover tightly and refrigerate for up to 3 days. Bring to room temperature before serving.

3. Fold each turkey slice in half and in half again to make quarters. Arrange on two large platters, lining up the folded corners and overlapping the slices in two or more rows down the length of the platters. Garnish with scallions. Accompany with bowls of cranberry salsa.

GINGER-GLAZED HAM WITH BRANDY

Most fully cooked, semiboneless hams are marketed with half the rind left on the shank end. Ask the butcher to cut it off (or you can do it easily yourself). This size ham normally serves 10 to 12 people for a regular dinner; with the other buffet food in this menu, bake two hams to serve 50.

25 Servings

10- to 12-pound fully cooked, semiboneless smoked ham

whole cloves

grated zest and juice of 1 orange and 1 lemon

½ cup brandy

3 tablespoons jalapeño jelly

2 tablespoons finely chopped candied ginger

1 tablespoon Dijon-style mustard

1. Preheat oven to 300°F. Trim the ham of excess fat and score the fat on top of the ham in a diamond pattern; the lines should be about 1 inch apart. Stick a whole clove into the center of each diamond. Place the ham in a roasting pan, fat side up. Bake 1 hour.

2. Sprinkle the top of the ham with the orange and lemon zest. Add the citrus juices to the pan. Return it to the oven for 1 hour, basting frequently.

3. In a small food processor or blender, combine the brandy, jalapeño jelly, ginger, and mustard and process until smooth. Transfer to a small bowl. Brush the glaze over the ham and continue baking until the ham is browned, about 30 minutes, basting frequently. Let the ham stand at room temperature for 10 to 15 minutes before slicing.

BLUEBERRY AND APRICOT CHUTNEY

If covered tightly, this will keep for four to six weeks in the refrigerator. Double the recipe for this menu.

Makes 3 to 4 cups

2 cups apple cider

¼ cup white wine vinegar

1 tablespoon sugar

1 tablespoon finely chopped candied ginger

1 small piece vanilla bean

2 jalapeño peppers, minced

1 cup chopped dried apricots

1 cup toasted pine nuts

2 cups fresh or thawed frozen blueberries

1. In a nonaluminum saucepan, combine the cider, vinegar, sugar, ginger, vanilla bean, and jalapeños and bring to boil. Lower heat and simmer 3 minutes.

2. Add the apricots and cook uncovered until the liquid thickens, about 8 minutes.

3. Remove from heat and add the nuts and blueberries. Toss well. Cool, then refrigerate overnight.

The Meat Table

CUCUMBER YOGURT RELISH

Just a spoonful alongside the ham adds a refreshing touch.

Makes about 12 cups

4 cucumbers, peeled, seeded, and cut into ¼-inch dice (about 6 cups)

4 apples (preferably Granny Smith), cored, peeled, and cut into ¼-inch dice

4 cups plain yogurt

2 cups golden raisins

2 cups thinly sliced scallions

2 red bell peppers, cored, ribs and seeds removed, cut into ¼-inch dice

¼ cup sugar

juice of 2 limes

1 teaspoon ground cumin

Combine all ingredients in a large bowl and toss well. Cover and refrigerate overnight.

SALAD TABLE

CHICKEN PECAN SALAD

This may be made ahead by two days, but do not dress the watercress until just before serving. When offered with other buffet food, triple this recipe to serve about 50.

10 Servings

6 tablespoons unsalted butter

3 pounds boneless, skinless chicken breast halves

salt and pepper

1 cup pecan halves

3 packets (4 ounces each) enoki mushrooms

¼ cup thinly sliced scallions

1 yellow or orange bell pepper, cut into ¼-inch dice

1 green bell pepper, cut into ¼-inch dice

¼ cup capers, drained

¼ cup white wine vinegar

¼ cup thinly sliced scallions

1 tablespoon Dijon-style mustard

⅔ cup vegetable oil

¼ cup finely chopped parsley

1 tablespoon finely chopped fresh tarragon or 1 teaspoon dried

2 bunches watercress, trimmed, rinsed, and dried

1. Divide the butter between two heavy skillets with lids and melt over moderate heat. Add chicken and turn to coat both sides with butter. Season with salt and pepper. Cover both skillets with buttered rounds of waxed paper and top with lids. Lower heat and cook until the chicken is done, about 12 minutes. Transfer chicken to a bowl.

2. Combine the chicken cooking juices in one skillet, scraping the other with a rubber spatula. Boil the cooking liquid over high heat until reduced to about ¼ cup.

3. Cut the chicken into thin strips. Return to the bowl and add reduced broth. Add half the pecans and all the mushrooms, scallions, peppers, and capers. Add salt and pepper to taste.

4. To make dressing, whisk together the vinegar, scallions, mustard, and salt and pepper to taste. Slowly add the oil, whisking until emulsified. Add parsley and tarragon. Pour ⅔ of dressing over the chicken mixture and toss.

5. Toss the remaining dressing with the watercress. Arrange on a large platter. Mound the chicken mixture on the center of the platter and garnish with the remaining pecans.

The Salad Table

Avocado, Pink Grapefruit, and Orange Salad with Lemon Pepper Dressing

The dressing, grapefruit, and oranges may be prepared several days ahead if covered tightly and refrigerated. Slice the celery hearts and store in a sealed plastic bag in the refrigerator overnight. Do not combine the fruit with the dressing until shortly before serving. Double this recipe to serve 50.

25 Servings

⅓ cup fresh lemon juice

⅔ cup fresh pink grapefruit juice

1⅓ cups olive oil

salt and freshly ground pepper

3 avocados, peeled, pitted, and thinly sliced lengthwise

10 oranges, peeled, pith removed, thinly sliced crosswise

6 pink grapefruit, peeled, pith removed, quartered lengthwise, and thinly sliced crosswise

2 cups thinly sliced celery hearts, including pale green leaves

½ cup chopped fresh mint leaves

1. Combine lemon and grapefruit juices. Slowly whisk in the oil until emulsified. Season with salt and a liberal amount of pepper. Cover tightly and store in the refrigerator; bring to room temperature before serving.

2. Arrange avocado in a flat glass or ceramic container. Spoon 3 to 4 tablespoons dressing over the slices, turning gently to coat both sides. Cover tightly and refrigerate up to one day.

3. When ready to assemble, overlap the orange slices in the center of a large platter. Overlap grapefruit slices around the oranges, reaching to 1 inch from the platter's edge. Outline edge of grapefruit with avocado slices. Sprinkle with celery. Spoon dressing over the salad and garnish with mint.

The Wedding Cake

The most important of cakes—the wedding cake. The most beautiful and the best tasting I've come across was made by Katherine Eisenhauer Thomas of Hingham, Massachusetts. Katherine is married and the mother of four, and one might rightly ask "Where does she find the time?" Here is how she makes her basketweave wedding cake.

Familiarize yourself with the whole recipe before starting. Though not really difficult, baking and decorating a wedding cake is a detailed, multistep procedure. You don't need any last minute panic at a time like this; be sure you have all the decorating supplies well ahead of time.

You will need to purchase the following items from a cake decorating supply store or through Wilton Enterprises, Inc., of Woodridge, Illinois.

- Separator plates: one 8-inch and one 10-inch
- One package of 12 wooden dowels, each 12-inches long and ¼-inch wide
- Cake rounds: one 6-inch, three 8-inch, and three 10-inch
- Five 12-inch cake rounds, stacked and taped together, or one 12-inch round cake board (for base)
- Two sets of 5-inch pillars
- Decorator's foil and cake lace for decorating base
- Approximately 16 ounces prepared decorator's filling in a flavor of your choice
- One 10- or 12-inch decorator's bag
- Coupler and decorator tips #48, #47, #46, and #21
- Icing spatula
- Wedding cake top (if you wish)

For floral decoration, choose about 3 dozen fresh or silk bridal roses, 2 dozen sprigs of assorted greens, and a few fresh or silk accent flowers. If possible, display the cake on a 2- to 3-inch-high wooden platform; cover it with a white cloth and twine one or two strands of ivy around it.

Recipe continues on page 168.

Basketweave Wedding Cake

GENERATION CHOCOLATE CAKE

Serves 50

Serving Size: 2 × 2-inch pieces

A 6-inch tier is reserved as a "keepsake cake" and there will be extra batter that can be used to make cupcakes or another 6-inch tier.

This cake can be made in advance, wrapped airtight and frozen; thaw it in the wrapping before icing. You will need to make the recipe three times, using two 6-inch, two 8-inch, and two 10-inch round pans, each 1½ inches deep. The 10-inch tier will serve about 30 and the 8-inch will serve 20. The 6-inch tier, as noted above, is reserved for the bride and groom.

It's best not to decorate the layers the same day they are made; they are easier to handle if you wrap them and store them overnight.

2¼ cups cake flour, sifted

2 teaspoons baking soda

½ teaspoon salt

½ cup unsalted butter, room temperature

2½ cups firmly packed light brown sugar

3 eggs

3½ ounces unsweetened chocolate, melted and cooled

½ cup buttermilk

1 cup boiling water

2¼ teaspoons vanilla extract

1. Preheat oven to 375°F. Butter the two 10-inch pans. Line the bottoms with circles of waxed paper. Butter the paper and lightly dust bottoms and sides of pans with unsweetened cocoa powder or flour. (The 8-inch and 6-inch pans will be prepared in the same way.)

2. Sift the flour, baking soda, and salt. Cream the butter in the large bowl of an electric mixer until fluffy. Gradually blend in the sugar. Add the eggs one at a time, beating well after each. Blend in the chocolate at low speed.

3. Add the dry ingredients alternately with the buttermilk, beginning and ending with the flour mixture, and blend well. Stir in the boiling water and vanilla. Divide the batter between the prepared pans, using about 4 cups batter for each layer and filling the pans half to three-quarters full; do not overfill.

4. Bake until a tester inserted in the center of the layers comes out clean, about 30 to 35 minutes. Cool in the pans on racks for 5 minutes, then turn the layers out onto racks, remove the waxed paper and cool completely.

5. Mix a second recipe of batter and divide between the prepared 8-inch pans, using about 3 cups for each layer. Bake until a tester inserted in the center comes out clean, about 25 to 30 minutes. Cool and turn out the layers as in step 4.

6. Mix a third recipe of batter and divide between the prepared 6-inch pans, using about 2 cups batter for each layer; use leftover batter to make cupcakes or another small layer. Bake about 20 to 25 minutes. Cool and turn out the layers as in step 4. When thoroughly cooled, wrap all six layers separately in plastic and let stand overnight.

Floral Centerpiece

DECORATOR'S ICING

You will need to prepare this recipe three or four times to decorate the cake completely. Be sure to keep the bowl of icing covered at all times with foil or plastic wrap to prevent a crust from forming on top.

If you use all or part butter, the heat from your hand will soften the icing as you decorate, so spoon only a small quantity of icing (about as much as would fit in the palm of your hand) into the decorating bag at a time. Think twice about using butter if the wedding will be outdoors in warm weather; shortening will hold its shape much better. You may wish to add meringue powder (available at cake decorating supply stores) to stiffen the icing if it will be exposed to high temperatures; add about 2 tablespoons to each batch.

1½ cups solid vegetable shortening or ¾ cup shortening and ¾ cup butter

8 cups (about 2 pounds) confectioner's sugar

½ teaspoon salt

2 teaspoons clear vanilla extract or other flavoring of your choice

¼ cup water

Combine all ingredients in bowl of electric mixer and beat at low speed until fluffy and smooth, about 5 to 7 minutes.

ASSEMBLY

1. Position one 10-inch layer at eye level on a plate or cake stand. Using a long serrated knife held horizontally, saw off the curved "crown" from the top of the layer. Brush off loose crumbs. Place layer cut side down on a 10-inch cake round. Using a spatula, spread with prepared decorator's filling, approximately ¾ cup on the 10-inch layer (the 8-inch layer will require about ½ cup and the 6-inch layer will require about ¼ cup). Do not overfill, or the filling will push out between the cake layers. Remove the crown from the second 10-inch layer in the same way and position the layer cut side down on the filling.

2. Stand a dowel next to the highest side of the filled layers and cut it to that height. Cut 3 more pieces of dowel to the same size. Insert dowels in a circle around the center of the cake to support separator plate (it is essential to have dowels in the 10- and 8-inch layers to support the weight of the top two tiers).

3. Spread an even layer of icing over the top of the cake with a spatula. Spread a translucently thin coating of icing over the sides to seal in crumbs and provide a base coat for the decoration; do not frost the sides thickly. Let the cake stand until the icing has formed a crust.

4. Repeat steps 1 to 3 with the 8-inch and then with the 6-inch layers, using the appropriate-size cake rounds; omit dowels from the 6-inch tier.

5. Insert the coupler in the decorator's bag and mark the bag at the point where the coupler will twist. Cut off tip of bag. Insert the coupler and fit with #48 tip. Half-fill the bag with icing and twist the top closed; keep the top twisted throughout the decorating process. Squeeze the bag over the icing bowl to release air bubbles. The icing will make a popping sound when all the air has been released; squeeze until you hear it.

6. (See Basketweave illustrations at right.) If you are right-handed, decorate from left to right. (If you are left-handed, go from right to left, following adjusted directions in parentheses.) Hold bag at a 45-degree angle with the tip lightly touching the side of the 10-inch tier, serrated edge up. With tip at the top of the cake tier and the bag in 6 o'clock position, squeeze evenly in a vertical strip from top to bottom. Stop squeezing at base of layer and lift tip away. With bag in 3 o'clock (9 o'clock for left-handers) position, squeeze out short horizontal bars across vertical bar. Leave a space the width of the tip between vertical bars. To expand the basketweave pattern, repeat this step. Be sure to work one vertical bar at a time and that each new set of horizontal bars is positioned in between the horizontal bars of the previous set. Be sure that the horizontal bars of icing are long enough so that the next vertical strip can cover their ends without breaking the evenness pattern.

THE BASKETWEAVE

FIRST STEP | SECOND STEP

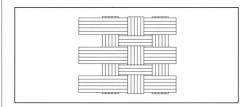

REPEAT PATTERN

7. Cover the 12-inch cake board or taped cake rounds with decorator's foil. Using icing, attach cake lace on to covered 12-inch rounds. The inside edge of lace should be under the 10-inch cake. Spread some icing in the center of the round to keep cake from sliding; position the 10-inch tier on it. Fit the decorator's bag with the #21 tip.

8. (See Shell Border illustration at right.) Practice the shell edging for the cake on a paper towel until you are comfortable with it. Hold the bag at a 45-degree angle at 6 o'clock position, slightly above the surface. Squeezing hard, let icing fan out generously as you lift the tip slightly. Gradually relax pressure on the bag as you lower the tip until it touches the surface. Stop squeezing and pull the frosting to a tail without lifing it off the surface, drawing the shell into a point. Continue all around the top and bottom edges of the cake. Set aside.

THE SHELL BORDER

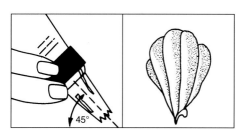

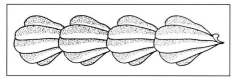

9. Tape two 10-inch cake rounds together and cover with decorator's foil. Spread some icing in the center and position the 8-inch tier on it. Decorate with the basketweave icing pattern, using the #47 tip. Finish the cake with shell edging as in step 8. Set aside.

10. Tape two 8-inch cake rounds together and cover with decorator's foil. Spread some icing in the center and position the 6-inch tier on it. Decorate with the basketweave icing pattern, using the #46 tip. Finish with shell edging and set aside.

11. When all three tiers are decorated, they can be assembled. If at all possible, transport the cakes to the wedding site before assembly; the finished cake will be heavy and difficult to move. To assemble, connect pillars to separator plates. Insert the pillars with the 10-inch separator plate into the 10-inch cake and top with the 8-inch cake. Insert the pillars with the 8-inch separator plate into the 8-inch cake and top with the 6-inch cake. No more than an hour before serving, decorate around the base of the cake and between the tiers with fresh flowers. Top the cake with a wedding cake top or more flowers.

Some housewarmings are impromptu affairs for people in the midst of a move—in which case the most welcome gifts are baskets of food and bushels of good wishes. But there are also more elaborate housewarming parties, when the movers, now established (or nearly so) in their new dwelling, want to share it with friends—and the obvious way is to invite them for food and drink.

A warm and happy way to do this is to cook Italian, for life in Italy is vibrant. The fields of deep red poppies and soft shades of lantana sweeping the Italian countryside suggest eternal springtime. In Italian kitchens one sees platters of roasted red and yellow peppers, slivers of pickled zucchini, roasts of lamb and veal, fresh fruit piled high in bowls, and cheeses oozing their freshness. The full-flavored aromas in the Italian kitchen and home say "welcome"—*benvenuto*.

A Housewarming

BUFFET MENU FOR 20

ANTIPASTO OF PROSCIUTTO,
ROASTED PEPPERS, SLICED
TOMATOES, SMOKED MOZZARELLA,
AND WARMED BEETS WITH OIL
AND BALSAMIC VINEGAR

FOCACCIA WITH OLIVES

HERBED STUFFED VEAL ROAST
WITH ONION MARMALADE

GREEN TAGLIARINI WITH FONTINA,
GORGONZOLA, AND PARMESAN

ZUPPA INGLESE

Antipasto

FOOD PREPARATION

1 day ahead:
- Make focaccia
- Make zuppa inglese
- Make onion marmalade (may be made 1 week ahead)

Serving day:
- Stuff and roast veal
- Prepare antipasto
- Prepare pasta

Note that the veal roast recipe may be prepared twice to serve 20; the two roasts may be baked together. Ask the butcher to bone the veal shoulders and prepare them for roasting. Tell him you plan to stuff them, and have him roll and tie them. Study the tie carefully, as you will need to unroll, stuff, and retie the veal—ask the butcher for more string in order to do this.

The zuppa inglese, similar to an English trifle, is very attractive in a beautiful glass bowl. Perhaps add a seasonal garnish—a few fresh strawberries or a sprig of holly. To serve 20, prepare the recipe twice.

WINE/BEVERAGE SUGGESTIONS

Serve cocktails and Chianti Classico Riserva di Marchese Antinori.

ANTIPASTO OF PROSCIUTTO, ROASTED PEPPERS, SLICED TOMATOES, SMOKED MOZZARELLA, AND WARMED BEETS WITH OIL AND BALSAMIC VINEGAR

This should be served on the largest platter available. Have all the components at room temperature except for the beets, which should be kept warm in a nonaluminum pan on top of the stove. Arrange all ingredients except the beets on the platter, adding the beets at the last moment. Other cured hams or cold cuts, such as Westphalian or country ham, capocollo, Genoa salami, or mortadella, may be substituted for the prosciutto.

20 Servings

2 pounds thinly sliced prosciutto

10 roasted red bell peppers (see page 193), sliced

6 large ripe tomatoes, thinly sliced

2 pounds smoked mozzarella cheese, thinly sliced

10 medium-size fresh beets

salt and pepper

½ cup olive oil

3 tablespoons balsamic vinegar

1 teaspoon chopped fresh thyme or ½ teaspoon dried

⅓ cup chopped fresh basil

1. Arrange the sliced meat on one end of the platter. Arrange the slices of roasted peppers at the other end.

2. Place the tomatoes along one side of the platter and the sliced mozzarella opposite them. Cover the platter and set aside.

3. Cut off all but 1 to 2 inches of the beet greens. Scrub the beets and place in a large saucepan. Cover with water. Bring to boil, cover, lower the heat, and simmer until tender, about 45 minutes; to test for doneness, pierce with the point of a sharp knife.

4. Drain the beets and drop into a bowl or pan of cold water. Slip off the skins. Slice thinly and place in a bowl. Season with salt and pepper.

5. In a small bowl, combine the oil, vinegar, and thyme, and blend well. Pour half the dressing over the beets and toss. While the beets are still warm, place on the center of the platter. Sprinkle the remaining dressing over the tomatoes and very lightly over the mozzarella. Sprinkle the chopped basil over all.

FOCACCIA WITH OLIVES

Makes one 14-inch round or 11 x 17-inch rectangular loaf

1 envelope dry yeast

1 cup warm water

3 to 3½ cups unbleached all-purpose flour

1½ cups oil-cured black olives, pitted and chopped

¼ cup plus 2 tablespoons olive oil

2 teaspoons coarse salt

1. Sprinkle the yeast over the warm water and stir. Let stand 10 minutes.

2. Place 3 cups flour in a large bowl and make a well in the center. Add the yeast mixture, 1 cup chopped olives, ¼ cup olive oil, and 1 teaspoon coarse salt. Work in the flour until a dough forms, then turn the dough out onto a floured work surface and knead until smooth and elastic, about 10 minutes, adding more flour as needed. Place the dough in a clean bowl, cover with a towel, and let rise until doubled in volume, which may take up to 2 hours.

3. Brush a 14-inch pizza pan or an 11 × 17-inch jelly-roll pan generously with olive oil. Punch down the dough and roll out lightly to fit the pan. Place the dough in the pan and brush all over with the remaining olive oil. Sprinkle with the remaining teaspoon of coarse salt and the remaining ½ cup of chopped olives. Let rise for 30 minutes.

4. Preheat oven to 350°F. Bake the focaccia until nicely browned, about 1 hour. Serve warm.

Focaccia With Olives and Stuffed Veal Roast

HERBED STUFFED VEAL ROAST WITH ONION MARMALADE

10 Servings

1½ cups fresh breadcrumbs

½ cup chopped parsley

2 tablespoons butter, melted

1 tablespoon chopped fresh tarragon or 1 teaspoon dried

1 tablespoon Marsala

2 garlic cloves, minced

1 teaspoon each salt and pepper

4-pound shoulder of veal, boned

1 cup dry white wine

1 cup chicken stock or broth

1. Mix all ingredients except the veal, wine, and stock in a large bowl and toss lightly but well.

2. Preheat oven to 425°F. Place the veal, unrolled, on a flat surface and spread evenly with the stuffing mixture. Roll the veal and tie it neatly, first lengthwise and then at 1-inch intervals along the roll, to help it keep its shape as it cooks.

3. Place the veal in a baking pan. Add half the wine and stock. Roast for 30 minutes, basting the meat with the pan liquids several times. Cover the veal with foil, lower the heat to 350°F, and continue roasting for 1½ hours, basting every 20 minutes and adding the remaining wine and stock as needed.

4. Remove the veal from the pan and let cool for 5 to 10 minutes before slicing. Arrange the slices on a platter and strain some of the pan juices over them.

ONION MARMALADE

Serve this as a condiment with the veal. It will keep, covered, in the refrigerator for a week.

Makes about 2 cups

¼ cup butter

2 pounds onions, thinly sliced

½ cup sugar

2 garlic cloves, minced

½ cup sherry vinegar

1 teaspoon dried rosemary, crushed

1. In a large skillet, melt the butter. Add the onions and sugar and cook, stirring every 2 to 3 minutes, until the onions are golden, about 10 minutes.

2. Add the garlic and cook 1 minute longer. Add the vinegar and rosemary, stir well, and cook until thickened, about 15 minutes, stirring every few minutes. Let cool before serving.

GREEN TAGLIARINI WITH FONTINA, GORGONZOLA, AND PARMESAN

Tagliarini are pasta strips cut ⅟₁₆ inch wide. Fresh is best (some shops will cut pasta sheets to size for you), but if you can't get fresh tagliarini, substitute dried linguine.

20 Servings

½ cup butter

⅓ pound fontina cheese, cut into small cubes

⅓ pound Gorgonzola cheese, crumbled

1½ cups grated Parmesan cheese

1 cup half-and-half or light cream

1 cup chicken stock or low-salt broth

white pepper

½ teaspoon freshly grated nutmeg

2 pounds fresh or dried green tagliarini

basil sprigs or chopped scallions or parsley (garnish)

1. Bring a large stockpot of salted water to boil for the pasta. Meanwhile, in a saucepan large enough to hold the pasta, melt the butter. Add the fontina and Gorgonzola and stir until melted. Fold in ½ cup of the Parmesan, the half-and-half or cream and stock and bring just to boil. Lower the heat and simmer 3 to 4 minutes. Add the white pepper and nutmeg and keep warm.

2. Cook the pasta until al dente; if it is fresh, it will not take more than a couple of minutes. Drain well. Add the pasta to the pan with the sauce and toss over medium-high heat for 1 to 2 minutes to coat the strands. Add more chicken stock or broth if needed.

3. Transfer the pasta to a large platter or bowl and garnish as desired. Serve the remaining Parmesan on the side.

Green Tagliarini With Three Cheeses

ZUPPA INGLESE

10 Servings

3 eggs

¾ cup sugar

½ cup all-purpose flour

6 tablespoons unsweetened cocoa powder

¼ cup butter

2 ounces semisweet chocolate

3 cups milk, scalded and cooled to lukewarm

juice of 1 lemon

½ pound ladyfingers

¾ cup sweet vermouth

¾ cup Marsala

1 tablespoon confectioner's sugar

1. Beat the eggs until foamy. Add the sugar and beat until the mixture is thick and pale yellow. Blend in the flour. Divide the mixture evenly between 2 saucepans.

2. Add the cocoa, butter, chocolate, and half the milk to one of the pans; bring to boil, beating constantly. Remove from heat.

3. Add the remaining milk to the other pan; bring to boil, beating constantly. Remove from heat; stir in the lemon juice.

4. Line the bottom of a 3- to 4-quart glass bowl with ¼ of the ladyfingers. Mix the vermouth and Marsala in a glass measuring cup and sprinkle ¼ of the mixture over the ladyfingers. Spread with half of the chocolate custard. Cover the custard with ¼ of the ladyfingers and sprinkle with ¼ of the wine mixture. Spread with half of the lemon custard. Repeat layering wine-soaked ladyfingers and custards, ending with the remaining lemon custard. Cover and refrigerate.

5. Just before serving, sift the confectioner's sugar over the top.

Zuppa Inglese

Welcome home. The expression itself conjures a feeling of warmth and caring, and so it was when I recently returned from visiting the hill towns of Tuscany. My dear friends Lydia and Steve Moss greeted me with a festive lunch that I would like to share with you. It is perfect for any welcome home celebration.

Welcome Home Luncheon

MENU FOR 4

ROASTED OLIVES

GRILLED PEPPERS WITH ANCHOVY
HERB SAUCE

PASTA PUTTANESCA

STRAWBERRIES WITH CITRUS SAUCE

Roasted Olives

FOOD PREPARATION

This is a simple menu that can be made in about two hours. However, you can prepare the olives two to three weeks ahead and the peppers up to a week ahead.

1 day ahead or longer:
- Make roasted olives
- Grill peppers

Serving day:
- Prepare strawberries
- Assemble pasta dish

WINE SUGGESTION

Serve Chianti Classico Riserva di Marchese Antinori.

ROASTED OLIVES

These can be refrigerated for several weeks.

Makes 1 pound

1 pound Gaeta olives

3 garlic cloves, sliced

4 sprigs fresh rosemary

⅓ cup dry white wine

Preheat oven to 400°F. Place the olives in a baking pan large enough to hold them in one layer. Add the remaining ingredients and bake for 15 to 20 minutes. Let cool before serving.

GRILLED PEPPERS WITH ANCHOVY HERB SAUCE

4 to 6 Servings

4 large bell peppers

1 can (2 ounces) anchovy fillets, drained

5 garlic cloves

3 tablespoons chopped mixed fresh marjoram, basil, and chives

6 tablespoons olive oil

freshly ground pepper

1. Grill or roast the peppers as directed on page 193. Let cool. Peel and remove the seeds. Cut the peppers into long strips about ¾ inch wide. Refrigerate until ready to use.

2. Combine all remaining ingredients in a food processor and blend well. Arrange the pepper strips on individual plates and top with the sauce.

Pasta Puttanesca

PASTA PUTTANESCA

Linguine is the pasta traditionally used for this dish, but any other string pasta works well too. *Puttanesca* sauce is supposed to have originated with certain women who received male visitors, offered them some pasta with a quickly prepared sauce, and were soon ready for the next customer.

4 Servings

2 pounds ripe tomatoes, seeded, coarsely chopped, and drained

¼ cup small capers, drained

¾ cup Gaeta olives, pitted and chopped

4 anchovy fillets, chopped

½ bunch Italian parsley, chopped

1 teaspoon chopped garlic

½ teaspoon red pepper flakes

salt and white pepper

½ cup extra virgin olive oil

1 pound linguine or other pasta

1. Place all ingredients except the pasta in the bowl of a processor and chop coarsely. Transfer to a large bowl and set aside for at least 30 minutes.

2. Cook the pasta according to package directions and drain well. Add to the sauce and toss well. Serve hot, lukewarm, or at room temperature.

Strawberries With Citrus Sauce

STRAWBERRIES WITH CITRUS SAUCE

This may be made several hours ahead.

4 Servings

1 cup fresh orange juice

¼ cup fresh lemon juice

½ cup sugar

1 teaspoon Marsala

1 pint fresh strawberries

Mix all ingredients except the strawberries. Pour over the berries and refrigerate until ready to serve.

The men that women marry,
And why they marry them, will always be
A marvel and a mystery to the world.
   —From "Michael Angelo"
   by Henry Wadsworth Longfellow (1807–1882)

Wedding anniversaries are recognized all over the world, but they are especially observed in the United States—perhaps to celebrate those marriages that endure against the odds of outrageous divorce statistics. One of the greatest joys I've had recently was attending the celebration of a 50th wedding anniversary; the celebrants were even fortunate enough to have the maid of honor and the best man in attendance! One might consider the advantages of this celebration over that of their wedding: there were three grown children present, all married and with their own children attending. The spirit of strong family ties filled the air and touched everyone deeply. And what a sight to see the happy couple dance the anniversary waltz.

Many people are serious about gift-giving on these occasions, and what to give on which anniversary has been widely promoted by merchants. Americans love to give gifts; unfortunately, many of them end up on the shelf. So, it's important to try to learn what people need and want. Traditionally, each anniversary year connotes a type of gift, as shown on page 184.

Anniversary Dinner

MENU FOR 6

STUFFED MUSHROOMS WITH
HAZELNUTS AND ROSEMARY

ROAST FILET OF BEEF WITH BRANDY
SHALLOT SAUCE

LEEK, ONION, AND CARAWAY
SEED CUSTARD

MIRABELLE MERINGUE PIE

BASKETS OF BERRIES

Roast Filet of Beef

FOOD PREPARATION

1 day ahead:
  · Prepare mushrooms but do not bake
  · Make brandy shallot sauce
  · Make meringue pie

Serving day:
  · Bake mushrooms
  · Bake leek custard
  · Roast filet
  · Arrange berry baskets

WINE SUGGESTIONS

Serve Gevrey Chambertin with the dinner
and champagne with dessert.

STUFFED MUSHROOMS WITH HAZELNUTS AND ROSEMARY

6 Servings

12 large mushrooms

2 tablespoons fresh lemon juice

salt and pepper

⅔ cup whole hazelnuts

1 tablespoon fresh rosemary or 1 teaspoon dried

¼ cup butter, melted

¼ cup fresh breadcrumbs

1. Preheat oven to 325°F. Carefully remove the stems from the mushrooms and discard or reserve for another use. Wipe each mushroom cap with a damp towel; do not rinse. Place the caps in a dish with the lemon juice, and salt and pepper, and toss well.

2. Place the hazelnuts and rosemary in a small baking pan and bake until the nuts are toasted, 5 to 10 minutes. Remove and cool slightly. Chop the nuts and rosemary and combine them with the melted butter. Turn the oven up to 375°F.

3. Fill each mushroom cap with the nut mixture. Sprinkle with the breadcrumbs. Bake until golden brown, about 12 to 15 minutes; the mushrooms should retain their shape. Serve hot.

Mushrooms Stuffed With Hazelnuts and Rosemary

ROAST FILET OF BEEF WITH BRANDY SHALLOT SAUCE

Ask your butcher to trim the filet of fat and ready it for roasting by tying it with string so it holds its shape.

6 to 8 Servings

3-pound whole filet mignon, room temperature

¼ cup butter, softened

⅓ cup chopped shallots

salt and freshly ground pepper

Brandy Shallot Sauce (see below)

6 watercress sprigs (garnish)

1. Preheat oven to 500°F. Spread the filet with butter on all sides. Season lightly with salt and liberally with pepper.

2. Roast the filet for 5 minutes. Reduce oven temperature to 400°F. Sprinkle the shallots over the beef and roast to desired doneness, about 20 to 25 minutes for rare. Let stand at room temperature for about 5 minutes before slicing.

3. To serve the filet, spoon some sauce onto a warm plate and top with a slice or two of the beef. Garnish with a sprig of fresh watercress.

BRANDY SHALLOT SAUCE
Makes about 3 cups

1½ cups beef or veal stock or broth

1 cup peeled, seeded, chopped tomatoes

1 cup sliced fresh mushrooms

⅓ cup cognac or brandy

⅓ cup Madeira

⅓ cup chopped shallots

1 tablespoon Dijon-style mustard

salt and pepper

1. While the beef is roasting, combine all ingredients for the sauce in a saucepan and bring to boil. Lower the heat and simmer briskly for 20 minutes.

2. Put the mixture through a food mill and keep warm. If you prefer a thinner sauce, add more stock by the tablespoon. If you prefer a thicker sauce, boil it longer to reduce.

LEEK, ONION, AND CARAWAY SEED CUSTARD

6 Servings

¼ cup butter

2 tablespoons vegetable oil

2 cups thinly sliced leeks

6 cups thinly sliced onions

1 teaspoon sugar

1½ tablespoons all-purpose flour

3 eggs

1½ cups heavy cream

pinch each of cayenne pepper and freshly grated nutmeg

¼ cup grated fontina or Gruyère cheese

1 teaspoon caraway seeds

salt and pepper

1. In a large skillet, heat the butter and oil. Add the leeks, onions, and sugar and toss well. Cover and cook over low heat until the leeks and onions are soft but not brown. Transfer to a large bowl.

2. In another bowl, combine the flour, eggs, cream, cayenne, and nutmeg and beat until smooth. Add the cheese, caraway seeds, and salt and pepper. Blend in the onion mixture.

3. Preheat oven to 375°F. Transfer the mixture to a buttered 2-quart baking dish. Place the dish in a larger pan and pour hot water into the larger pan to come halfway up the custard dish. Cover with foil. Bake until set, about 1 hour, removing the foil for the last 15 minutes. Serve hot.

MIRABELLE MERINGUE PIE

This is a simple, delicious pie made with a meringue crust. Mirabelle is a delicately flavored plum liqueur. Use it if at all possible, but the pie also works with other liqueurs, such as kirsch, Poire William or Triple Sec. Serve iced champagne with this dessert.

Serves 8 to 12

MERINGUE SHELL

4 egg whites, room temperature

pinch each of cream of tartar and salt

¼ teaspoon vanilla extract

¾ cup sugar

1 tablespoon vegetable oil

1. Beat the egg whites until frothy, about 1 minute. Add the cream of tartar and salt and beat another minute. Add the vanilla and beat in the sugar a tablespoon at a time; the whites will be shiny with firm peaks when the beaters are raised.

2. Preheat oven to 200°F. Spread the oil over the entire inside surface and rim of a 9-inch glass pie dish. Using a rubber spatula, scrape the meringue out of the mixing bowl into the pie dish. Spread the mixture to form a pie shell.

3. Bake on the center oven rack for 2 hours. Cool on a wire rack.

MIRABELLE FILLING

4 egg yolks, room temperature

½ cup sugar

1 tablespoon fresh lemon juice

3 tablespoons mirabelle liqueur

1 cup heavy cream, whipped

1. Combine the yolks and sugar in the top of a double boiler, mixing well with a wire whisk. Place over simmering water and stir constantly until smooth and the consistency of thick mayonnaise, 7 to 10 minutes.

2. Remove from over water and stir in the lemon juice and liqueur. Set the pan in a larger pan of ice water to speed the cooling process. Fold in the whipped cream. Spread the filling in the cooled pie shell and refrigerate for at least 3 hours.

BASKETS OF BERRIES

6 Servings

2 pints fresh seasonal berries

mint leaves

Choose any 2 pints of raspberries, strawberries, blueberries, or other seasonal berries. Pick them over for soundness and refresh under cool water. Drain well. Divide between 2 decorative pint baskets, leaving the caps on 2 or 3 strawberries and adding a mint leaf here and there. Place on the table as part of the decoration or pass with the dessert.

Traditional Anniversary Gifts

1st	Paper	13th	Lace
2nd	Cotton	14th	Ivory
3rd	Leather	15th	Crystal
4th	Linen	20th	China
5th	Wood	25th	Silver
6th	Iron	30th	Pearl
7th	Copper, wool	35th	Coral
8th	Bronze	40th	Ruby
9th	Pottery	45th	Sapphire
10th	Tin	50th	Gold
11th	Steel	55th	Emerald
12th	Silk	60th	Diamond

Mirabelle Meringue Pie

Most businesses and governmental organizations have policies governing retirement: at a certain age or for a given reason, a particular person will be replaced by another. Some workers like this and others abhor it, but the passage into retirement is with us, and in most cases it is a cause for celebration. For many people, retirement means the start of a second career—or the time to do something that one has always wanted to do.

A retirement party calls for a special meal. Most people of retirement age watch what they eat, but perhaps this is one time to take certain liberties and enjoy lobster with melted butter . . . why not? Filet mignon with a superb wine sauce? But of course! Thick-sliced delicious potatoes? *Mais oui.* Real ice cream . . . I just can't say no. If one refuses beef, why not a delightfully easy fish substitute—fish fillets with a lemon and caper sauce. A retirement celebration is a once-in-a-lifetime occasion.

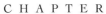

Retirement Party

DINNER MENU FOR 6

COLD LOBSTER WITH HOT BUTTER

BEEF TENDERLOIN WITH HERB
CRUST AND PORT SAUCE *OR*
FISH FILLETS WITH LEMON
AND CAPER SAUCE

POTATOES IMPERIALE

GREEN BEANS BALSAMIC

RUM-POACHED PEARS WITH
STRAWBERRIES

Cold Lobster With Hot Butter

FOOD PREPARATION

1 day ahead:
- Prepare lobster if using fresh
- Make port sauce
- Prepare potatoes to step 2
- Prepare green beans
- Make pear dessert

Serving day:
- Complete potato and lobster dishes
- Prepare beef tenderloin and heat sauce, *OR*
- Make fish dish

WINE SUGGESTIONS

Serve Puligny Montrachet with the lobster and William Hill Winery Napa Valley Cabernet Sauvignon Reserve (with beef) *OR* Sancerre de la Loire (with fish).

COLD LOBSTER WITH HOT BUTTER

Lobster meat may be bought fresh or frozen; if you have a good source for it, save time by not cooking your own. Still, preparing lobster is quite easy, as explained here.

6 Servings

2 live lobsters
(about 1 ½ pounds each) or
1 pound fresh or frozen lobster meat

juice of 1 lemon

½ cup butter, melted

¼ cup chopped parsley

salt and pepper

shredded lettuce leaves (optional)

1. To cook live lobsters, bring a large stockpot of water to boil. Plunge in the lobsters head first and return the water to boil. Lower the heat, cover, and simmer until the lobsters turn pink, about 3 minutes. To avoid overcooking, immediately drain the lobsters and plunge into a pan of cold water. Drain and cut in half lengthwise. Pick out all the meat, being sure to discard the sandy sac near the eyes and the intestinal vein. Toss the meat with the lemon juice. Cover and refrigerate.

2. Heat the butter until it bubbles. Remove from heat and add the parsley and salt and pepper.

3. To serve, place the lobster meat in a bowl and accompany with the hot butter. Alternatively, divide the lobster meat among 6 individual plates lined with shredded lettuce. Pass the butter separately.

Note: Some prefer to kill a lobster humanely—that is, instantly. To do this, place the lobster on a cutting board and plunge the tip of a large, sharp knife between the eyes. Then proceed as above.

BEEF TENDERLOIN WITH HERB CRUST AND PORT SAUCE

6 Servings

2½ cups fresh egg-breadcrumbs

2 cups chopped parsley

3 tablespoons chopped fresh basil or 2 teaspoons dried

¼ cup butter, melted

salt and pepper

6 1-inch-thick beef tenderloin steaks (about 8 ounces each)

3 tablespoons olive oil

Port Sauce (see next page)

1. Combine the breadcrumbs and herbs in a large bowl. Pour the melted butter over and mix lightly. Add salt and pepper to taste. (May be prepared 2 days ahead, covered, and refrigerated.)

2. Salt and pepper the steaks on both sides. In a heavy skillet, heat the olive oil and brown the steaks about 4 minutes per side. Remove from heat and let stand about 20 minutes.

3. Preheat broiler. Press some of the breadcrumb mixture lightly on top of each steak, covering completely. Broil until the crumbs are browned, being careful not to burn.

4. Preheat oven to 450°F. Place the steaks on a baking sheet and bake 10 minutes.

5. Nap the steaks with the sauce and serve.

PORT SAUCE

This may be made four to five days ahead, covered, and refrigerated. Reheat just before use.

Makes about 1 ¼ cups

1 shallot, chopped

1 cup tawny port

1 cup beef stock or canned consommé

2 tablespoons water

1 tablespoon arrowroot

1 tablespoon fresh lemon juice

grated rind and juice of 1 orange

2 tablespoons currant jelly

½ teaspoon dried tarragon

3 drops Tabasco or other hot pepper sauce

salt and pepper

1. Boil the shallot with ½ cup port until reduced to 2 tablespoons.

2. Heat the stock or consommé. Combine the water and arrowroot in a small bowl. Mix in a little of the warmed stock and stir to combine. Return mixture to the remaining stock and simmer for 2 minutes.

3. Add the reduced port, citrus juices and rind, currant jelly, and tarragon and simmer 5 minutes. Stir in the remaining port, hot sauce and salt and pepper. Bring to boil and simmer 2 minutes. Serve hot.

FISH FILLETS WITH LEMON AND CAPER SAUCE

6 Servings

6 fillets (6 ounces each) of white-fleshed fish, such as sole, flounder, bass, or snapper

salt and pepper

3 tablespoons olive oil

3 tablespoons butter

3 tablespoons fresh lemon juice

3 tablespoons small capers, drained

2 tablespoons each finely chopped parsley, basil, and tarragon

1. Rinse and dry the fillets. Salt and pepper both sides.

2. Heat the oil in a large skillet and sauté the fillets on both sides just until opaque, about 2 minutes per side depending on thickness. Place on individual plates.

3. In a small skillet, heat the butter until slightly browned. Remove from heat and add the lemon juice and capers. Pour over the fish and sprinkle the herbs over.

Beef Tenderloin With Port Sauce and Vegetables

POTATOES IMPERIALE

My sister Louise Imperiale is an excellent cook; this is her recipe.

6 Servings

4 large baking potatoes

salt and pepper

¼ cup butter

¼ cup olive oil

1. Preheat oven to 450°F. Bake the potatoes on the center rack until not quite cooked, 35 to 40 minutes. Let cool for 10 minutes. Refrigerate at least 3 hours or overnight.

2. Peel the potatoes and grate them on the large holes of a hand grater. Add salt and pepper and toss lightly.

3. Heat an 8- or 9-inch skillet. Add the butter and oil and heat until bubbly. Add the potatoes and cook for 10 minutes, using a spatula or plate to press down on them. Invert the potato cake onto a plate, then carefully slide back into the pan uncooked side down, adding a little more butter and oil first if necessary. Cook until the bottom is crisp and golden, about 10 minutes longer.

4. Serve hot, cutting the cake into rectangles or wedges.

GREEN BEANS BALSAMIC

6 Servings

1 ½ pounds fresh green beans, ends trimmed

salt

½ cup olive oil

3 tablespoons balsamic vinegar

½ teaspoon Dijon-style mustard

1 onion, finely chopped

1 garlic clove, minced

pepper

½ cup grated Parmesan cheese

1. Rinse the beans well. Bring a large pot of water to boil. Add a sprinkle of salt and the beans; cook for 6 minutes or until the beans are crisp-tender. Drain well and pat dry on paper towels. Transfer the beans to a serving plate or platter.

2. In a bowl, blend the oil, vinegar, and mustard. Add the onion, garlic, salt, pepper, and cheese. Check the seasoning, adding more salt and pepper if needed. Pour the dressing over the beans, tossing lightly but thoroughly. Serve warm or at room temperature.

RUM-POACHED PEARS WITH STRAWBERRIES

Ideally, these should be refrigerated for two or three hours, but they may be made the day before and kept overnight.

6 Servings

1 cup dark rum

1 cup water

1 cup firmly packed dark brown sugar

1 cinnamon stick

6 pieces orange zest, cut into julienne

6 firm-ripe Anjou or Bosc pears

whipped cream

18 strawberries with stems, rinsed and dried

1. In a saucepan large enough to hold the pears upright, combine the rum, water, sugar, cinnamon, and orange zest. Bring to boil, lower heat, cover, and simmer 5 minutes.

2. Peel and core the pears, leaving stems intact. Cut a thin slice from the bottom of each pear so it can stand upright. Carefully place pears in the saucepan, cover, and poach over low heat until just tender, about 15 minutes. Transfer the pears to a shallow glass dish.

3. Increase heat to high and boil the poaching liquid until reduced to sauce consistency. Pour over the pears. Cover and refrigerate for several hours or overnight, basting the pears occasionally.

4. Divide the pears among individual plates. Spoon some cream to the side. Place 3 strawberries around the base of each pear to form a triangle. Serve immediately.

Rum-Poached Pear With Strawberries

34

Kitchen ABCs:

Appetizers, Basic Recipes, and Conversion Tables

BASIC RECIPES

BECHAMEL SAUCE

Makes about 2 cups

2 tablespoons butter

¼ cup all-purpose flour

2 cups hot milk

1 parsley sprig

1 bay leaf

1 celery stalk with leaves

1 small piece of carrot

¼ onion

salt and white pepper

1. Melt the butter in a medium saucepan. Add the flour and whisk until blended. Cook over low heat for 2 minutes.

2. Slowly add the heated milk, whisking until blended. Add the herbs and vegetables and cook over low heat for 15 minutes. Put the sauce through a fine strainer, season with salt and pepper and serve.

BROWN SAUCE

This is a shortcut method that uses canned beef broth. Of course, if you have a rich homemade beef stock, use that instead—but the sauce is still good made as below.

Makes about 1½ cups

3 scallions, thinly sliced

6 tablespoons butter

1 cup dry red wine

1 can (10½ ounces) beef broth

¼ teaspoon dried thyme

3 tablespoons all-purpose flour

salt and pepper

1. In a saucepan, sauté the scallions in 3 tablespoons of the butter until they soften and begin to color.

2. Add the wine and broth and bring to boil. Add the thyme and boil until the liquid is reduced by half.

3. In a small saucer, work together the remaining 3 tablespoons butter and the flour with fork.

4. Whisk ⅓ of this butter/flour paste, or beurre manié, into the reduced sauce. Whisk in the remaining beurre manié in 2 additions. Season to taste with salt and pepper. Strain the sauce before serving.

CLARIFIED BUTTER

Melt about one-third more whole butter than you will need of the clarified butter called for in the recipe. When it is melted, spoon off the white foam that rises to the top. Then pour off the yellow liquid, leaving behind the whitish milk solids at the bottom of the pan. The yellow liquid you pour off is clarified butter, which will keep in the refrigerator for several weeks.

FISH STOCK
Makes about 8 cups

2 pounds fish bones, rinsed

1 medium onion, chopped

1 carrot, sliced

1 celery stalk, including leaves, sliced

1 bay leaf

6 peppercorns

6 cups water

2 cups dry white wine

1. Combine all ingredients in a large saucepan, cover, and simmer for 40 minutes.

2. Strain the stock through a fine sieve, discarding the bones and vegetables. Use right away or cool and refrigerate for several days; freeze for longer storage.

PATE BRISEE
Makes one 9- or 10-inch pie or tart shell

1 ¼ cups all-purpose flour

6 tablespoons cold butter, cut into ¼-inch pieces

2 tablespoons cold vegetable shortening

pinch of salt

3 tablespoons ice water

1. In a large bowl, combine the flour, butter, shortening, and salt and blend until the mixture resembles coarse meal.

2. Add the ice water and toss with a fork just until the water is incorporated. Form the dough into a ball, flattening it somewhat. Dust lightly with flour. Wrap in plastic or waxed paper and refrigerate for 1 hour.

3. On a floured surface, roll the dough out into a ⅛-inch-thick circle. (If you prefer, roll the dough between 2 pieces of waxed paper.) Fit into a 9- or 10-inch pie or tart pan. Trim any excess dough and, if you are using a pie pan, crimp the edge decoratively. (If using a tart pan, trim the dough even with the edge of the pan.) Chill for 1 hour.

4. For a baked pie shell, preheat oven to 425°F. Line the shell with waxed paper and fill with raw rice, dried beans, or pie weights. Bake on the lowest oven rack 10 minutes. Remove the weights and paper and bake until the pastry is light golden, about 10 minutes longer.

Note: This may be made in a food processor. Combine the flour and salt in the processor bowl and blend for 3 seconds. With the machine running, gradually add the butter and shortening through the feed tube, blending just until the mixture resembles crumbs. Add the ice water and stop the machine as soon as the dough starts to cling together. Remove from the bowl and shape the dough into a flattened ball; flour lightly. Wrap in waxed paper and proceed with step 3 above.

PEELING TOMATOES

1. Bring a saucepan of water to boil. Immerse the tomatoes two at a time and count to 10; then transfer the tomatoes to a bowl of very cold water using a slotted spoon.

2. Cut out the core of each tomato, and then use the edge of a knife to pull away the skin. To seed, cut the tomatoes in half crosswise and squeeze gently to eject the seeds.

ROASTING PEPPERS

1. To roast any number of bell peppers, preheat broiler. Place the peppers on their sides on a baking sheet and broil 4 inches from the heat source until blackened on one side. Turn a quarter-turn and broil again. Continue until all sides are blackened.

2. Remove the peppers from the oven and place in a brown paper bag. Close the bag and let stand for about 10 minutes.

3. Core the peppers and peel away the black skins. Remove the seeds and visible ribs. (It is often easiest to rinse the peppers to get rid of the skin and seeds. If you do this, be sure to dry well with paper towels before continuing.) Cut the peppers into strips as directed in the recipe.

VINAIGRETTE
Makes 1 cup

¾ cup olive or vegetable oil

¼ cup white wine vinegar

1 teaspoon sugar

1 teaspoon Dijon-style mustard

salt and pepper

Mix all ingredients until well blended. Use right away or refrigerate in a tightly covered jar.

ZEST OF LEMON OR ORANGE

The zest is the colored part of the rind, with almost no pith (the white, bitter layer under the skin). Special zest peelers are available and work well, but you can easily use an ordinary vegetable peeler without cutting deeply into the pith. Use the zest as fresh as can be—that is, as soon as it is peeled away and minced, use it in the recipe. Dried zest works well, too, but the flavor is more pungent if the zest is fresh.

APPETIZING EXTRAS

Though the menus in this book incorporate appetizers, first courses, and hors d'oeuvres, it might be helpful to add a few extra choices you can use as you wish. Some of these are served cold, some hot, and some at room temperature. Most are simple to make.

BARQUETTES

These are made with prepared frozen pastry or puff pastry forms (usually 2 inches long and 24 or 36 to a box), sold in many markets. They may be filled with a variety of items—for instance, frozen broccoli (or spinach or any other) soufflé, thawed, spooned into the pastries, topped with grated Parmesan, and baked; or pizza topping consisting of a small spoonful of stewed tomatoes, a thin piece of mozzarella, some herbs, and a drop of olive oil, baked until the cheese melts. Serve the barquettes hot from the oven.

ROASTED NUTS

Almost any kind of nut will work here, and in large quantities. Think of using almonds, pecans, walnuts, and/or cashews, singly or together. I have suggested nuts with rosemary (page 46) and with curry (page 58), but they can also be roasted with such herbs as tarragon, oregano, or thyme, or with salt and pepper, cumin, or celery or mustard seeds.

CHEESE SQUARES

Trim the crusts from a loaf of extra-thin-sliced firm white bread. Cut each slice in half and then in half again to make 4 squares from each slice. Combine an 8-ounce package of softened cream cheese, ¼ cup soft butter, 3 tablespoons mayonnaise, and 3 thinly sliced scallions in a bowl. With additional butter, butter each square of bread and arrange the squares buttered side up on a broiler pan. Broil until lightly toasted. Turn over and toast the unbuttered side. Thickly spread some of the cream cheese mixture on the toasted buttered side, sprinkle with grated Parmesan and broil until bubbly. Serve right away.

Variation: Replace ⅓ of the cream cheese with Gorgonzola, Stilton, or other blue cheese.

BACON AND WATER CHESTNUT CRUNCH
Makes about 24

Use an 8-ounce can of whole water chestnuts, drained and patted dry. Marinate in ¼ cup light soy sauce for 1 hour; drain. Cut 6 slices of bacon in half crosswise and then in half lengthwise (this is easy to do with a pair of poultry shears). Wrap each water chestnut with a piece of bacon and spear with a pick. Broil about 5 inches from the heat source, turning once, until the bacon is done. Or to microwave, place the wrapped water chestnuts around the outer edge of the carousel and cook on High (100%) for 6 minutes. If there is no carousel, set them around the edge of a shallow dish in the microwave and turn once or twice during cooking.

REFRIED BEAN APPETIZER
Makes about 4½ cups

In a saucepan, combine 1½ cups refried beans, 1 cup sour cream, 1 cup shredded cheddar cheese, 1 cup mild or hot chunky salsa, ¼ cup milk, and a 1.9-ounce envelope of dehydrated vegetable soup mix. Heat slowly, being careful not to scorch. Serve hot with tortilla chips.

BELGIAN ENDIVE WITH BRANDIED GORGONZOLA
Makes about 1 cup

Combine 4 ounces softened Gorgonzola cheese, 3 ounces mascarpone or softened cream cheese, and 2 tablespoons brandy or cognac. Add about 1 tablespoon milk or cream if needed to make mixture spreadable. Fill washed and dried leaves of Belgian endive with the mixture.

SMOKED TURKEY AND HAZELNUT BUTTER CANAPES
Makes about 36

Place ½ cup hazelnuts in a pan and toast in a preheated 300°F oven for 15 minutes. Transfer to a coarse sieve and rub the nuts to remove their skins. Place the nuts, 6 tablespoons butter, and black pepper to taste in a food processor and grind to a paste. Refrigerate for about 2 hours. Spread the mixture on 10 to 12 thin slices of pumpernickel bread. Top with 6 ounces thinly sliced smoked turkey. Trim the edges and slice the bread into thirds. Dust with a little more black pepper.

MEASUREMENT CONVERSIONS: UNDERSTANDING THE U.S., METRIC, AND BRITISH SYSTEMS

In the metric system the *kilogram*—1,000 grams, equivalent to 2.2 pounds—is the fundamental unit of weight. The *liter*—slightly less than 1 quart—is the fundamental unit of volume. It is divided into milliliters (ml); 5 ml is equivalent to 1 teaspoon.

WEIGHT CONVERSION

Ounces	Grams
1	28.4
4 (¼ pound)	113.4
8 (½ pound)	226.8
12 (¾ pound)	340.2
16 (1 pound)	453.6

VOLUME CONVERSION

Tablespoons	Cups	Milliliters	Liters
1		15	
4	¼	60	
5⅓	⅓	80	
8	½	120	
16	1	236	
	2	450	.5 (approx.)
	4	950	1 (approx.)

LINEAR MEASURES

The *meter*—a little more than a yard—is the fundamental unit of length in the metric system. It is divided into *centimeters* (cm) and *millimeters* (mm).

1 meter = 39.37 inches
1 cm = 0.39 inch
1 mm = 0.039 inch
1 inch = 2.54 cm or 25.4 mm
1 yard = 91.44 cm

BRITISH MEASURES

Do not confuse the British (imperial) system of weights and measures with the metric system. Though many British units of measurement have the same names as U.S. measures, not all are identical. In general, weights are equivalent, but British measuring cups and spoons are about one-quarter larger than those used in the United States and Canada.

DRY MEASURES

Outside the United States, the following items are measured by weight. When using this table, bear in mind that measurements will vary depending on the ingredients' exact variety and moisture content. Cup measurements are loosely packed; flour is measured directly from the package (presifted).

	U.S. Customary	Metric	Imperial
Flour (all-purpose)	1 cup	150 g	5 oz.
Cornmeal	1 cup	175 g	6 oz.
Sugar			
granulated	1 cup	190 g	6½ oz.
confectioner's	1 cup	80 g	2⅔ oz.
brown	1 cup	160 g	5⅓ oz.

TEMPERATURE CONVERSIONS

To convert Fahrenheit into Celsius (also known as centigrade) temperatures, subtract 32, multiply by 5, and divide by 9.

$350°F - 32 = 318$
$318 \times 5 = 1590$
$1590 \div 9 = 177°C$ (approximately)

To convert Celsius into Fahrenheit, multiply by 9, divide by 5, and add 32.

$200°C \times 9 = 1800$
$1800 \div 5 = 360$
$360 + 32 = 392°F$

These conversions can be summarized in the following two simple equations:

Fahrenheit = 9/5 Celsius + 32
Celsius = 5/9 Fahrenheit − 32

OVEN TEMPERATURE EQUIVALENTS

Fahrenheit	225	300	350	400	450
Celsius	110	150	180	200	230
Gas mark	¼	2	4	6	8

CONVERSION TABLE FOR SOLID MEASURES

For cooks measuring items by weight, here are approximate equivalents, in both imperial and metric units. To avoid awkward measurements, some conversions are not exact.

	U.S. Customary	Metric	Imperial
Butter	1 c.	225 g	8 oz.
	½ c.	115 g	4 oz.
	¼ c.	60 g	2 oz.
	1 Tbsp.	15 g	½ oz.
Cheese (grated)	1 c.	115 g	4 oz.
Fruit (chopped fresh)	1 c.	225 g	8 oz.
Herbs (chopped fresh)	¼ c.	7 g	¼ oz.
Meats/chicken (chopped, cooked)	1 c.	175 g	6 oz.
Mushrooms (chopped, fresh)	1 c.	70 g	2½ oz.
Nuts (chopped)	1 c.	115 g	4 oz.
Raisins and chopped dried fruits	1 c.	175 g	6 oz.
Rice (uncooked)	1 c.	225 g	8 oz.
(cooked)	3 c.	225 g	8 oz.
Vegetables (chopped, raw)	1 c.	115 g	4 oz.

CHAPTER

35

The Elements of Style

INVITATIONS

Always extend invitations well in advance. If you invite guests by telephone, you'll get a fast acceptance or rejection; if it's the latter, you can quickly move on to someone else if you wish. When written invitations are sent, some people wait until the last minute to decline—and what could be more rude? For important occasions, take the trouble to send reminder cards after phone invitations have been made. As a general rule, the more formal the occasion, the more formal the reminder or invitation.

Printed invitations, while impressive, are not usually necessary. Most card shops offer attractive preprinted cards on which you fill in the date, time, and other pertinent information. Again, the more formal the event, the more formal the card.

Whenever food is to be served, it is important to add an RSVP. For large cocktail parties, some hosts request "regrets only." In either case, you need to know how many will be in attendance in order to prepare for them properly. Always spell out whether dinner or a meal is to be offered—say, something like "Cocktails, 6 to 8 p.m." (almost everyone knows that this means drinks and hors d'oeuvres only) or "Drinks and dinner, 7:30 p.m."

Often it is more fun to make your own invitations. When I planned a cookout for friends visiting from England, I wrote the invitation in the center of a colorfully bordered paper plate. Would you believe that several people answered in the same manner? That was fun!

Invitations should be answered as soon as possible, and in answering always mention the time and date of the event. If a mistake was made on the part of the host or hostess, or if you misread something, there is still an opportunity to correct it.

STOCKING THE BAR

A knowledge of wines and spirits as well as a knowledge of food is necessary for today's hosts. Such beverages have a traditional place in American hospitality, and an understanding of their proper use is necessary for successful entertaining. Here are some major types.

• **Bourbon** (American whiskey) is made from a mash of corn, rye, and barley malt, with the corn predominating.

• **Rye** (American whiskey) is made from a mash of rye grain and either rye malt or barley malt, with the rye grain predominating.

Both bourbon and rye whiskies are classified under two general categories:
1. Straight whiskey—those which are "bottled in bond," aged for four or more years and exactly 100 proof, and those which do not conform to those age and proof requirements.
2. Blended whiskey—the label of every bottle has to tell the percentage and type of the whiskies and spirits forming the blend.

• **Scotch whisky** (the "e" is omitted in the Scottish spelling) is made from fermented malted barley mash. The distinctive flavor of scotch results from drying the malt over a peat fire, which gives the finished liquor its smoky taste.

• **Irish whiskey** is made from fermented mash of barley and unmalted grains of various kinds. These whiskies do not have the smoky flavor of Scotch.

- **Dry gin** is made of distilled spirits with flavoring from juniper berries and many other aromatic substances, including coriander seeds and angelica root. Sloe gin is made by steeping sloeberries in dry gin, which produces a deep cherry color with the flavor of wild plum.

- **Vodka** was originally distilled from fermented wheat mash but now may also be made from a mash of rye, corn, or potatoes.

- **Rum** is distilled from the fermented juice of sugar cane, molasses, or a mixture of the two. It is made all over the West Indies and is of two types: the dark Jamaican variety and the lighter Cuban and Puerto Rican versions.

- **Brandy** properly refers to a liquor distilled from natural wine; sweetened products are more correctly called liqueurs or cordials. The most famous brandy comes from the Cognac region in France.

- **Cordials** are made by distilling or infusing various fruits, berries, and aromatic substances with pure alcohol or with brandy, and then sweetening the mixture. Among the many flavorings used are herbs, roots, cocoa, mint, orange peel, caraway seed, and so on.

- **Wine**, basically and simply, is the fermented juice of freshly pressed grapes. Its varieties are almost infinite. **Fortified wines**, such as sherry and port, are natural still wines to which has been added brandy distilled from the same type of wine. Genuine sherries come from Andalusia in Spain; port wines are from the area of Oporto, Portugal. Port is not served during a meal, but usually afterwards, or between meals.

- **Sparkling wines** are made in the same way as still wines, except that the last stages of fermentation take place in the corked bottle. The result is that some carbon dioxide gas is retained in the liquid and effervesces when the bottle is opened. The name "champagne," by French law, may be applied only to those sparkling wines actually produced in the region of Champagne, France.

THE CARE AND SERVING OF WINES

Store wine bottles on their side so that the cork remains wet, thereby keeping the cork swollen and excluding air. Keep the wine at an even, cool temperature and don't shake it. Since mature full-bodied red wines often contain some sediment, older bottles of vintage wine should stand upright for a few days before serving to allow the sediment to settle to the bottom.

Glasses should not be filled more than half-full. Most red wines are best served at room temperature, although some prefer to chill Beaujolais and other young, light-bodied types. White and sparkling wines are served chilled. Fortified wine may be recorked in its bottle or kept in a decanter with a stopper.

Too many of us get lost in the myriad rules that are supposed to govern wine drinking. I learned a long time ago to follow the French and Italian custom of picking a wine that suits my taste and enjoying it with whatever food I wish. Perhaps this would be the best plan for you and your guests also.

Still, there are guidelines as to whether a particular wine will "go with the food." A good principle to follow is that the wine should be at least as full-bodied as the food it is served with. As a guide, I am suggesting three white and three red groups, "A" representing the lightest, "B" the medium-bodied, and "C" the heaviest wines. For example, a Muscadet might be served with broiled whitefish, California Chardonnay with roast stuffed chicken, California Merlot with grilled pork, and Brunello di Montalcino with filet mignon.

WHITE WINES

Group "A" (Light): Non-Riesling German; German, Austrian, and American Rieslings; dry Rieslings; Soave; Chenin Blanc; Vouvray; Muscadet; champagne

Group "B" (Medium): Chablis; Sancerre; Pouilly-Fumé; Pouilly-Fuissé; Mâcon; Gewürztraminer; white Bordeaux; Sauvignon Blanc

Group "C" (Heavy): Puligny-Montrachet; Chassagne-Montrachet; Meursault; white Rhône; California Chardonnay

RED WINES

Group "A" (Light): Beaujolais; Côte de Beaune; Rioja; Dolcetto; Valpolicella; Chianti Classico

Group "B" (Medium): Côte de Nuits; Médoc; Pomerol; Barbera; California Merlot and Pinot Noir; Zinfandel

Group "C" (Heavy): Rhône; Syrah; California Cabernet; Barbaresco; Barolo; Brunello di Montalcino

WHICH GLASSES SHALL I USE?

It isn't necessary to buy many different kinds of glasses; the selection of an exact glass for each use is not all that important. Personal preference and budget are usually the deciding factors.

Six- and eight-ounce glasses are in good taste and are suitable for many uses. Filled no more than ⅓ full, the 6-ounce glass may be used for sherry, Madeira, Marsala, port, and other fortified wines. For cordials or brandy, the glass should be filled only ¼ full.

The 8-ounce glass is perfect for red and white wines but it may also be used for beer, water, champagne, and other sparkling wines. Except for beer and water, do not fill more than half-full.

Wine glasses must be thin, clear, and untinted in order for the color of the wine to be fully appreciated. The wine's bouquet can be enjoyed more when the glass is not filled. Choices include 4-ounce claret glasses, 3- or 4-ounce Rhine or Moselle glasses, 3-ounce sherry glasses, and 1 to 2 ½ ounces for cordials or brandy.

When serving more than one wine on formal occasions, place the glasses in a row to the right of the water goblet in the order of their use, the first one farthest to the right. Each glass is removed after it is used. Glasses intended for after-dinner drinks are never put on the table during dinner.

There are various stemmed glasses for cocktails, all 3 or 3 ½ ounces in size. The best choices are neat and simple designs in clear crystal. Colored glasses should not be used.

Old-fashioned glasses in sizes from 4 to 7 ounces are a practical addition to most bars. They should be sturdy enough to allow mashing a lump of sugar in the glass with a wooden muddler. I prefer the larger 7-ounce glasses for looks and style.

Taller glasses for highballs, Collins-type drinks, or scotch and soda usually come in 8-, 10-, and 12-ounce sizes. The best of the lot are the 10-ounce, which can easily suffice for all uses.

A few words of advice to the home bartender:

• Always use immaculately clean glasses, and never handle them by the rim—pick them up either by the stem or at the base of the glass.

• Pouring freely by hand when mixing cocktails or long drinks can have disastrous effects. Use a jigger to measure liquor, even if you are offering more than 1 ounce per drink.

• Always use fresh fruit and citrus juices. It is difficult to make a good drink with bottled lime or lemon juice.

• Use bitters sparingly, as you do herbs and spices in cooking. Grenadine is added principally for color, not taste, although it does add a little sweetness.

• Club soda, sparkling wine, and other effervescent ingredients should be added last so the drink retains its sparkle.

• Useful items include a 1-ounce jigger, a cocktail shaker, a strainer, a juicer for citrus fruit, an ice crusher, a wooden muddler, an ice bucket with tongs, spears and skewers, coasters, a bottle opener, a corkscrew, cloth and paper towels, cocktail napkins, and a tray.

SPECIAL CELEBRATION DRINKS AND PUNCHES

The first three punches average out to about two 3-ounce servings per person. Increase or decrease the ingredients as necessary, holding the proportions constant. Use clear glass punchbowls and glasses, not ceramic mugs.

ARTILLERY PUNCH

For 25 people

¾ cup sugar

juice of 4 lemons

1 ½ tablespoons bitters

1 750-ml bottle dry red wine

1 750-ml bottle sherry

1 750-ml bottle scotch, bourbon, or rye whiskey

1 750-ml bottle brandy

3 cups club soda

2 cups ice cubes

Mix all ingredients except ice in a large punchbowl. Add the ice cubes and stir well.

VODKA PUNCH

For 20 people

3 750-ml bottles vodka

3 750-ml bottles sparkling water

juice of 3 lemons

juice of 6 oranges

½ cup maraschino or sloe gin

1 cup sugar

ice

Combine all ingredients and add ice to chill.

RHINE WINE PUNCH WITH STRAWBERRIES

For 10 people

*1 quart fresh strawberries
(use the little wild ones called*
fraises de bois *if at all possible)*

2 cups sugar

¼ cup water

*3 750-ml bottles chilled Rhine or
Moselle wine*

1. Hull and rinse the strawberries and place in a bowl. Add the sugar and water and toss well. Cover the mixture and refrigerate for 8 hours.

2. When ready to serve, transfer the strawberry mixture to a punchbowl and add the chilled wine.

SANGRIA

For 4 to 6 people

1 orange, sliced

1 lemon, sliced

1 750-ml bottle red wine

3 tablespoons cognac

*½ cup fresh or frozen sliced
peaches (optional)*

*¼ cup fresh or frozen cherries
(optional)*

1 cup cold sparkling water

ice cubes

Combine all ingredients except the sparkling water and ice in a pitcher and chill. At serving time, add sparkling water and ice cubes. Serve in large wine glasses.

HAMMERSLEY'S PLANTER'S PUNCH

In the 1950s, the island of Tortola in the British Virgin Islands was still relatively undiscovered. In those days, the Fort Burt "hotel," owned and operated by Chris and Millie Hammersley, was about a mile west of Roadtown. The scent of evening jasmine and the special Planter's Punch guaranteed a full night's sleep on a straw mattress. A case of Mount Gay rum cost $10 in those days.

1 Serving

2 teaspoons sugar

2 dashes orange bitters

¼ teaspoon grenadine

1 tablespoon sparkling water

⅓ cup dark rum

crushed ice

1 orange slice

1 pineapple stick

1 maraschino cherry with stem

Mix the sugar, bitters, grenadine, and sparkling water in a double old-fashioned glass until the sugar is dissolved. Add the rum and fill with crushed ice. Decorate with the fruit.

ALL ABOUT THE TABLE

DRESSING THE TABLE

Next to the food, probably the most important indicator of the host or hostess's personality is the table setting. The setting offers an unusual opportunity to create something special. The menu will, of course, dictate the essentials, such as silverware, number of plates, number and types of glassware, and so on; but tablecloths, placemats, napkins, china, centerpieces, location of the table, candles, flowers, and many other components create the ambience that in some cases will be charming and in others chic, tasteful, or sophisticated.

When our parents and grandparents set the table for an important dinner, the style was fairly consistent: usually white damask, matched china (remember those china sets that came in 144 pieces?), and a formal floral arrangement as centerpiece. Today's tables are infinitely more adventuresome. Designers and product manufacturers have flooded the market with items that make it easy to create excitement on the tabletop.

Here are some items to keep in mind for constructing more interesting and attractive tablesettings.

• Different kinds of pitchers—not necessarily glass.

• Decanters and cocktail shakers.

• Large oval and round platters, some white and simply styled, others colorful, some antique. Look for these in flea markets, bazaars, and antiques shops.

• Wooden boards and trays. Use a wooden pizza peel, lined with green leaves, to serve a variety of cheeses. These boards have handles, so they are easy to pass around the table.

• China, glass, and ceramic bowls of all sizes. Believe it or not, a magnificent 10-inch glass bowl is available at Tiffany's for about $40; it may be used for punches, fruit salads, cold rice and pasta salads, and many other dishes.

• Chafing dish—attractive for buffets and to warm appetizers.

• Covered tureens are useful for soups and stews, and can be used to serve breads, muffins, and biscuits.

• Cake stands add an elegance that ordinary plates cannot. They are useful for tarts (dessert and others) and add drama to your presentation.

• Baskets of all descriptions, for many uses—filled as centerpieces, for breads and rolls or for fruit. Small ones can be used for one kind of fruit or berry: for example, fill one small basket just with raspberries, one with strawberries, one with blueberries.

• Candlesticks and other candle holders, including votive glasses and hurricane chimneys, are important to the glamour of the table, creating atmosphere and a soft glow. Make some luminarias (see page 104), or set a votive candle at each place, or arrange three hurricane chimneys, with candlesticks and candles inside, down the center of a large party table.

• Use jumbo brandy snifters for after-dinner drinks and for some desserts. The idea is to have a large glass only partially filled.

• Colorful Italian and French earthenware casseroles are great enhancements to a buffet. Lift the covers with a dramatic flourish and watch the steam rise. Belshazzar rides again!

• For sheer elegance, it is difficult to improve on the tiered display piece known as an epergne. Whether crystal, silver, or ceramic, each tier can hold a different goodie—cookies, cakes, candies, fruit, marzipan.

• Oversize enamelware plates make terrific underliners or service plates. I have some in bright yellow and others in marbled cerulean blue and white that have been used again and again. They are sturdy, inexpensive, and extremely decorative, whether the party is indoors or out.

• Tablecloths and napkins of various descriptions are indispensable. I have used sequined Indian squares for curry and Christmas dinners; solid green table skirts draped with green floral squares for a spring lunch; Gucci cotton scarves patterned with flowers, birds, and grapes over table skirts for a celebration. Oversize white damask napkins gave the setting additional sparkle and added a note of freshness. Quilts make fabulous table covers—red and white ones for Christmas, pale green and pink ones for a spring wedding, and so on. Use attractive flat-weave cotton towels for napkins; they are inexpensive and machine washable. Canvas and straw mats are as versatile as table accessories can be.

NAPKIN FOLDS

Here are four simple but effective ways to fold napkins for most meals, and three fancier folds.

1. *The Simple Rectangle:* Fold the napkin twice to make a square, then fold again to make a rectangle. This is placed with the closed side next to the plate. If the napkin is decorated or monogrammed, the motif should appear at the lower left of the open side of the napkin.

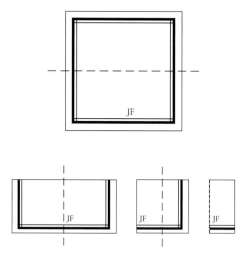

2. *Two-pointed Napkin:* This is best for smaller napkins with a decoration or monogram. Simply fold under two opposite corners of the folded square, leaving two points in view.

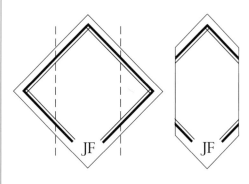

3. *One-pointed Napkin:* This is the same as the two-pointed one, except that the top point is folded under first, and then the two sides are folded under.

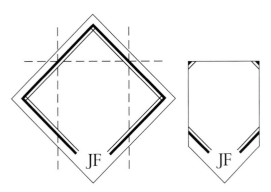

4. *The Flower-bed Fold:* One of the prettiest folds, this requires fresh flowers or leaves for each napkin. First fold the napkin in a square. Position it with the four free points facing you. Fold down and in half to make a triangle. Bring the long ends of the triangle together, tucking one into the other. Turn the napkin over and fold over the top point to make a pocket or "flowerbed." Insert a small fresh flower or pretty green leaf into the pocket.

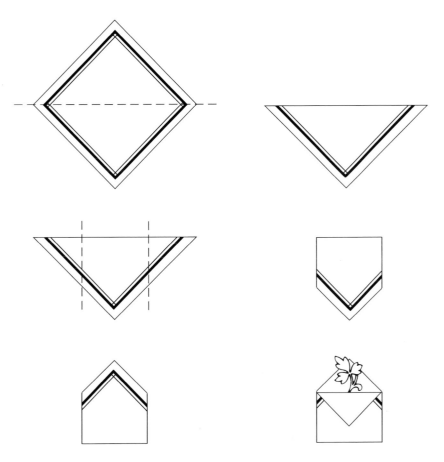

5. *The Bouquet Napkin:* Fold the napkin twice to make a square and position with the four free points at the top. Turn up the opposite point (the one closest to you) to reach about ⅓ the distance to the top point. Gather the bottom edge to make soft folds and hold the folds together with a simple napkin ring. Insert a flower or leaf spray in the ring to finish it off.

6. *The Bordered or Fringe Roll (some call this a firecracker):* This works best on a napkin with a fancy border—lace, fringe, or decorative hemstitch, for example. Open the napkin wide and fold in the side closest to you not quite to the center. Do the same with the opposite side. Press the napkin shut with both hands; turn it over. Roll up the napkin starting from an unfolded edge. The roll will resemble a sort-of-firecracker, encircled by two fancy edges.

7. *The Lotus Flower:* Open the napkin wide and fold each of the four corners to meet at the center. If the napkin is large, do this again. Carefully turn over the napkin and fold over the four corners to the center. Holding down the center, get under and pull out the corners below to make petals and form the lotus.

SETTING THE TABLE

Formal or Informal Lunch: The napkin is placed to the left or in the center of the placemat. The fork is at the left of the plate; the knife is at the right of the plate with the sharp edge facing the plate. If a shrimp or oyster fork is required for a first course, it is always placed to the right of the knife. The water glass is placed above the knife and the wine glass, if any, is placed to the right of the water glass.

If coffee is to be served at an informal lunch, the coffee spoon is placed to the right of the knife. A cup and saucer may be placed on the table to the right of the setting, but it is better to bring in a tray with cups, saucers, and spoons when ready to serve the coffee.

Informal Dinner: The table is set as for lunch, except that if the first course or salad requires a fork, it is placed to the left of the dinner fork. Again, if a shrimp or oyster fork is required, it is placed to the right of the knife.

Formal Dinner: For the rare times that there will be a soup, a fish, and a meat course, the fish fork is placed to the left of the dinner fork at the left side of the place setting. The fish knife is placed to the right of the dinner knife, the soup spoon to the right of the fish knife. Salt and pepper are placed on the table; it is most convenient to have one set for every two people. The water glass is at the right above the dinner knife, the red wine glass is to the right of the water, and the white wine glass is to the right of the red wine. Do not set cigarettes or ashtrays on any table; this is simply out of style. Formal dinners usually require service plates (placed at each setting to receive the first courses, such as soup; then both first course and service plates are removed), and the napkin is almost always placed on top of the service plate. The napkins should be large ones. Fancy tablecloths are most often used but white linen or lace placemats will work also.

It is difficult to vary these established patterns of table setting simply because no one has found a better way of doing it. But traditional or not, here are two additional rules that work for me.

1. Whether lunch or dinner is formal or not, bring in the dessert flatware with the dessert. There is usually just too much already on the table, and quite frankly it bores me to see silverware that will not be used until the end of the meal sit there.

2. Do not set the first course on the table before guests are seated. Fish or salad-type first-course dishes always seem fresher if they come directly from the kitchen, and it really only takes a few steps more to do it this way. Also, not having food on the table gives people a chance to settle themselves and to get to know the person to the left or right, rather than gobbling a shrimp the moment they sit down.

The Buffet: Rules for buffets are not as rigid as they are for formal sit-down lunches or dinners; no doubt that's one reason why the buffet is such a popular form of entertaining in this country. The food need not be set on a dining table. I have set buffet food on library tables, cabinets, benches on the back porch, long garden tables, kitchen countertops. Often I display the main dishes in one place and the dessert items in another, sometimes with coffee cups in a third location. If space allows, give some thought to a centerpiece on the main buffet table.

Plates and flatware don't have to be placed on the table with the food. If people are assigned seats at one or more tables, the plates, glasses, and flatware may be set there. On the other hand, if seats are not assigned, a separate table near the food can hold utensils, including wine and glasses if there's not enough room in the food-serving area.

Sometimes it is pleasant to have a first course, if there is one, served in another location, such as a porch. If the buffet is a really large one, such as the wedding buffet in Chapter 29, consider using more than one table for food and grouping like foods together: fish on one table, meats on another, and so forth.

CREATIVE CENTERPIECES

The table setting is important but it's the centerpiece that will make a table shine. There is almost no limit to the creativity that can explode here; even floral arrangements can be boring unless some thought is given to them. One attractive display I saw recently was country-type baskets filled with different summertime flowers, set on tables with different tablecloths. But floral arrangements do not always have to be in the form of a centerpiece. An individual small container can be made for each person as part of the place setting, or consider using the flower bed napkin fold discussed earlier. In any event, remember not to make any arrangement so high or wide that people cannot see each other across the table, or that branches are poking into wineglasses.

Here are some ideas to play with:

• Use a group of Staffordshire lambs at Eastertime, or ceramic pigs for a charcuterie party.

- Place an oversize shell filled with "pearls" or glass balls in the center of the table for a fish dinner. The pearls can be of the dime-store or Christmas-bazaar variety.

- Fill an oversize fish platter with lemons, some of them quartered (seeds removed), and present with fish that is served on individual glass fish plates.

- Serve lobster stew or fish soup in individual lobster tureens. Use a matching large tureen as a centerpiece, overflowing with fresh sprays of a specific herb used in the dish.

- Build a pyramid of apples as a centerpiece for a curry dinner, especially if cut-up apples are among the condiments.

- Use ceramic or bisque hens and chickens as centerpieces for egg-based dishes.

- Arrange a number of different-size candles to make an interesting centerpiece. Inexpensive votives make a big show, but do not use perfumed candles.

- Instead of one floral centerpiece, group three or four vases of various sizes with different flowers.

- Use a magnificent antique as a centerpiece—one that complements the food, plates, or table linens. This could be a china tureen, a silver bird, a silver or glass epergne, an old clock at New Year's.

- Use baskets of all descriptions, filled with almost anything. In the spring try fresh broccoli and bunches of spring onions in a pretty basket. For a summer gathering use a basket filled with fresh herbs, strawberries, and lovely apricots.

- Fill attractive decanters with various cordials to make a centerpiece. The cordials may actually be used over a dessert of fresh fruit or ice cream.

- At Christmas, use an elegant scarf as a table covering, with a gingerbread house for a centerpiece. Flank the centerpiece with two innovative candlesticks. Additional Christmas decorations can be added to the base of the house, and changed to pick up a theme for a New Year's Eve party.

- Top a basket of flowers with photos of a birthday celebrant at various ages. Or put the photos on small easels, with several roses strewn at their bases. The easels should face different ways so everyone around the table can enjoy the centerpiece.

All of this said, let me add that some people go overboard on centerpieces in the sense that they spend many hours to make them, often at the expense of other important details. There is no need to fall into this trap. Your home probably has many items that can be the basis for an ideal centerpiece. The main trick is to take some time to think about it, for it can add so much spirit to your table.

SEATING THE GUESTS

It is customary for the hostess to sit at one end of the table and the host at the other, but that is not always the case these days; happily, the makeup of dinner groups no longer suffers from the old "boy, girl, boy, girl" syndrome. Today if there are more men than women or vice versa, the seating arrangement may have to be more innovative. The important thing to remember, however, is that the male guest of honor (if there is one) sits to the right of the hostess, and the female guest of honor to the right of the host. But even this doesn't work if there are 8 in the group (or 12 or 16 or 20), because two women or two men will end up sitting next to each other (if there are the same number of men and women). If that is the case, the solution is for the hostess to move one place to the right, giving up her place at one end of the table. With this arrangement, then, the host is at one end and the male guest of honor is at the other. (See the illustration at right.) There doesn't always have to be a guest of honor, although these seating principles are helpful in seating those to whom a bit more attention may be in order, such as an older person, a visitor from afar, or whatever the case may be.

If a woman is giving the dinner alone and there are 8 or 12, she may sit at the head of the table. I never seat husbands and wives together, but I always do young couples who are going steady or engaged.

Yet despite all these guidelines, I often try simply to figure out who would enjoy sitting with each other and let that determine the seating arrangement. When there will be more than one table, I try to have a person "head" each, asking them about this ahead of time. If there are several tables, the male guest of honor would sit to the right of the hostess at her table, and the female guest of honor would sit to the right of the host at his table. I almost always use place cards for a dinner of 8 or more, and always for more than one table. This prevents confusion as people come to the table, and it shows that some thought went into the planning. When the guests are ready to be seated, I usually help direct them to their places by referring to a card with the seating plan that I keep readily available in the dining room or in my pocket. In other words, I make the plan and try to execute it with as little fuss as possible.

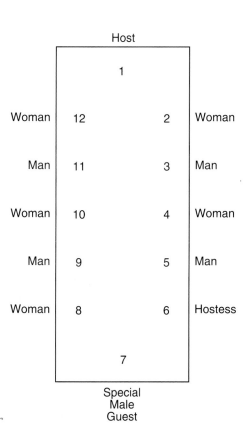

Index

C